Fight on!

[signature]

Jossey-Bass Books by Edward E. Lawler III

Corporate Boards: New Strategies for Adding Value at the Top (Jay A. Conger, Edward E. Lawler III, and David Finegold)

Creating High-Performance Organizations: Practices and Results of Employee Involvement and TQM in Fortune 1000 Companies (Edward E. Lawler III, Susan A. Mohrman, and Gerald E. Ledford Jr.)

Designing Performance Appraisal Systems: Aligning Appraisals and Organizational Realities (Allan M. Mohrman Jr., Susan M. Resnick-West, and Edward E. Lawler III)

Doing Research That Is Useful for Theory and Practice (Edward E. Lawler III, Allan M. Mohrman Jr., Susan A. Mohrman, Gerald E. Ledford Jr., Thomas G. Cummings, and Associates)

From the Ground Up: Six Principles for Creating the New Logic Corporation (Edward E. Lawler III)

High-Involvement Management: Participative Strategies for Improving Organizational Performance (Edward E. Lawler III)

Large-Scale Organizational Change (Allan M. Mohrman Jr., Susan A. Mohrman, Gerald E. Ledford Jr., Thomas G. Cummings, Edward E. Lawler III, and Associates)

The Leader's Change Handbook: An Essential Guide to Setting Direction and Taking Action (Jay A. Conger, Gretchen M. Spreitzer, and Edward E. Lawler III)

Motivation in Work Organizations (Edward E. Lawler III)

Organizing for High Performance: The CEO Report on Employee Involvement, TQM, Reengineering, and Knowledge Management in Fortune 1000 Companies (Edward E. Lawler III, Susan A. Mohrman, and George Benson)

Organizing for the Future: The New Logic for Managing Complex Organizations (Jay R. Galbraith, Edward E. Lawler III, and Associates)

Rewarding Excellence: Pay Strategies for the New Economy (Edward E. Lawler III)

Strategic Pay: Aligning Organizational Strategies and Pay Systems

Tomorrow's Organization: Crafting Winning Capabilities in a Dynamic World (Susan A. Mohrman, Jay R. Galbraith, Edward E. Lawler III, and Associates)

The Ultimate Advantage: Creating the High-Involvement Organization (Edward E. Lawler III)

Treat People Right!

Treat People Right!

How Organizations and Individuals Can Propel Each Other into a Virtuous Spiral of Success

Edward E. Lawler III

JOSSEY-BASS
A Wiley Imprint
www.josseybass.com

Published by Jossey-Bass
A Wiley Imprint
989 Market Street, San Francisco, CA 94103-1741   www.josseybass.com

Jossey-Bass books and products are available through most bookstores. To contact Jossey-Bass directly call our Customer Care Department within the U.S. at 800-956-7739, outside the U.S. at 317-572-3986 or fax 317-572-4002.

Jossey-Bass also publishes its books in a variety of electronic formats. Some content that appears in print may not be available in electronic books.

Library of Congress Cataloging-in-Publication Data

Lawler, Edward E.
   Treat people right! : how organizations and individuals can propel each other into a virtuous spiral of success / Edward E. Lawler III.—
1st ed.
        p. cm.
Includes bibliographical references (p.) and index.
      ISBN 0-7879-6478-6 (alk. paper)
   1. Personnel management.   2. Success in business.   3. Organizational effectiveness.   I. Title.
      HF5549 .L289 2003
      658.3—dc21

                                                                        2002154861

Printed in the United States of America
FIRST EDITION
HB Printing   10 9 8 7 6 5 4 3

Contents

Part One: The New Relationship Between Organizations and Individuals

Part Two: The Seven Principles of Treating People Right

Acknowledgments

My wife, Patty, helped me from the beginning with this book. She encouraged me to write it and contributed ideas to it. Once I started working on it, she provided editorial help. But most of all, for all the years we have been together, she has provided me with love and support. Thank you, Patty. I love you.

Rick Benzel worked closely with me on the final preparation of the manuscript. His analytical and writing skills were an enormous help to me. He asked the right questions and made my ideas sharper and more user-friendly. Thank you, Rick.

Last year I was fortunate enough to receive the Michael Losey Award from the Society for Human Resource Management. The financial support this award provided helped me free up time to work on this book.

Finally, writing this book was greatly facilitated by the help I received from the members of the Center for Effective Organizations. Special thanks to Dan Canning, Arienne McCracken, and Patty Trinidad for their help in preparing the manuscript.

E.L.

Preface

Today's business environment is tougher than ever. Organizations everywhere are struggling to be competitive, and the path to success seems harder and harder to find and travel. That said, I think I have found a path that can lead to both individuals and organizations reaching their goals. It is to "treat people right."

You may think that treating people right sounds naive or worse yet, out-of-date. You may think I am going to espouse a variety of feel-good ideas about how organizations need to be generous to their employees and cater to their needs and whims in order to make them happy and productive. You may even fear that I am yet another management guru arguing that organizations must provide good working conditions, fair supervision, and good pay in order to be profitable—a premise that you doubt is true.

Let me reassure you that this is not a feel-good book. Treating people right is a fundamental key to creating organizational effectiveness and success. It also is easier said than done. Treating people right involves a highly complex set of actions on the part of both organizations and employees. Organizations must develop ways to treat their employees so that they are motivated and satisfied; employees must behave in ways that help their organizations become effective and high-performing.

Both organizations and people need to succeed; one can't succeed without the other. To provide people with meaningful work and rewards, organizations need to be successful. And to be successful, organizations need high-performing individuals. The challenge is to design organizations that perform at high levels and treat people in ways that are rewarding and satisfying.

Treating people right is not about being generous. Rewarding people generously may please them, but it does not necessarily lead to greater levels of either motivation or satisfaction, nor does it guarantee increased organizational performance. The challenge—and it is a significant one—is to identify and implement organization designs and practices that are good for *both* individuals and organizations.

Treating people right is not easy to implement. It takes visionary leadership and skilled management. It requires a wide range of well-thought-out structures, programs, and practices that are oriented toward motivating people to perform at their *highest* levels. It takes effort and patience to implement and monitor the practices that make organizations and their people highly effective in achieving their goals. And it takes commitment and dedication to create an environment where management and employees genuinely respect and value each other.

A False Conflict

At the core of many people's concern about the wisdom of treating people right is a belief that there is an irreconcilable conflict between what is good for a business and what is good for employees. Although it would be foolish for me to argue that there is never or seldom a conflict between satisfying these two outcomes, the fact is that when people are treated right, the potential for such conflict is greatly reduced.

The reason for this is that treating people right actually produces substantial positive long-term payoffs for both organizations and employees. For organizations, the payoffs come in the form of being able to attract better people, retain them longer, and motivate them to achieve excellence. The payoffs for people come in the form of more interesting work, more control of their careers, and increased rewards. Especially in the chaotic business world of the early twenty-first century, such payoffs can make the difference in the success of organizations and individuals faced with changing markets, globalization, fickle customers, and a volatile investment climate.

For individuals and organizations to succeed, they each need to understand how the other operates, and they need to make informed decisions about their relationship. Simply put, they need to actively manage their relationship (no matter how short or long) based on mutual understanding and shared information. This can happen only if organizations commit themselves to practices that are good for both their performance and their employees.

Treating people right is a two-way street. Just as the organization must adopt new attitudes and programs that respect its people, individuals must also recognize that they have a responsibility in this new world of organizational high performance. They have to take greater responsibility for their knowledge, skills, and career. They must effectively manage their development and performance in order to enjoy success.

Virtuous Spirals of Success

When both individuals and organizations achieve more and more of their goals, I call this relationship a "virtuous spiral." Virtuous spiral relationships come about when an organization values and rewards its people, and as a result, they are committed to performing well. Through their performance, people propel the organization to higher levels of accomplishment, and as a result it is able to reward them better and to attract and retain highly talented people. This in turn spirals the organization's performance to higher and higher levels.

Developing and maintaining a virtuous spiral requires going far beyond simply being nice to people and treating them fairly. It means developing a wide array of human capital management practices that motivate people to excel and reward them when they achieve high levels of performance. And it takes people making greater commitments to their organization and becoming responsible for their behaviors.

Overview of This Book

My goal in this book is to provide organizations with a blueprint for treating people right and creating a virtuous spiral. Along the way, I will also have advice of a much more personal nature about the implications of the principles enumerated in this book for your career and for achieving your own virtuous spiral of career success.

Part One presents the strategic and conceptual foundation for the book. I begin Chapter One with an explanation of the rationale for why today's organizations must focus on their people. I discuss numerous important changes that have occurred over the past few decades in the world's economy, politics, and business climate. These changes leave organizations no choice other than to treat their people right in order to gain competitive advantage. I then show how treating people right involves seven principles that lead to creating a virtuous spiral.

Chapters Two and Three present fundamental concepts about organizations and people. You need to understand these because they are critical to the development, implementation, and utilization of the seven principles. Chapter Two focuses on the elements of organizational effectiveness, that is, the factors that must be present to ensure a high-performing organization. Chapter Three focuses on the elements of individual effectiveness, summarizing what researchers have found about what makes people motivated and able to perform at high levels. These two chapters are crucial in educating you about the underpinnings of organizational designs and management systems that are needed to attract and retain the best people while motivating them to perform at their highest levels.

Part Two of the book is where you will find the substance of how to treat people right. Chapters Four through Ten set out the programs and practices that are the nuts and bolts of the seven principles of treating people right. The principles cover every aspect of organizations, from locating the best talent to developing leadership throughout an organization.

Each of these seven chapters opens with a discussion of the fundamental concepts that drive the chapter's principle. This is followed by detailed descriptions of specific programs and "best practices" that are based on years of research on the world's leading organizations, some of which, in my view, have already established virtuous spirals. In this way, the chapters in Part Two form a comprehensive and practical guide for creating a virtuous spiral in your organization.

Let me add that in selecting the best practices for inclusion in this book, my goal was to choose only those practices that have the greatest cost-benefit impact from both an organizational and an individual point of view. For organizations, this means selecting practices that maximize employee attraction, retention, development, motivation, skills, knowledge, and organizational effectiveness. For individuals, this means practices that increase job satisfaction, development, reward levels, and informed decision making.

Finally, Chapters Four through Ten each end with a section that discusses the implications of that virtuous spiral principle for individuals. These discussions are written in a very personal way and contain specific information about how the seven principles of virtuous spirals affect your career. As you will see, you may be required to make changes in your personal attitudes, experiences, and development in order to manage yourself and your career and enjoy a virtuous spiral of success.

This book ends with an Epilogue that looks to the future of treating people right and virtuous spirals. It identifies what organizations need to do to maintain their virtuous spirals and how more virtuous spiral organizations can be built and thrive in our rapidly changing world.

Who Can Benefit from This Book

The fundamentals of how people and organizations need to relate to each other pertain to all people who work for organizations. So whether you are a corporate executive, a middle manager, veteran employee, or a recent graduate in your first job, you can benefit by analyzing how you want your organization to manage its people, as well as by understanding how you will need to manage your career in the coming years. In short, I hope the recommendations provided in this book will find their way into cubicles and corridors of all sizes and shapes.

My Background

My interest in how people and organizations can best serve each other is more than a passing fancy or a recently acquired conviction. For those of you who know me, you are aware that I have been studying, teaching, and writing about human resource management and organizational effectiveness for more than forty years. During four decades of observation and learning, I have done many research studies that show how and why people perform well and what is fundamental to organizational success.

For the past twenty-five years, I have been the director of the Center for Effective Organizations in the Marshall School of Business at the University of Southern California. The center and its staff perform research in many fields of management, leadership, and organizational effectiveness. Many of the recommendations and research findings that I mention in this book are drawn from the work of the center.

I have chosen to write this book now because four changes have occurred that make it possible and timely.

1. Decades of research and theory have established an excellent foundation of knowledge covering individual and organizational effectiveness. This work clearly points to some "must do's" for individuals and organizations.
2. The experimentation and innovation that some organizations engaged in during the past decade have produced a number of best practices that can be widely applied to improve organizational performance and individual well-being in many other organizations.
3. We now live in a complex world of rapid and unpredictable change, with an increasing reliance on high technology and human capital and growing global competition. Because of this, human capital and its effective utilization have become, in many situations, the key source of competitive advantage for organizations.
4. The traditional relationship between individuals and organizations has been destroyed by repeated downsizing, corporate fraud, executive excess, and an increasingly competitive business environment. A new relationship is needed, one that individuals will believe in and that creates effective organizations.

In short, we are at a point in history where we have both a good supply of knowledge about how to create virtuous spiral organizations and a clear need to create them.

January 2003   EDWARD E. LAWLER III
Los Angeles, California

Part One

The New Relationship Between Organizations and Individuals

Chapter One

Why Treating People Right Pays Off

We are entering a new era in the relationship between organizations and their employees. The world of work is sharply altering most of the century-old understandings between employers and employees. No longer can organizations think of people as either loyal "family members" or as easily replaceable resources when it comes to accomplishing their business objectives.

In this new era, people need to be respected and treated as precious human capital, more essential to an organization's effectiveness than its financial capital. People can now be the primary source of a company's competitive advantage in most businesses. To put it bluntly, how people are treated increasingly determines whether a company will prosper and even survive.

In the past, arguments about the importance of how people are treated have largely fallen on deaf ears in the executive offices and boardrooms of most organizations. Yes, there are many companies that claim that their people are their most important asset, and they even put pictures of them (always smiling) in their annual reports. But most of these companies do not behave like their people are their number one priority. All too often, they treat them as replaceable parts that add little value.

But today, a number of powerful and compelling factors are coalescing into a new reality: to be effective, organizations must excel in organizing and managing their people. In the twenty-first century, treating people right is not an option; it is a necessity.

The Compelling Forces of Change

Every reader of this book knows that the business environment of the twenty-first century is different from what it was twenty or thirty years ago. In fact, the business world today is vastly different from what it was just five years ago. There can be no doubt that the world is changing more rapidly and has become more chaotic, demanding, and competitive than ever before.

But let's get specific about how the world is now different. Let me invite you to take a step back for a moment and consider the business environment throughout most of the second half of the twentieth century.

For organizations, the business environment was relatively stable and predictable and offered numerous opportunities for growth. An organization was assured of at least a degree of success and profitability as long as it produced moderately good products or services and made productive use of its employees. It could gain competitive advantage with relative ease by controlling its sources of raw materials or by obtaining low-cost financial capital and physical assets. Some organizations also gained competitive advantage because they had government-created protection from competition.

For people, too, the old environment was also relatively stable and secure. Most employees who worked for governments or large corporations lived under a "loyalty contract," a tacit agreement with their employers that if they were loyal, they could have a comfortable life with that organization. They had not just a job but a career that included the security of a regular paycheck, benefits, and retirement income. Even for employees not covered under a loyalty contract, the growth and power of the union movement provided many of them with benefits and protections that guaranteed a good quality of life.

Now contrast that with today's business environment.

For most organizations today, the sense of stability and assured success is in question. It is no longer easy to find competitive advantage and, once found, to maintain it for very long. New threats seem to come from everywhere: start-ups, international competitors, legal changes, new technologies. Most organizations must fight tooth and nail to secure their profits and continue their growth. Most also regularly struggle to find qualified people for their leadership and knowledge work jobs. As a result, the past decades have seen the downfall of many venerable companies, as well as the overnight birth and death of many seemingly smart start-ups—witness the many failed dot-coms that originally seemed destined for success.

For most people, the new environment is equally insecure. The promise of a steady job has all but disappeared, with millions of workers downsized, furloughed, laid off, or voluntarily choosing to move from company to company. Many people have found that they simply don't have the skills needed to compete in the marketplace, having lost their personal competitive advantage and their value as human capital. Many of today's workers are finding that although they still have jobs, they are falling behind the business, scientific, and technical needs that organizations have.

These starkly contrasting sketches of the business environment are the result of four major changes:

- The globalization of competition
- The rapid development of scientific and technical knowledge
- The death of the loyalty contract
- The scarcity of skilled employees

Of course, not all of these have affected or will affect every organization in the same way, but most organizations have felt or will feel the impact of at least several of them. Most people, too, will feel the impact of several of them at some point during their careers.

Let's explore these forces in greater detail so that you can understand how each affects organizations and people.

Globalization of Competition

The old days of limited competition are over. With the disappearance of communist and totalitarian regimes in many parts of the world, more and more countries are opening up to foreign business and trade. While this increasing globalization has created new markets and growth opportunities for many existing organizations, it has also dramatically elevated the level of competition in nearly all industries.

Many new competitors exist. Over just the past decade, we have seen the emergence of a coalition of Western European countries into a major new economic power, the emergence of India as a global competitor in software and technology, the entrance of the formerly socialist or communist Eastern European bloc countries into the world market, the awakening of the Chinese and Southeast Asian dragons, and the adoption of the North American Free Trade Agreement. Each of these developments has created competitors searching for profits, dominance, and new markets. Many of these newer competitors have distinct advantages in areas ranging from geographical proximity to important markets to high-skilled, relatively low-wage workforces to large storehouses of financial capital with which to buy new plants and equipment as well as to acquire other companies.

While some organizations have found expanded profits in the new global markets, many others have struggled or suffered due to increased competition and the complexities involved in operating on the global stage. Globalization has also had a negative impact on millions of people whose jobs have been transferred to foreign countries where the labor is cheaper. They have been forced either to find new jobs, often at lower pay, or to retrain themselves to compete in new industries. If it hasn't already, at some time in the future, globalization is likely to dramatically affect your career, and you will face some important choices about how to manage your career in this new era of global competition.

Greater Scientific and Technical Knowledge

In the past several decades, the bar has been significantly raised with respect to the level of scientific and technological knowledge that organizations need in order to compete. And there is every reason to believe that the growth of new knowledge will continue to accelerate.

The amount of knowledge now required to be competitive has altered the core of what organizations do, the types of products they produce, and how they operate, as well as where they can find competitive advantage. Entire industries, including communications, entertainment, consulting, housing, banking, finance, retailing, and manufacturing, have been forced to rethink their strategies and how they go about their business.

Changes in technology have also caused many of the world's most venerable companies to completely change their direction or invest large amounts of capital to develop new products or to acquire new technologies. And like dinosaurs, a few historic companies (Polaroid and Westinghouse, for example) have been vanquished by faster, smarter competitors who were able to invent or adopt new technologies.

Perhaps the most vivid example of the rapid evolution of technology and its impact on organizations is the Internet. In the blink of an eye, the Internet created a host of new competitors that served customers in new and different ways. While many Internet companies accomplished little other than the expenditure of huge amounts of investment capital, many others truly succeeded in changing the world (think of Amazon.com and eBay), creating the need for competitors to adopt new business models.

Meanwhile, the demand for increased scientific and technical knowledge has put significant pressure on workers everywhere. Increasingly, today's employees in developed countries must have highly sophisticated skills with respect to managing information, developing knowledge, and dealing in abstract concepts. They need to have the ability to think, analyze, and problem-solve. Fewer workers are needed to do the mind-numbing, repetitive manual tasks that formerly dominated the work scene. These are being done by machines or sent to low-wage economies. Needless to say, it has become absolutely clear that people who cannot keep pace with scientific and technological change are quickly losing their value as employees.

Death of the Loyalty Contract

Throughout most of the twentieth century, organizations maintained a tacit agreement with their workers that as long as they were generally productive, their jobs and a reasonable pension plan were guaranteed. This was often referred to as the "loyalty contract."

However, globalized competition, the rise of technology, and the increasing demand for knowledge workers with state-of-the-art skills has made maintaining the loyalty contract unrealistic in the case of most companies. More and more organizations have realized that buying their workers' long-term loyalty is simply not a good investment.

Despite its honorable tradition, today the loyalty contract is in many ways counterproductive. By providing employees with a relatively secure and comfortable lifestyle, it serves to attract and retain only those people who want secure, predictable employment situations. It does not attract or retain those who want to be part of an entrepreneurial organization or who want to be part of a rapidly changing, technologically advanced, or knowledge-intensive organization. A loyalty relationship also does little to encourage individuals to learn new skills, keep up with technology changes, and keep the company financially competitive.

Beginning in the 1980s, more and more companies ended their loyalty contracts. Such revered organizations as General Electric, IBM, and AT&T shattered their contracts by laying off thousands of employees. In retrospect, it is clear that most of these organizations had no choice. At that time, laying off their workers was the best way these firms could adapt to the dramatic changes in their businesses. To have done otherwise would have been fatal for them.

The death of the loyalty contract has had enormous repercussions in today's business environment. One of its major effects has been on the cost, availability, and attitudes of good labor. Most people, especially younger workers, understand and accept that loyalty to their organization is largely a losing proposition. As a result, many of them are no longer willing to be dependent on their employers or amenable to accepting practices and decisions that are not advantageous to them. Without the benefits of the old loyalty contract, today's employees are demanding substitutes such as challenging work, opportunities for learning, and substantive rewards. And when they do not get what they want, today's workers are quick to move on to more attractive employment situations.

The change is significant: organizations can no longer count on their members' loyalty, so they must continuously compete for talent. They have to focus on attracting and hiring the most talented people and retaining their existing talent. Because of the increased mobility of individuals, organizations need to change the fundamental way they think about their employees. They need to look for approaches to managing them that are advantageous to both themselves and their employees.

Scarcity of Skilled Employees

Two powerful forces are contributing to an increasing shortage of knowledgeable skilled employees: workforce demographics and education.

First, many industrialized countries are facing the burden of an aging population.[1] Increasingly in the United States, Europe, and Japan, a high percentage of the workforce is approaching or has attained the traditional age of retirement. This demographic shift is a result of a combination of relatively low birth rates, especially in countries like Japan, Italy, and Germany, as well as longer life expectancies. Although many potential retirees can remain in the workforce, they have to be sold on the idea of continuing to work. They also may not be able to meet the needs that organizations have for employees with knowledge.

The other force behind the growing scarcity of skilled labor in the United States is an underperforming educational system. It is accepted in the business world that our schools simply do not produce enough well-educated students who are capable of doing the type of complex knowledge work that is increasingly needed in today's world. Fewer and fewer new graduates leave school ready to handle the challenges and intricacies of today's competitive jobs. Particularly lacking are people who can problem-solve and do cutting-edge technical and engineering work.

When it comes to human capital, you must not underestimate the importance of a highly skilled workforce. As tasks become more complicated, the difference between an average performer and a good performer rises dramatically. If you examine a simple, repetitive assembly line job, the difference between the best performer and the worst may only be a few percentage points in productivity. However, the difference between an outstanding knowledge worker and an average one can be 1,000 percent or more.

In the old competitive environment, many jobs did not require highly effective performance for an organization to be successful, so the demand for highly talented people was relatively limited. Many organizations simply did not need to make it a priority to fill jobs with highly talented individuals, other than at the very senior levels of management and in a few key technical areas. In most cases, organizations were satisfied to fill jobs with people who could perform at a "good enough" level because the work was not particularly challenging or difficult and how well it was done did not have a significant impact on the organization's overall performance.

But in the new competitive environment, the situation is radically different. There is now an undeniable need for highly knowledgeable, skilled people, and many corporations are having trouble finding enough of them. With more and more technically difficult and personally demanding jobs, creating an extraordinary workforce is a constant challenge, while the payoff from staffing with top performers can be tremendous.

You may be wondering if the shortage of skilled human capital is just a temporary phenomenon; after all, it did ease after the dot-com bust. I am convinced that the problem is here to stay. While the ups and downs of birth rates and economic cycles will affect the labor market over short time spans, the shortage of highly qualified human capital is likely to remain a reality for decades. The reason is simple: the growth of knowledge and technology continuously creates higher demands for an educated workforce.

The New Competitive Advantage

The four major changes we have just reviewed show every sign of continuing. There is little question that we will experience a further globalization of business and even more competition. The demand for scientific and technical knowledge workers will continue to grow as organizations need to commit more resources to developing and delivering new and more complex products and services. And there is no stopping the increasing need for skilled people to handle more and more complex business management issues, products, and decision making. In light of the increasing demand for talent, people are more and more likely to see themselves as free agents.

In the future, organizations will undoubtedly need to meet new challenges if they are to survive and thrive. To do this, organizations must learn how to attract, retain, motivate, organize, and manage talented individuals. People are the key to helping organizations stay ahead of change and to having a competitive advantage. This calls for a new type of relationship between organizations and people, one that recognizes the true importance of *human capital.*

How should organizations recognize the importance of human capital? History has some important lessons to teach us about what not to do. One thing not to do is to put the human assets on the corporate balance sheet. If human assets truly matter, the argument goes, they should be valued and accounted for. Yet efforts at human asset accounting have failed, largely because they are based on flawed thinking—people are not comparable to the assets already appearing in corporate accounting statements. Assets are owned and can be bought, sold, and manipulated. But people cannot be owned; they make their own decisions, and they have their own unique competencies and capabilities that make managing and organizing them far more complex and challenging than managing buildings, equipment, and other corporate assets. In short, it is a serious mistake to think of people as assets.

However, from an organizational point of view, it is valid to consider people as human *capital* and at least as important as an organization's financial capital. Like financial capital, people need to be treated with care, respect, and commitment if the organization expects them to stay invested. It must also provide them with the returns they need. Just as in managing financial capital, organizations cannot afford to waste their human capital or risk having it go to places where it can get a better return. Like financial capital, human capital needs to be carefully allocated, utilized, and managed.

I recently heard a radio ad that illustrates the erroneous thinking behind the traditional approach to the role of human capital in organizations. The ad was for a company that specializes in outsourcing human resource management for corporations, and the ad ended with the jingle, "We take care of your people so you can take care of your business." This sounds great, but it actually is the opposite of how a company should think about its people. A more appropriate slogan would be something like, "We take care of your people so *they* can take care of your business." As my revision of this slogan indicates, it is the people who must deal with the business in today's world because they are the business and the best source of competitive advantage.

Talented People and Well-Designed Organizations

Let me clarify one point about treating people right and the importance of human capital. I am not suggesting that having the right people alone will make organizations effective. Treating people right is not just about talented people; it is also about strategies, practices, designs, and policies that make organizations into places where people want to perform well and can work effectively. Extraordinary results can be obtained only by having talented people *and* well-designed organizations with the best management systems.

In fact, opinions differ regarding the importance of talent. Some academics such as Charles O'Reilly and Jeffrey Pfeffer argue that companies can gain competitive advantage and achieve extraordinary results with ordinary people.[2] In their view, if you have the right systems, you don't have to worry about having the best people.

Others have argued that talent is all that counts. For example, Secretary of State Colin Powell, in many of his speeches on leadership, has argued that "organization does not really accomplish anything. Only by attracting the best people will you accomplish great deeds."

My position is that both are wrong. Achieving the competitive advantage needed today requires *both* great people and great organizational practices. It is misleading to claim that organizations can get extraordinary results with ordinary people, just as it is misleading to argue that organizations can get extraordinary results with ordinary management practices. To be effective, organizations need both outstanding people and outstanding management systems because that is what produces world-class results for both individuals and organizations.

Outstanding individuals and organizational practices tend to reinforce each other and seek each other out because of the momentum they create. Effective organizational practices attract outstanding people, and outstanding people create effective structures and practices. Treating people right is all about identifying and implementing the things organizations can do that are good for organizational performance and individuals.

The Ultimate Goal: A Virtuous Spiral

In the Preface, I alluded to the fact that treating people right leads to powerful win-win virtuous spirals of success. Virtuous spirals occur when organizations treat people right by implementing the effective practices needed to motivate them and enable them to perform well. Virtuous spirals are actually the ultimate competitive advantage—powerful and hard-to-duplicate sources of positive momentum and higher and higher levels of performance.

A virtuous spiral begins when an organization takes intelligent, strategy-driven, conscious actions to attract, retain, motivate, develop, and effectively organize committed, high-performance individuals. This generates a high-performance organization. It boosts the rewards for employees, which increases their motivation and commitment. The more challenging and rewarding environment that results further reinforces the organization's ability to attract, retain, and develop effective employees, who further positively affect performance. Thus a virtuous spiral forms and expands, carrying the organization and its members to greater heights. Figure 1.1 captures this in graphic form.

To successfully develop a virtuous spiral, organizations need to emphasize ever-increasing levels of performance, higher rewards for individuals, and increasingly competent employees. As they achieve these goals, a positive performance momentum develops that feeds on itself and provides a powerful competitive advantage.

Virtuous Spiral Organizations

Let me present a few examples of organizations that have achieved impressive results due to their dedication to treating people right. Because I have studied and consulted with these organizations, I can state with considerable confidence that their success is very much due to their ability to create and sustain virtuous spirals.

Microsoft is one of the most impressive examples of a company that has profited from a virtuous spiral relationship with its people for decades. Since the early 1980s, the company has had an environment in which its employees have done well and the company has done well. The employees have had challenging work and, of

Figure 1.1. Virtuous Spiral.

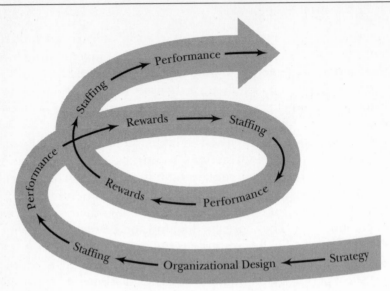

course, one of the most highly rewarding stock plans around. Microsoft has been an enormously attractive place to work, especially for high performers. As a result, it has attracted some of the country's top software engineers and marketing executives.

Because of its relationship with its human capital, Microsoft has been able to generate a powerful dynamic in which success begets success, which begets more success. The company's seemingly unstoppable growth began to slow down only in the late 1990s, when it faced a rapidly changing competitive environment along with government challenges to its growing power. But even in the market downturn of the early years of the new century, Microsoft has continued on a virtuous spiral of increasing growth and success.

Another organization that has clearly enjoyed a virtuous spiral of success for decades is General Electric. Even before Jack Welch became CEO in the early 1980s, GE had already established an environment where highly talented individuals wanted to work because of the opportunities the company offered for career development and financial rewards. Able to attract and retain highly talented individuals, GE has enjoyed decades of enviable growth in profits and as a result has attracted more and more talented individuals. GE is a clear example of a cycle of successful performance leading to successful recruitment and motivation of individuals, which in turn produce even more successful performance.

Southwest Airlines is a third example of an organization that has managed to maintain a virtuous spiral for decades. From its very beginning, Southwest was a human capital–focused organization that sought a high-quality relationship with its employees. Its founder, Herb Kelleher, stressed from day one that the company's competitive advantage is its people. The result has been excellent customer service and an absence of the hostile labor relationship characteristic of every other major airline. Despite being highly unionized, Southwest has never had a strike and is frequently mentioned as one of the best places to work.

Like many other organizations that have created virtuous spirals, there is no one secret to Southwest's success. The company has emphasized the careful selection of employees, building a employee-friendly work environment, giving employees freedom to control their jobs and work environment, profit sharing and stock ownership for all employees, and the opportunity for employees to grow, develop, and advance in the company.

Procter & Gamble is yet another example. Though the company is over one hundred years old, the past forty years of its existence have been marked by many forward-thinking efforts to establish a virtuous spiral relationship with its employees based on employee involvement and the development of leaders throughout the company. P&G was an early adopter of employee involvement practices in its manufacturing plants. It also has a stock ownership plan that has placed over 30 percent of its stock into the hands of its employees.

Other examples of virtuous spiral organizations are worth noting quickly:

• Johnson & Johnson has had a long-term virtuous spiral relationship with its employees. Key to its success are numerous separate business units that allow for a high level of autonomy and a clear mission vision and statement of ethical standards. It, like Procter & Gamble, also has a high level of stock ownership by its employees and has done an outstanding job of instituting employee involvement practices in many of its manufacturing locations.

- Capital One, the financial services firm, is a relatively new firm that has had a virtuous spiral relationship with its employees since its founding. Its human resource management system focuses on the development of people, and most employees own Capital One stock.

- Harley-Davidson recovered from near extinction in the 1970s by building a strong cooperative relationship with its unions and using employee involvement to improve quality and productivity. It continues to be a market leader both in its business sector and in the way it treats its people.

- Medtronic is a leading manufacturer of medical equipment that has grown rapidly by creating innovative lifesaving products. It goes out of its way to involve all employees in the mission of the company, which is to improve the quality and length of people's lives. As a result, employees profit both financially and intrinsically as a result of working there.

- Applied Materials is the world's leading producer of semi-conductor manufacturing equipment. It is frequently listed as one of the best places to work despite the fact that it is in a highly cyclical business. It deals with this by using slowdowns to train and develop people, and it uses stock to be sure that everyone wins when the business is strong.

When Organizations Don't Treat People Right

Organizations that do not attempt to treat people right and to initiate a virtuous spiral are susceptible to the opposite result, the *death spiral.*

Death spirals occur when organizations mistreat their human capital, and as a result, their performance declines, causing repercussions that lead to further declines and in many cases death. When organizations experience declining performance, they are perceived to be in trouble. As a result, they cannot attract the right human capital to fix their situation or the financial assets and the customers they need to reverse their decline. They soon become a place no one wants to be associated with. They become less and less of a competitor and ultimately die. Death spirals can last decades or just a few days.

Perhaps the most recent dramatic example of a death spiral is the complete collapse of Arthur Andersen. In a very short period of time, it went from being one of the world's five premier accounting firms to oblivion. In essence, it lost the reputation of its brand and its attractiveness as an employer. Both customers and employees began leaving the company, and in just a matter of months, its ability to function ended.

The collapse of Arthur Andersen illustrates an important point about death spirals. Organizations like Andersen whose market worth is in its intangible assets, such as its reputation, brand, and human capital, are extremely vulnerable to sudden death spirals. Many knowledge work firms, like consulting firms and publishers, have intangible assets that represent more than 75 percent of their market value; only a small portion of their assets are in their plant, equipment, and financial assets. When such organizations lose their attractiveness as an employer or their reputation as a good place to do business, they can plunge, much like an airplane that has lost its forward momentum. Their performance decreases so quickly that almost overnight they go out of business.

Rapid death spirals rarely happen to old-economy companies in industries like steel, automobiles, and energy because they have more tangible assets. As a result, it usually takes longer for them to fail. They can even defy gravity and exist in a zero-momentum condition if they have significant tangible assets and operate in a forgiving environment. For example, most public utilities have been able to maintain a steady-state existence because of their monopoly power. But when they have been deregulated, they rarely do well: witness the declines of AT&T, Nortel, and Lucent.

Several major organizations today are in a slow death spiral. General Motors has been for decades and has had great difficulty reversing its downward momentum, losing market share year after year. Two of the great retailers in American history, Montgomery Ward and Sears, have both declined, although at different rates. Montgomery Ward has already gone into bankruptcy, while Sears continues to lose market share. It has new, fierce competitors—namely Wal-Mart, Target, Lowe's, and Home Depot—that continue to take market share away from it in part because they have developed virtuous spirals.

Without exception, organizations that are in death spirals have failed to fully recognize and respond to the compelling forces of change in the world today. None has adequately altered its strategy and management practices to fit the new world or changed its relationship with employees in ways that can reverse the death spirals. These companies are no longer seen as good places to work and have increasing difficulty attracting the kind of human talent that they need in order to be effective.

The world of professional sports provides an excellent juxtaposition between actions that create a virtuous spiral and those that lead to a death spiral. In the 1980s, one of my consulting clients, the NFL, reached an agreement with its players' union that effectively created a virtuous spiral relationship. In essence, it assured labor and management that each would share in any revenue improvements that took place in the business. This resulted in a virtuous spiral relationship that has enriched both the owners and the players. Strikes became a thing of the past, and the game of professional football has grown in popularity and revenue; today it is the most popular spectator sport in the United States.

Just the opposite has happened in professional baseball. Labor and management have never been able to agree on an acceptable revenue-sharing relationship. Instead of creating the kind of virtuous spiral relationship that pro football enjoys, it has created a death spiral. Contract negotiations with the union have been highly acrimonious. There have been eight work stoppages since 1972, one of which led to the cancellation of the World Series. In 2002, after months of hostile negotiations, a contract was reached without a strike, but it did little to forge a cooperative labor-management relationship. TV ratings for the 2002 World Series reached an all-time low, in part because fans were turned off by the threat of a strike. Instead of both sides winning, both management and labor have ended up losing relative to what might have been.

The Seven Principles for Treating People Right and Creating a Virtuous Spiral

By now, I hope that the rationale for treating people right and creating a virtuous spiral is clear. The only question that remains is how to do it. What steps do organizations need to take to treat people right and potentially launch a virtuous spiral?

To be competitive in this new world, an organization must attract and retain highly talented, high-performing individuals. It needs to encourage people to develop the skills and knowledge that the organization needs in order for them to perform effectively. It needs to motivate them to perform their work well and to commit themselves to the success of the organization. Finally, it needs to create an organization design and a leadership capability that lead to effective organizational performance.

Creating a virtuous spiral is something most organizations can do. Through my research and study of many leading organizations, I have identified seven principles that are key to organizations' developing virtuous spirals. These seven principles guide a wide assortment of specific practices that I have seen implemented in exemplary organizations with positive results.

These seven principles are summarized in Exhibit 1.1 and will be explored in depth in Part Two of this book.

Your Own Virtuous Spiral

Before we examine these seven principles in detail, let me point out that there are a number of important implications of treating people right that you need to consider if you work with or for an organization.

On the positive side, just as organizations need to view you as human capital, you need to begin seeing yourself as human capital, not an asset. Consider your time, energy, intelligence, and skills. You have the opportunity to invest your knowledge and skills in any organization you want, and you can choose to withdraw it from one organization and invest it elsewhere if better returns are offered. In today's highly competitive world, you are a valuable resource for organizations. If you manage your career right, you will be in demand, and organizations will vie for your services more than they vie for investment dollars. In fact, the more you improve your skills and knowledge and invest in your personal development, the more you can build your own personal virtuous spiral of career success. Figure 1.2 depicts the type of virtuous spiral that you can create. It shows that increased skills and performance can lead to better jobs and higher rewards.

Exhibit 1.1. Seven Principles for Treating People Right and Creating a Virtuous Spiral.

---

1. Attraction and Retention
Organizations must create a value proposition that defines the type of workplace they want to be so that they can attract and retain the right people.

2. Hiring Practices
Organizations must hire people who fit with their values, core competencies, and strategic goals.

3. Training and Development
Organizations must continuously train employees to do their jobs and offer them opportunities to grow and develop.

4. Work Design
Organizations must design work so that it is meaningful for people and provides them with feedback, responsibility, and autonomy.

5. Mission, Strategies, and Goals
Organizations must develop and adhere to a specific organizational mission, with strategies, goals, and values that employees can understand, support, and believe in.

6. Reward Systems
Organizations must devise and implement reward systems that reinforce their design, core values, and strategy.

7. Leadership
Organizations must hire and develop leaders who can create commitment, trust, success, and a motivating work environment.

Figure 1.2. Virtuous Career Spiral.

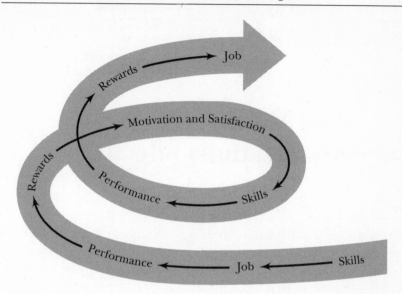

For you to have the best opportunity to develop a virtuous career spiral, your organization needs to be in a virtuous spiral. Organizations cannot thrive unless their people prosper, but at the same time, people cannot thrive unless their organizations prosper. Although Figures 1.1 and 1.2 show separate spirals for organizations and individuals, in practice they are intertwined. They depend on each other and feed off each other.

This suggests that you too need to continuously increase your commitment, dedication, and value to any organization you work for. With the death of the loyalty contract, however, you must also behave and think as a free agent, because no matter where you work, your organization may not be able to keep you employed indefinitely. You need to learn how to negotiate for what you want while getting it because of what you can offer.

As we review each of the seven principles of treating people right, I will provide the specifics of how each principle can affect your career.

Chapter Two

What Makes Organizations Effective

In order for organizations to design systems and practices that serve as a foundation for treating people right, they first need to know what factors contribute to organizational effectiveness. It makes no sense to develop and implement management practices if those practices do not ultimately improve your organization's performance and results.

To help you understand the complexities of organizational effectiveness, I have developed a model I call the Diamond Model that identifies the key factors that determine organizational effectiveness (see Figure 2.1). The Diamond Model establishes four fundamental determinants of organizational effectiveness—strategy, organizational capabilities, core competencies, and the environment. They anchor the four corners of the diamond. Inside the diamond are four elements of organization design—people, structure, rewards, and processes—that are shaped by the four determinants of effectiveness. The more tightly these elements fit with the four corners of the diamond and each other, the stronger the diamond will be, which is to say, the more effective the organization will be.

Strategy: The Leading Edge

Strategy identifies what must be done in order for an organization to be successful. It refers to the master plan that the organization establishes for all aspects of its existence: its goals, purpose, prod-

Figure 2.1. The Diamond Model of Organizational Effectiveness.

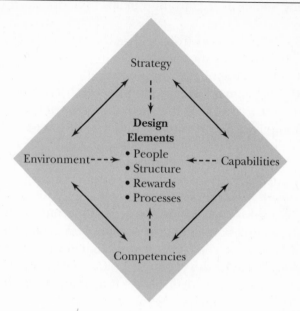

ucts and services, business model, structural design, and so on. Strategy is about what the organization does, as well as why and how it expects to win with its business model. A complete strategy for an organization needs to cover five points:[1]

1. Where the organization will be active—what type of products and services it will offer, what markets it will serve
2. How it will operate—where it will develop or get its products and services
3. How it will win—what its competitive advantage will be
4. What its moves will be—how it will change and grow
5. How it will be profitable—what business model it will follow

Strategy cannot be formulated in a vacuum. The organization must consider its competencies, capabilities, and the environment—the other three corners of the Diamond Model. These factors inform an organization about what challenges it faces and what resources it has that will help it compete and change. Effective strategy formulation involves not just assessing the existing conditions but also recognizing what the organization needs to do to be successful in the future.

Of course, no matter how brilliant a strategy is, it is only as effective as the organization's ability to implement it. Many more strategies fail because of poor implementation than because they are flawed. In fact, many organizations develop strategies that they cannot implement because they lack the organizational capabilities and competencies that are needed to implement it.

For example, a very common mistake occurs when organizations decide to move into a new business area without an accurate assessment of their resources or their strengths and weaknesses. This happened to a number of traditional companies that tried to start doing business on the Internet. Many struggled and failed because they didn't have people with expertise in the on-line arena or the right reward systems to attract the talent needed to operate Internet businesses or the capability to deliver the quality of customer service that was needed. These companies experienced poor execution of their strategies because they failed to match their strategic goals to their ability to execute their strategies.

Traditionally, most organizations have formulated strategy only at the top, relying on their senior leadership. However, in my view, this does not have to be so, nor should it be so. In fact, many organizations are now opening up the strategy formulation process to include multilevel employee involvement.

Regardless of how many people are involved in strategy formulation, it is critical that organizations develop practices that help all employees understand that strategy, especially in terms of how they are supposed to perform their jobs. In fact, the greater the understanding of strategy among employees, the less hierarchical structure an organization needs, and the greater the potential for individuals throughout the company to become leaders.

Organizational Capabilities

The second corner of the Diamond Model of effectiveness is organizational capabilities. To be successful, organizations must have capabilities that allow them to coordinate and focus their behavior in order to produce the levels and types of performance that their strategy requires.

Organizational capabilities are not amorphous; they are clearly identifiable kinds of performance. For example, capabilities include the ability to focus on quality, operate on a global basis, be a low-cost operator, manage knowledge, develop new knowledge, respond quickly to the business environment, speed products to market, focus on customers,—and do many other things that provide organizations with a competitive advantage.

Organizational success today frequently requires not just a single world-class organizational capability but a combination of several. It may take two or three that are exceptional and a number of others that are at least at a world-class level.

One of the important points to remember about organizational capabilities is that they do not exist in only one practice or place, in the heads of a few technology gurus, or in a small set of patents. In reality, they reside in the many systems and relationships that exist in an organization. They lie in a synergistic combination of individuals and systems that combine to form the organization's way of operating. Because they are embedded in a complex matrix of practices and systems, they are hard to develop, duplicate, and copy.

Consider 3M, which for decades has been a prime example of a company that is able to innovate. Much of the company's success and growth over the years has to do with its organizational capability to create, develop, and market new products, such as Scotch tape, Post-it notes, and thousands of other products.

The reasons for 3M's capability to innovate go far beyond the company's technical expertise in the chemical properties of materials. It results from a range of companywide systems, practices, and structures. One very specific behavior that 3M has fostered is experimentation. The company has developed a number of policies and practices that give employees time to experiment, and its reward system recognizes innovative work.

Most people who visit 3M to study how it maintains such an outstanding record of innovation have the same reaction: what 3M does cannot be duplicated in most other companies. They correctly recognize that 3M's organizational capability to innovate does not rest in a single or limited set of practices that other organizations can easily copy.

Motorola also developed an important capability that is not easily copied, though many companies are trying to imitate it and an increasing number are succeeding. Motorola's Six Sigma quality capability represents the product of all of its systems and structures, including its employee selection process, training programs, corporate vision statement, and senior management's behavior. It is not based on any one system or practice but permeates the organization. The capability was developed as an integral part of Motorola's corporate strategy, making it difficult to copy and giving the company a competitive advantage.

Once the company recognized its value, Motorola began selling its Six Sigma capability. It offered training programs through Motorola University and sold written materials. It found a number of buyers, including GE, which ended up developing a successful Six Sigma capability of its own.

Maintaining Capabilities

Another important point about capabilities is that they require ongoing attention and maintenance. Motorola, for one, learned this the hard way. During the late 1990s, the company decreased its focus on its Six Sigma quality program and as a result fell behind the competition in several of its key businesses, including cell phones and semiconductors.

Ford Motor Company has also mismanaged its quality capability through lack of attention. Starting in the 1970s, it invested heavily in building a quality capability and enjoyed some success. Do you remember, "Quality Is Job One"? When it acquired Jaguar, it successfully transferred its quality knowledge to Jaguar, with impressive gains. Jaguar's quality improved so much that it went from being just ahead of the Yugo, considered the world's worst car in quality during the 1980s and early 1990s, to being one of the top cars in the world in terms of manufacturing quality.

However, while Ford was successfully transferring its quality capability to its newly acquired Jaguar subsidiary, it lost much of its quality capability in its U.S. manufacturing operations. What happened in the United States? Essentially, Ford took its eye off the ball. Like Motorola, it failed to maintain a focus on its quality capability, and as a result, quality deteriorated in its U.S. manufacturing and design facilities.

Importance of the Ability to Change

Today, the ability to change rapidly is perhaps the most critical capability for organizations to have. Being able to alter strategies and capabilities quickly enables organizations to stay ahead of their competitors and meet the increasingly higher performance standards that today's unpredictable environment demands.

Admittedly, the capability to change can be very difficult to develop and maintain. One reason is that major organizational change often requires changes in human capital, either in the workforce's skills or careers. Another challenge is that sometimes the change must be far more dramatic than the organization is prepared to accept, such as developing a new capability or core competency. For example, it is not easy to go from a company that has had generous budgets to one that is a low-cost producer. But even when the change is subtler, it still can be challenging for an organization to continually be ready and able to change.

Creating an organization that has a change capability requires that it be designed with change clearly in mind. The organization must have people who like to learn and are willing to try new things, structures that can be easily adapted and modified, and reward systems that reward growth and the development of new skills. Finally, the organization must also have budgeting and other processes that support innovation and the start-up of new products and services.

In sum, organizations today need to be "change-ready" and, I would add, capable of high-velocity change. They need to be able to alter their capabilities and core competencies whenever they are forced to develop new strategies in response to the environment. Finally, the most effective and successful corporations are often those that are able to develop new capabilities while maintaining their existing ones.

Core Competencies

Core competencies are crucial to organizational effectiveness and are the third corner of my Diamond Model. In their influential 1990 *Harvard Business Review* article, Gary Hamel and C. K. Prahalad defined core competencies as a combination of technology and production skills that underlie the product lines and services of an organization.[2]

Consider Sony. Sony's core competency lies in miniaturization technology, which allows the company to make the Walkman, video cameras, notebook computers, and a host of other products. Similarly, Honda's ability to produce gasoline engines is crucial to its success in selling motorcycles, lawn mowers, outboard motors, and automobiles. 3M's core competency in understanding chemical processes and materials has helped the company develop a wide range of products from ordinary tape to exotic bonding materials for the aerospace industry.

Getting the Most from Your Core Competencies

Like capabilities, core competencies need to be an integral part of a company's strategy. Organizations need to know what their core competencies are when they develop their strategy. It is much easier to create new products and services when they make use of existing competencies. To properly implement strategies that require mastering new core competencies is often difficult but can pay large dividends if it leads to innovative products that are hard to duplicate.

How long an organization can derive a competitive advantage from its core competencies depends on where these competencies are and how easy they are to copy. For example, anyone can easily duplicate core competencies that are contained in the minds and skills of a small number of employees. These core competencies walk out the door every night, and when they are not treated right, they may not come back.

Xerox once had a significant technological lead in the personal computer business. It developed the first office PC. However, it lacked the organizational capabilities to capitalize on its technological core competencies, and as a result, it is not in the computer business today. Apple, by contrast, still is because it obtained key competencies by hiring the people from Xerox's Palo Alto, California, research facility who developed the software operating system for Xerox's innovative personal computer, Star. They helped develop Apple's core competency in computer design.

Of course, employees may also leave on their own and take core competencies with them in order to start their own businesses. One of the most dramatic examples of this occurred with Fairchild Electronics, which in the 1970s pioneered the development and production of semiconductors.

Fairchild had a high level of technological competency but a well deserved bad reputation when it came to the way it managed and treated employees. This made it difficult for Fairchild to maintain its technological advantage. The pioneering development work it did on semiconductors was lost. Employee after employee simply took the knowledge that was part of Fairchild's core competency in semiconductors when they left and used it to start competing businesses that were better managed. The new companies—Intel, AMD, and others—are now among the most successful semiconductor firms in the world today, while Fairchild is out of business.

Finally, sometimes new technologies come along that make a company's core competencies obsolete. The Polaroid Corporation is a classic example of an organization that was never able to change its competencies to adapt to new market conditions. It does not appear that Polaroid's problem was a lack of awareness that its chemical-based instant photography products were rapidly becoming obsolete. In fact, Polaroid frequently issued statements saying that the company was changing its business strategy and moving to electronic still photography. Instead, Polaroid's problem was transferring its strategy into action.

Not only did it lose out in instant still photography, but just when Polaroid created instant movie film, a truly impressive accomplishment, Sony and others began selling video cameras. Polaroid's instant movie film quickly became a museum piece.

Beyond Technology Competency

In the twenty-first century, there is no doubt that it is essential to acquire, develop, and protect core technological competencies. One key to this is definitely treating people right. But I advise you not to overlook the fact that technology is neither sufficient by itself for success nor necessarily the best source of a sustainable competitive advantage. Organizations also need organizational capabilities oriented toward understanding their customers and speeding technology to market with the best possible quality at a reasonable cost. This is precisely why the Diamond Model shows that organizational effectiveness requires both the right competencies and the right capabilities.

The Environment

Environment is in the fourth corner of the Diamond Model of organizational effectiveness. A number of environmental issues are critical determinants of an organization's performance, including the business climate, the condition of the economy, the availability of human capital, the development of new technology, the political environment, and the physical environment. These features of the environment all need to be taken into account when organizations set out to formulate their strategy and develop their competencies and capabilities.

In some cases, environmental factors are givens, and there is little an organization can do except develop a strategy that takes them into account. In other situations, organizations can change the environment, and this may need to be part of their business strategy.

Let me discuss the major environmental factors individually, starting with the business environment, which can have a major impact on the effectiveness of an organization. In formulating strategy, organizations need to consider both what their competitors will do and what demand will exist for their products and services. I have seen many seemingly excellent strategies fail because management makes erroneous assumptions about its business environment.

In the 1990s, a number of companies believed there was going to be worldwide explosive growth in the market for fiber optic and broadband communication technology. This led Corning, for one, to completely change its business model so that it focused on fiber optics rather than its wide variety of traditional glass products. Similarly, it led Nortel and Lucent to project dramatic growth in the sales of Internet communications equipment. When the expected growth did not materialize, the financial performance of these companies suffered tremendously. They went from being leading performers to posting enormous financial losses.

A second environmental factor is the condition of the general economy. It must play a critical role in how organizations implement their strategies and what types of business performance they commit to achieving. A rising economy calls for very different actions than a declining one does.

For instance, when the economy is in a growth mode, a common obstacle that interferes with even the best strategies is that the right people cannot be found to develop or expand an organization's competencies and capabilities. However, in a declining economy, the issue is often how to protect the organization's existing competencies and capabilities. And when the economic environment is wavering between up and down, it can be challenging to determine what changes to make in a strategy.

The availability of qualified human capital is yet another element of the environment that must be considered. If an organization develops a strategy but the human capital necessary to develop and maintain the right mix of core competencies and organizational capabilities is not available, the strategy is clearly dead in the water. This is why organizations need to realistically assess their environment before developing expectations about what additional human capital they can attract and retain.

One point to keep in mind is that you can attract particular kinds of human capital only if they exist. This might seem like an obvious point, but it is often overlooked. For example, if schools are not turning out engineering graduates in a particular area of expertise, it does little good for organizations to open up jobs for such engineers or to have a strategy that calls for developing a core competency that requires this type of expertise.

In my view, organizations need to become actively involved in shaping their human capital environment to ensure themselves the kind of talent they need to succeed. For example, they can approach universities and prod them to produce the type of talent needed for the products and services they offer.

In fact, many employees lack an understanding of the basic economics of business, as well as problem-solving, group process, and decision-making skills. These are usually not skills that students learn in most K–12 educational settings. As a result, companies need to encourage schools to build more self-management skills training into their curriculum and more education that focuses on economics and on how businesses operate.

One way that organizations can find the skilled people they need is to take a global perspective. Some skills are simply more available in certain countries than in others. Those organizations that are willing and able to move their work to where the skills are can increase their strategic options as well as their performance. Indeed, one implication of globalization is that people are increasingly competing for work in a worldwide labor market. There is often tough competition from people in other countries who will work for less money or who have better skills.

Another environmental force to consider, perhaps one of the most powerful in the past half-century, is technological change. Entire industries have been altered, eliminated, or created because of the invention of new technologies. Semiconductors have replaced vacuum tubes; cell phones are everywhere; Internet equipment manufacturing has become a major industry. Other examples of technological change abound, but the point is clear: an organization's business strategy must articulate well with whatever technology exists in the environment. In fact, an organization's strategy must be able to change at least as fast as the underlying technology changes. In the best-case scenario, organizations should anticipate technology changes before they happen.

An additional environmental issue that affects organizations is the political situation and the legislative rules that affect how they can do business. A new wrinkle is the growing importance of global political changes. More and more companies operate in multiple countries, and so they need to take into account a variety of legal and political circumstances when putting together marketing, manufacturing, and product development strategies.

One last environmental element that cannot be neglected when formulating a business strategy is the physical environment—climate, location, natural resources, and the transportation and communications infrastructures in an area. Organizations should plan for the likelihood and potential impact that a natural disaster could have on them. Fires, earthquakes, and floods can severely disrupt a corporation's business. Of course, today organizations also need to account for any impact they themselves have on their physical environment. There is a growing focus in many countries on the effects that businesses have on the environment, from pollution and traffic to the health of their employees.

As you can see, the environment can have an impact on an organization's effectiveness in a multitude of ways. The performance of most organizations can benefit from proactive planning and in some cases active environmental management. The environment should be treated as a critical determinant of a company's business strategy. Companies should also be prepared to change in response to it. Indeed, given the difficulty in predicting change, more and more companies are focusing on responding quickly to change rather than trying to predict what changes will occur.

Organization Design Elements

As noted earlier, the interior of the Diamond Model contains four organizational design elements whose interactions give the diamond strength. How an organization implements and manages these elements determines whether it can develop the competencies and capabilities it needs to execute its strategy and successfully compete in its environment. Here is an overview of these four design elements; they will be discussed further throughout the rest of this book.

People

Organizations must be staffed with people who perform at high levels. I am going to discuss the factors that make people high performers in Chapter Three, but for now, a good starting point is an equation that I learned when I first studied psychology:

$$\text{Performance} = \text{ability} \times \text{motivation}$$

In this equation, both ability and motivation can vary from 0 to 100 percent of the amount needed to perform effectively. As a result, high levels of individual performance only occur when people have the right knowledge, skills, and competencies and are motivated to perform well. Achieving this requires well-designed human resource management systems, as well as well-designed jobs and work processes.

Structure

Structure is a second element of design that organizations must focus on in implementing their strategy. Structure refers to how people are grouped together, including who reports to whom, how tasks are assigned, and the nature of the jobs within the organization. Even if an organization does not have a formal hierarchy, reporting structure, or traditional job descriptions, it must still determine how to group people together, how major decisions are made, how many levels of management are needed, and a variety of other structural issues. These determinations must be closely aligned with the organization's overall strategy. These decisions significantly influence the kinds of people the organization needs to attract, so people and structure must be looked at together.

Rewards

Another important element of an organization's design is its reward system. How the organization compensates its people must fit closely with its overall strategy, in terms of the types of people it needs to attract and motivate and in terms of the methods it uses to reward employee behaviors. The reward system must be designed with a solid knowledge of how people are motivated, what rewards make them work harder and smarter, and what types of rewards are required to get the right people to join and stay with an organization. We will discuss the psychology of rewards in greater detail in Chapter Three, but for now keep in mind that people differ greatly in the rewards they value, so an organization's reward strategy is often a complex piece of the puzzle.

Processes

Processes refer to the management systems that an organization puts into place to control, manage, inform, and direct its members' behavior, both individually and collectively. Management processes include information and communication systems, budgeting and financial measurement systems, and the behavior of managers, particularly those involved in decision making and setting direction for the organization. An organization must design these processes (or revise the processes it already has) so that they support the strategy and fit with the other three elements—people, structure, and rewards.

Organizational Culture and Effectiveness

The organization design elements of people, structure, rewards, and processes lead us to another important characteristic of organizations: corporate culture. To a large extent, culture results from the confluence of all these elements. It can have a significant impact on an organization's effectiveness and potential performance. Culture consists of what people in an organization think they should do, how they believe they should perform, and what they think will be rewarded.

It can be very helpful to analyze an organization's culture, particularly in regard to how the culture supports the corners on the Diamond Model. For example, we can ask questions such as these: Does the culture value the behaviors needed to implement the strategy? What is the relationship of the organization's culture to its capabilities? Does the culture value developing the skills needed to support the organization's competencies? Does the culture attract the right employees? Is the culture a good fit with the environment?

Once we understand these facets of an organization's culture, we can begin to figure out how to change the culture to enhance organizational effectiveness. However, you need to be aware than organizations cannot directly control their culture to the same extent that they can manage the four design elements. Culture can be influenced by altering the design elements of people, structure, rewards, and processes, but it is not hard-wired to them.

The importance of an organization's culture cannot be underestimated. Many organizations have failed to perform effectively over time because of dysfunctional cultures. One common problem occurs when people sign up to work in an existing culture and then resist the changes required to create a culture that fits a new strategy.

Fit and Performance

My goal in this chapter has been to provide a model to help you understand the basic elements of effective organizations. Treating people right is meaningful and in the long term possible only in the context of creating a high-performing organization. To treat people right, organizations must prosper. Success requires a tight fit among the four elements of strategy, capabilities, competencies, and environment. If they are not aligned and supported by the right organization design elements, it is impossible for the organization to enjoy a virtuous spiral of success. Thus the focus in Part Two will be on organization design practices that treat people right and create a fit among them.

| **What Makes People Effective**

Now that we have focused on what makes organizations effective, we are ready to consider what makes people effective contributors to organizational performance. After all, if organizations are going to treat people right, they need to know what motivates them and what determines how well they can perform. A virtuous spiral can exist only if people are willing and able to take responsibility for providing the upward momentum.

The fact is, people influence all the important aspects of organizational performance in one way or another. People conceive and implement the strategy. An organization's capabilities are contained in the mix of its people and its systems. Competencies are primarily a function of the skills and knowledge of an organization's human capital. And a major feature of the environment is its ability to supply qualified high performers who can implement strategy.

In short, organizations can accomplish little without capable people. To be successful, they must commit themselves to attracting, retaining, and motivating the best and the brightest.

But who are the best and the brightest? What makes some people capable of performing at high levels while others do not? What motivates people to perform well and be committed to organizations?

Answering these questions requires us to delve briefly into the psychological literature on motivation and performance capability. There are numerous conflicting theories that attempt to explain why people make certain choices concerning their work, why they seek particular rewards, and why they are satisfied or dissatisfied with their work and rewards. But there are also some commonly accepted truths.

I will summarize what most modern researchers in psychology and human resources generally accept about motivation and the development of knowledge, skills, abilities, and personality. Some academic researchers, like myself, have written entire books on the topics I will cover in this chapter. By summarizing, I run the risks of being accused of oversimplifying a complex topic and of falling completely out of favor with my academic colleagues.

I think they are risks worth taking. While not every theorist will endorse my summary, I believe it represents a useful and valid overview of the thousands of research studies available. I am also confident that it can help you understand the causes of human performance so that your organization can design strategies, structures, rewards, and processes that treat people right and contribute to creating a virtuous spiral.

The Causes of Performance

As noted in Chapter Two, people's performance is captured by the equation

$$\text{Performance} = \text{motivation} \times \text{ability}$$

Of course, this equation oversimplifies some very complex issues, but it reinforces a fundamental truth that performance depends on two factors, not one. People need both motivation and ability. Highly motivated workers will not achieve results if they do not have the skills, expertise, and personality the organization needs. Similarly, expertise, knowledge, and skills will not produce great results if employees are unmotivated.

That being true, we need to explore each of these factors to understand what makes for effective, high-performing people.

People and Motivation

The most widely accepted explanation of why people are motivated to work and perform is rooted in what psychologists call expectancy theory.[1] Expectancy theory argues that people are mostly rational decision makers who think about their actions and act in ways that satisfy their needs and help them reach their goals. The theory recognizes that we sometimes have misperceptions about reality, make mistakes in our assessment of the likelihood that something might happen, and badly misread situations.

But overall, the core of the theory states that people generally try to deal rationally with the world as they see it and to direct their behavior in productive ways. The theory views people as proactive, future-oriented, and motivated to behave in ways that they believe will lead to valued rewards.

Expectancy theory is popular because it is useful for understanding how people are motivated in many aspects of their lives, including relationships, family, and work. The theory accepts the view that there are large differences among people in their needs and as a result in the importance they attach to rewards.

As the name implies, expectancy theory points to the fact that people are motivated by the promise of rewards. This has not escaped the attention of most organizations and managers. They constantly experiment with offering a wide range of rewards in the hope of finding those that motivate employees the most.

In fact, the rewards offered by corporations in recent years have become truly diverse, if not downright amusing. In addition to the usual ho-hum rewards of interesting work, recognition, fringe benefits, cash, stock options, and big offices, some corporations have given out private rodeos with mechanical bulls, fly fishing on western ranches, flights in a fighter plane, river rafting, sabbaticals, forty-two different free drinks, and a lifetime supply of Ben and Jerry's ice cream. The book *1001 Ways to Reward Employees* even became a best-seller in the 1990s.[2]

Which rewards truly matter when it comes to motivating performance? That depends on reward attractiveness, which is a large discussion in itself.

What Makes a Reward Attractive?

Research has shown that the attractiveness of a reward depends on at least two major determinants: (1) how much of it is being offered and (2) how much the individual values the particular type of reward being offered. The more an individual values the type of reward and the more of it that it is offered, the more motivational potential there is.

If you live in a state with a lottery, you can readily understand what I mean about the amount of a reward being a significant factor. Think about what happens when your state lottery prize goes up. A $100 million payoff attracts many more players than a $1 million payoff. When the prize is big enough, a surprising number of people are willing to endure traffic jams and standing in line for hours just for a minuscule chance to be the next big winner.

Regarding the second determinant of attractiveness, research shows that the perceived value of a reward is related to a person's needs. The noted psychologist Abraham Maslow, whose theories are still well accepted, established that most of us have the same basic needs and that these arrange themselves into a hierarchy of importance. At the bottom, we all have fundamental physiological survival needs (food, water, shelter, security), followed by the need for social interaction, then respect from others, then self-esteem, and finally a need for personal growth and development.[3]

People's feelings of satisfaction or dissatisfaction are largely the result of the rewards they receive. The more dissatisfaction people feel with respect to a given need, the greater the importance they place on rewards that satisfy that need. As a need becomes satisfied, it tends to weaken. For example, people seem to need only so much food, water, and social interaction. However, the same may not be true at the highest level of needs: self-development. The more people experience it, the more they want of it.

According to Maslow, people first aim to satisfy their most basic, lowest-level needs for security, food, and water. Only after they satisfy them are the needs higher up in the hierarchy (social interaction, esteem, personal development) likely to come into play.

Satisfying needs is a constant. When one need is partially or fully satisfied, it is replaced by a new need, so people always want to obtain rewards. They may want more of a reward to satisfy the same need or one that satisfies a newly important need. This reality means that in order to experience a virtuous career spiral, people need to receive more of certain rewards and to receive new kinds of rewards over the course of their careers.

I need to mention that Maslow's theory does not include a need for spirituality and meaning in one's life. The closest he came to this was his statement about the need for personal growth and development. However, recent thinking suggests that the neglect of spirituality is a significant oversight in Maslow's work. It seems clear that many people want to understand their life experiences in the context of a supreme deity or another set of beliefs about their lives and that these beliefs are an important determinant of their behavior.

Intrinsic rewards count too. Maslow's higher-level needs remind us that people can also give themselves rewards in the form of self-esteem as well as feelings of achievement and growth. Individuals can literally reward themselves for certain kinds of behavior because they feel they have accomplished something worthwhile, achieved a personal goal, learned a new skill, or experienced excitement or intellectual stimulation.

Furthermore, there does not seem to be any canceling out or interference effect between intrinsic rewards and key extrinsic rewards such as money. That is to say, if performance is tied to extrinsic rewards, as in a pay-for-performance plan, any intrinsic rewards individuals may give themselves for performing well will *not* disappear. In fact, it seems that the greatest amount of motivation is present when people perform tasks that are both extrinsically and intrinsically rewarding. This argues for designing organizations in which high performance leads to both types of rewards.

Two Other Factors Affecting Reward Attractiveness

In addition to Maslow's hierarchy of needs, several other factors seem to influence how strongly a person is attracted to a reward. Two of these are the environmental and cultural conditions that color an individual's experience.

Maslow did not focus on the ability of external stimulation to increase the strength of needs. However, there is good reason to believe that one's environment, at least temporarily, can have a strong influence on the attractiveness of a reward. Just as the smell of food can stimulate the desire for food and viewing attractive pictures of the opposite sex can increase the desire for a relationship or for sex, watching somebody achieve something significant or talking about achievement can increase the need for achievement. This explains in large part the success of "motivational speakers" who are able to stimulate people's desire to develop and achieve.

Cultural conditioning can also play a role in determining the attractiveness of rewards. That is why international companies have learned that they may need to use different reward systems in the various countries in which they have employees. The same reward systems that work for American workers are not necessarily respected or appreciated by non-American workers because their cultural upbringing is infused with different values. As a result, workers in different countries may view a reward that is highly valued by most Americans (such as tickets to a sports event or a company golf outing) as not particularly attractive, preferring a reward that fits their culture (for example, a day off or a plaque of honor).

Gender and Age in Connection with Reward Attractiveness

Finally, research shows that gender, age, and maturity can also be factors in determining the strength of people's needs. A whole industry has grown up around studying the importance that people of various ages place on different kinds of rewards. There are an ever-increasing plethora of research reports that attempt to explain how generations differ in what they value.

For instance, some studies have claimed that the members of Generations X and Y are different from baby boomers in what they value and appreciate. In my view, such differences exist, but they are minor. In analyzing any generation, it seems more accurate to say that the differences between generations are less important than the similarities among them. You should also remember that people who are in their fifties and sixties are different from those in their twenties not necessarily because they grew up in different eras but because aging simply changes people and their needs.

Large Individual Differences

Perhaps the best general conclusion that can be reached about how people value rewards is that organizations must recognize that tremendous individual differences exist. These differences are the result of their environment, culture, age, generation, and many other factors. This explains why different people attach different degrees of importance to rewards such as money, recognition from a supervisor, and a ride on a mechanical bull.

The importance of individual differences should not escape those in organizations who design reward systems. When it comes to rewards, a manager who wishes to respond accurately to what his or her employees value must take individual differences into account. This is particularly true when the workforce is diverse and global or when different kinds of employment relationships exist within the organization, such as temporary workers versus key technical "hot talent."

Why Not Just Ask?

The most obvious way to find out what people want would seem to be simply to ask them what rewards they value. And indeed, many companies administer surveys that do just that.

Unfortunately, people's answers to questions assessing reward importance are often misleading. For a variety of reasons, it is difficult for most people to state what is important to them.

First, they may not know themselves well enough to respond accurately. Often they do not know how they will feel about something until they have experienced it.

Second, in some cases, social desirability, peer pressure, and modesty can prevent people from reporting their feelings accurately. This is particularly true in discussing money. In many societies and organizations, it simply does not make a good impression to admit, "I work for the money." As a result, people sometimes understate its true importance to them. Some employees also fudge their answers because they are trying to send a self-serving or self-enhancing message to the organization.

Another reason that surveys aren't good indicators is that they usually obtain different results depending just on the wording used in the questions. For example, studies that ask about the importance of "fair pay" often confirm that pay is indeed rated as one of the most important features of jobs, if not the most important one. However, studies that ask about the importance of "getting rich" or having "high pay" often report that the importance of pay is less than the importance of career opportunities, the challenge that a job offers, and other features of work.

Recent research by three of my colleagues from the University of Southern California illustrates that serious incongruities can arise in using surveys to assess what people truly value. It also highlights the point that people are complex. Whatever they may say about the importance of various rewards found in the workplace, their behavior at work, commitment, and willingness to stay with a company (called retention) often prove otherwise.

In a study of knowledge workers in a variety of American companies, my colleagues Susan Mohrman, David Finegold, and Gretchen Spreitzer asked about the importance of a variety of factors.[4] As you might expect, there were clear age differences in the answers. For example, career advancement was much more important to people under thirty years of age than it was for employees over fifty. They found one strong point of agreement among all age groups, however: all said that work-life balance was the most important feature of the workplace to them.

Despite this answer, there was very little correlation between satisfaction with work-life balance and the indicators of employee commitment and retention. Workers who said they were satisfied with their work-life balance often had high levels of turnover. Actually, the best predictor of retention for the under-thirty crowd was satisfaction with career advancement. In second place was satisfaction with pay for organizational performance. Satisfaction with pay for performance also showed up as a strong predictor of commitment to the organization even though it was not rated as highly important. Job security was highly rated, but people who were satisfied with their job security did not show higher levels of either retention or commitment.

Finally, there was little relationship between age and what type of satisfaction best predicted retention and commitment; it was the same for all age groups. This, of course, supports my argument that generational differences are often given more importance than they deserve. Overall, the data for all age groups clearly reinforce the idea that what individuals say about reward importance is often not a good predictor of critical behaviors such as remaining with an organization and behaving in a committed way.

I highly recommend that you avoid acting on the latest study that touts a specific reward as the most important. Whether it identifies pay, career, family time, interesting work, or having a good boss, most of this research suffers from fatal methodological problems and should not be taken seriously. Problems with the ability of people to accurately report on what is important to them also argues against taking seriously studies that attempt to rank the importance of such working conditions as supportive supervision, interesting work, high pay, job security, and development opportunities. You will be better off if you simply accept that these rewards are likely to be important to most individuals, but not all, and that their attractiveness to particular individuals is likely to change over time.

What Determines Satisfaction

As mentioned earlier, a reward is more attractive when there is more of it. The quantity of a reward is also a key factor in determining whether people are satisfied with the rewards they receive. As you might imagine, the general rule is, the more of a reward people receive, the more satisfied they are.

However, some funny quirks of human nature come into play here. People can be unpredictable and change rapidly when it comes to being satisfied with their rewards. For example, a basketball player who signs a record-setting contract of x million dollars may be very satisfied until another player signs one for $x + y$ million dollars. Suddenly, x million does not look as good.

A key aspect of satisfaction is how a reward amount compares to a hypothetical "standard" that people develop in their mind about what amount is fair. If their reward amount meets that standard, they are satisfied; if it falls short, they are dissatisfied and look for ways to increase the amount.

On the few occasions when a reward exceeds their standard, people can even end up feeling guilty about being overrewarded. However, it appears that feelings of being overrewarded are short-lived. People seem to quickly rationalize the excess and decide that they are in fact fairly rewarded or even underrewarded.

On rare occasions when even after reflection, people still feel overrewarded, they may actually reduce their reward level by declining rewards or giving them away. But the important point to keep in mind is that when individuals feel underrewarded, they try to obtain additional rewards and to improve their situation, thus reducing their feelings of dissatisfaction.

Rational and Irrational Comparisons

How can organizations understand and assess the standards against which their employees measure rewards? The answer comes from research indicating that people set up standards by comparing what others who are similar to them receive. These "similar others" are selected according to a variety of factors: performance, training, background, and other personal characteristics. For comparison purposes, people are likely to choose the characteristics of themselves that they think are particularly outstanding and to think that these same characteristics should be the basis on which they are rewarded.

For example, if they are well educated, they compare themselves to people with similar education levels, and they think that education should be a major criterion in determining reward levels. If they perceive themselves to be high performers, as most do, they tend to compare their rewards with the rewards of other high performers and of course are strong advocates of basing rewards on performance.

The reward comparisons that individuals make can sometimes be irrational, especially as they move up the chain of command. For example, executives who are highly paid compared to others in their organization often look outside at other organizations for their comparisons in order to find people who are paid more. And if they can't find other executives who are paid more, they look elsewhere. I have heard CEOs compare their reward levels to those of star athletes and entertainers. Time and time again, I have heard CEOs and senior executives say, "Well, I'm worth at least as much as Michael Jordan or Tom Cruise."

To say the least, this is an apples and oranges comparison. A more valid comparison would be to contrast their pay with that of Michael Jordan's coach when he was a player with the Bulls or with that of the president of the Bulls or with that of Tom Cruise's business manager. These would be much better comparisons from a work content and skills perspective. These lower-paid individuals are doing administrative, leadership, and coaching activities that are more similar to what CEOs do than what Jordan and Cruise do. But the reason CEOs and other executives often compare themselves to Jordan and Cruise is not because of the similarity of their work or skills but because they are using "high rates of compensation" as their comparison factor.

Even though some individuals make irrational comparisons, not all do. Production workers typically do not compare themselves with CEOs, and sales representatives typically do not compare themselves with vice presidents of human resources. It is perfectly possible to find sales representatives and production workers who are just as satisfied with their rewards as CEOs and vice presidents of human resources are, even though they are paid much less. Because of this, it is very possible for organizations to satisfy most, if not all, of their employees if they treat them right.

The Perception of Fairness

Another factor that influences whether people are satisfied with their rewards has to do with the perceived fairness of the method of distribution. It is difficult to state exactly what makes people believe that "procedural justice" in reward distribution has occurred, but several factors usually contribute to the perception of fairness and feelings of satisfaction.

First, openness about the decision-making process is one way to build trust and a perception of a fair process. A second key is believing that the "right" individuals were involved in the decision-making process. The process must include people who are viewed as trustworthy and who have integrity and valid information on which to make reward distribution decisions. Third, reward distribution is more likely to be seen as fair when clear criteria are stated in advance and are used for the distribution. Fourth, people are more likely to feel fairly treated when they have had a chance to participate in the decision-making process. And finally, fairness is more likely when an appeal process exists that allows individuals to safely challenge decisions that they think were unfair, uninformed, or unreasonable.

How to Make Rewards Motivate Performance

Now that you understand how people value rewards and what makes them satisfied, the next issue we need to tackle is how rewards actually motivate people to perform well.

Expectancy theory points to the fact that the promise of future rewards is what motivates people to behave in ways that support an organization's business strategy and performance needs. As a result, a critical issue in developing a virtuous spiral is the need to establish what is often called a clear *line of sight*. This means that organizations must clearly make a connection between the promise of a reward and the behavior required to obtain it.

I prefer to think of this as a *line of influence* because it highlights the fact that to be motivated in a work situation, people must see how their behavior influences a performance measure that in turn drives the allocation of a reward, or rewards, they value.

Whichever term we use, the concept is simple: if people see valued rewards as being tied to a particular performance or behavior, the organization is likely to get more of that behavior. The complement is equally true: if a particular behavior is not rewarded, the organization is likely to get less of it.

Expectancy theory also helps explain people's job choices. In fact, it is particularly useful because it leads to another simple conclusion: people choose to join and remain members of organizations that offer them the best mix of the rewards they value.

Given this conclusion, the issue of attracting and retaining employees becomes quite straightforward and can be reduced to a simple principle: Organizations that offer a very attractive mix of rewards will find that many individuals want to work for them. This explains why organizations that create virtuous spirals can increasingly attract and retain the people they need.

Becoming an Observer of Behavior

An important implication of what we have said so far about motivation is that there is much to learn by looking at people's behavior concerning rewards. The skillful manager needs to be a careful observer of how individuals respond to the opportunity to receive various rewards. By watching behavior, it is possible to develop a rewards value profile for anyone.

It is particularly useful to provide people with a choice between two or more rewards. Providing choice yields two useful benefits. It avoids giving individuals a reward that they don't particularly value—a common error in organizations—and it provides information about what individuals really value so that in the future, you can better target the rewards that are offered.

For example, instead of giving an employee a vacation to Hawaii without questioning whether such a trip is the best use of incentive money, it might be better to offer a choice between the vacation and the cost of the vacation. This not only provides important clues about what will motivate that employee's behavior in the future, but it also avoids giving the person a reward that may in fact be valued less than it costs the organization to purchase.

All too often, managers are not skillful at choosing the right rewards for their reports, so organizations end up spending far more to buy a reward than it is worth to the person who receives it. This is particularly true today with the very heterogeneous workforces that exist in most organizations. It is often true, for example, that many of the symbolic rewards that organizations give, such as clocks or plaques, are not valued in proportion to what they cost.

Finally, it is critical that managers be keen observers of how people respond to situations where rewards are tied to performance. When people are not motivated in these situations, it may very well be because they do not see a line of sight. An effective manager needs to determine why this has happened and figure out how to change the situation. Sometimes it is simply an information problem, because people have not been told about how they will be rewarded. Other times, people may see obstacles that will prevent them from being rewarded even if they perform well.

The Impact of Goals on Motivation

Expectancy theory places great emphasis on the importance of goals in motivating people. Research backs this up by showing that when individuals commit themselves to a goal, they are highly motivated to achieve it.[5] One reason is often that their self-esteem and sense of self-worth are tied to accomplishing the goal. People may also be motivated to achieve goals because there are financial or other extrinsic rewards tied to them.

A perennial question exists about goals: Can they can be set too high and become too difficult for people to meet? Expectancy theory provides an interesting way of thinking about this. It argues that if the goal difficulty gets too high, people may see a low probability of achieving it. This in turn weakens or destroys their motivation to work toward the goal, since the receipt of a reward becomes very unlikely.

However, this is not to suggest that people never try to achieve very hard goals. As long as two conditions exist, people may still be motivated to reach a difficult goal. First, the connection between achieving the goal and the rewards is clear; in other words, the line of sight or line of influence is strong. Second, the amount of reward associated with accomplishing the goal is very large. Conversely, if there is a low probability of achieving a goal and the rewards are small, it is almost certain that individuals will not put forth the effort that is needed to achieve it.

The research on goal difficulty leads to a somewhat contradictory and paradoxical conclusion related to the impact of intrinsic rewards. Some evidence suggests that as goal difficulty rises, people end up feeling a greater sense of accomplishment and achievement when they achieve a goal. Under certain conditions, they become more motivated to achieve difficult rather than easy goals, even though the probability of achieving them is low. In essence, what may be happening is that the intrinsic rewards associated with accomplishing something significant and difficult become so large that people are willing to put out extraordinary effort to achieve them.

Finally, I need to raise a caution flag about very difficult goals. When very difficult goals are combined with very large rewards for achieving them, some people will do whatever it takes to reach them. Unfortunately, "whatever it takes" sometimes includes cheating, unethical behaviors, and falsifying performance measures.

Consider the scandals that have enveloped Enron, WorldCom, Global Crossing, Adelphi, and other companies where corporate fraud has occurred. In these companies, the executives had extraordinarily large stock option grants whose worth depended on their producing increasingly higher levels of corporate performance. When for a number of reasons these levels became unachievable, instead of forgoing the rewards, the executives chose to falsify the books, cash in their stock options, and reap millions of dollars of rewards. Obviously, organizations need to show increasing vigilance in ensuring that such events do not happen when high goals and high rewards are at stake.

Job Satisfaction and Performance

Many managers believe that job satisfaction is an important determinant of motivation and performance. This is more a myth than a truth. In fact, the opposite may be true.

In the view of expectancy theory, motivation is based on anticipated rewards and future satisfaction, not on present satisfaction. Anticipated satisfaction causes rewards to be viewed as important and a potential source of motivation. Job satisfaction may be the result of performance when performance leads to rewards that in turn fulfill needs, but job satisfaction does not directly *cause* motivation or performance.

Nevertheless, there are several points about the impact of job satisfaction that are important to remember. First, job satisfaction is a function of rewards, in that it is actually determined by how satisfied individuals are with the total package of rewards they receive as a result of working for an organization.

Second, as we have seen, what is satisfying for one person may not be so for another. Given the existence of large individual differences in what people value, it is futile to debate whether, for example, money, recognition, interesting work, or promotion opportunities is the most important determinant of job satisfaction. For some people there is little doubt that money is the most important; for others the work itself is key. For still others it is the social relationships or maybe the opportunity to learn new skills that is the most important determinant of job satisfaction.

Third, over time, people tend to gravitate to work situations that meet their needs, and as a result, their overall job satisfaction goes up. This bodes well for organizations that try to retain their people and develop a virtuous spiral relationship. The longer people stay with the company, the more satisfied they are likely to be.

Fourth, increasing job satisfaction is unlikely to have a positive effect on performance. In fact, it may have a negative effect because, at least temporarily, people will cease to seek additional rewards because they will be satisfied with their reward level. In most cases, the effect is temporary, however, because they either try to satisfy other newly important needs or they decide they want more of the reward they thought they had enough of!

The Importance of Satisfaction

The fact that satisfaction does not drive individual motivation and performance does not mean that it does not influence organizational performance. When employees are not satisfied with their jobs, they are saying that they do not see positive consequences associated with coming to work and remaining part of an organization. Their current dissatisfaction is thus an indicator of their anticipated state of dissatisfaction in the future.

It is therefore hardly surprising that dissatisfied employees typically begin to look elsewhere for employment and ultimately leave when they find a situation that offers a better mix of rewards. If they do not leave, they become disgruntled employees who often seek to change their current situation by organizing and voting for a union, becoming activists, filing lawsuits, or engaging in other actions that they think will improve their lot.

In addition, while job satisfaction does not have a direct impact on the job performance of most individuals, job *dissatisfaction* can have a serious impact on absenteeism and turnover. Turnover can be a particularly costly item for organizations. While it is relatively inexpensive to replace unskilled labor, knowledge workers and highly skilled employees can be very costly to replace, particularly when qualified replacements are scarce.

Estimates vary considerably, but most studies put the cost of replacing skilled employees at six to twenty times their monthly salary.[6] Costs increase as the level of complexity of the work rises and as the scarcity of workers with the right skills increases. Because turnover destroys the social fabric that enables people to effectively work together, costs are particularly high when work is interdependent and people need to work in teams.

Job satisfaction is also quite important in the case of relationship-oriented service employees, such as stockbrokers, real estate agents, hair stylists, and most others in personal and professional service situations. Customers end up feeling a sense of commitment to a particular service provider and have confidence in that person. As a result, job dissatisfaction–caused turnover can lead to a loss of customers. What is more, research has shown that people prefer to do business with organizations that have satisfied employees because their customer experience is more enjoyable. Customers would rather deal with employees who are satisfied and are not complaining about how they are treated by their organization.

Part of the success of the Nordstrom department store chain is due to its emphasis on building relationships between the sales staff and customers. Nordstrom does a number of things to be sure this happens. It pays its employees well in order to keep turnover low, and it tracks customer and employee satisfaction so that it can identify and resolve problems.

In service situations that are primarily transaction-oriented (as opposed to relationship-oriented), job satisfaction may be less important. For example, customers going into a 7-Eleven do not particularly want to make friends with the cashier; they simply want to be served by a person who quickly completes their transaction, with or without a smile. The same applies to many fast-food restaurants, as well as to toll takers, parking lot attendants, and a host of other transaction-oriented sales situations.

In the long run, though, because dissatisfaction leads to turnover, customer loss, and a host of other negative impacts on organizational performance, it is almost always important to pay attention to employee job satisfaction.

A Recap of Rewards

Motivation and satisfaction are at the same time both complicated and simple topics—complicated because of the enormous individual differences that exist and the complexity of human beings. They are simple in that there are some key "truths" that can be used to guide the design of effective organizations when it comes to treating people right. These are worth repeating here because they are fundamental to the remainder of the book:

- Rewards must be important to be motivators.
- Individuals differ in the relative importance they attach to rewards.
- People value both extrinsic and intrinsic rewards.
- People give themselves intrinsic rewards.
- People may not know how important something is to them until they have experienced it.

- People may not be willing or able to accurately report on what is important to them.
- People are motivated to perform when they believe they can obtain rewards they value by performing well.
- People are attracted to jobs and organizations that offer the best mix of the rewards they value.
- Job satisfaction is determined by how the rewards individuals receive compare to what they feel they should receive and how the rewards are distributed.
- Satisfied employees are unlikely to quit and be absent.
- Customers prefer to deal with satisfied employees.

Ability: The Other Half of Performance Effectiveness

The other half of the equation that produces effective individual performance deals with ability, which refers to the knowledge, skills, competencies, and personality a person brings to the table. The research on what determines whether an individual can actually perform a task is vast and complex. A great deal of it makes the important distinction between the underlying characteristics of people that enable them to learn and perform and the specific skills and knowledge they have developed during their lives.

If we were to compare a person's ability to perform a task to an iceberg, specific skills and knowledge are the above-water portion. When a task is performed, specific skills and knowledge are relatively easily measured and addressed because they are visible. Below the water, though, are the underlying competencies that individuals have. These are harder to measure, but they have a big impact on what skills and knowledge people can develop.

In today's complex and rapidly changing business world, competencies are often as important to maintaining virtuous spirals as the skills and knowledge that people bring to their jobs. In fact, they are becoming even more critical since they are the foundation that enables new skills and knowledge to develop. If an organization's employees are regularly expected to learn new skills and knowledge, what they can learn and how quickly they can learn it may ultimately be more important than what they can do at any point in time.

Competencies can be categorized into a relatively small number of categories. The major ones are cognitive (thinking), motor (physical), and perceptual (recognizing patterns). Each of these contains a number of similar competencies (for example, cognitive competency includes memory, reasoning, logic, and so on). It often takes all three types of competencies for an individual to learn and perform a skill.

Furthermore, people who have a high level of one type of competency (such as cognition) tend to have high amounts of all the various competencies of that type (memory, reasoning, and so on). In other words, people seem to have either good or bad cognitive competencies in general. The same thing tends to hold true for motor competencies and perceptual competencies.

Other Factors That Influence Ability

In addition to the difference between competencies and learned knowledge and skills, here are some other parameters that organizations need to consider in understanding the ability of individuals to perform:

Early Environment

There is a never-ending debate about the degree to which people's abilities are determined by heredity (passed down genetically from their parents) or by the environment (formed by their family upbringing, education, friends, and other external influences). Researchers have never reached a definitive conclusion other than to assert that both heredity and environment are important.

One precept that is widely accepted, however, is that people's competencies are generally well established by the time they reach adulthood. This means that by the time someone enters the workforce, their competencies are relatively fixed and difficult to change. This is particularly true in the cognitive area.

Individual Differences

From the early days of IQ testing to the present, study after study has found that individuals differ enormously in their cognitive, motor, and perceptual competencies. Some individuals simply move more quickly, learn faster, solve problems quicker, think faster, paint better, and so on, than others do.

Because of the large individual differences that exist, organizations need to place a great deal of emphasis on determining which people to hire and which tasks to assign them to work on. Not only do organizations need to select people who are competent and able to learn new skills, but they also need to be sure that there is a good fit between the tasks that individuals are assigned and their skills and competencies. Skill deficits can be made up by training classes and other training experience, but deficits in competencies usually cannot. For this reason, the selection and placement of people is crucial in creating a high-performance organization.

As I mentioned earlier, in traditional companies that have well-designed, relatively simple jobs, the differences between good performers and poor performers may be relatively small, even if ability differences are large. For example, a good performer may produce only 20 or 30 percent more than a poor performer.

However, in work situations that are ambiguous, creative, and self-managing and where large amounts of ability are needed, the difference between an average performer and an outstanding one can be enormous. For example, in writing software code, doing research and development, or solving complex business strategy issues, top performers are often many times more effective than poor performers.

Because individual differences in abilities can make a vast difference in performance, organizations need to focus on finding individuals who can perform their critical tasks at the highest level.

Training and Development

Although people's underlying competencies are crucial in determining what they can do, it is also true that organizations can have a significant impact on the knowledge and skills of their employees, particularly through on-the-job training and formal training programs that teach a variety of skills (motor, intellectual, and conceptual). Employee training of all kinds is becoming increasingly easier to accomplish, due to the many programs offered via the Internet and in classroom settings.

Perhaps the most prevalent form of training is on-the-job mentoring. A knowledgeable coworker or manager can often do an excellent job of helping individuals develop the kind of task-specific knowledge that is needed to perform a particular job. As for management and leadership training, a great deal of evidence indicates that the most effective training results from assigning people challenging work that forces them to stretch themselves.[7]

Some organizations take the position that they can hire people with the skills and knowledge that are needed to perform a job. Obviously, this may be a very cost-effective solution to staffing jobs because it means that someone else has paid the cost of training individuals to do the tasks required, but the proposition can be risky.

The danger with relying on this solution is that many people may not be as qualified as expected, and the organization may have to pay very high premiums in order to attract skilled people. However, as will be discussed further in Chapter Five, hiring pretrained talent is certainly an important option that organizations need to increasingly consider given the speed with which business moves and the time it can take for people to develop the right job-related skills and expertise.

Personality and Performance

Personality traits predispose people to feel certain emotions, experience different types of reactions to situations, and behave and perform differently on the job. A large body of research indicates that five dominant personality traits have an important influence on behavior:

- Degree of extroversion or introversion
- Emotional stability
- Agreeableness
- Conscientiousness
- Openness to experience

Personality traits can determine many aspects of job performance, from the ability to learn to job satisfaction to the type of customer interactions that occur. Just as with competencies, large individual differences exist in personality, and an individual's personality is determined long before joining the workforce.

It may be even harder to change a person's personality than to change his or her competencies. Whereas training can often alter people's knowledge and skills, it is unclear that training can significantly influence people's personalities. As a result, organizations need to focus on assessing personality traits as part of the process of selecting people and determining what types of jobs to place them in.

The Right People

As with motivation and satisfaction, ability and competency are both complicated and simple topics. They are complicated because of the enormous individual differences that exist and the complexity of human beings. And they are simple in that there are some key truths that can be used to guide the design of effective organizations. These truths are worth repeating here because they are fundamental to the remainder of the book:

- It is important to distinguish between the underlying competencies of individuals and the skills and knowledge they have.
- Skills and knowledge are usually more on the surface and therefore more easily identified and measured.
- Underlying competencies are harder to observe but critical to performance and learning.
- Individuals have a variety of competencies, but they can be grouped into three general types: cognitive, perceptual, and motor. By the time individuals enter the workforce, their competencies are relatively fixed.
- Organizations facing rapid change need to select individuals who have the ability to learn new skills and knowledge; this often means that cognitive competencies are critical.
- Organizations can influence the skills and knowledge that individuals have through both formal training and job experiences.
- Often individuals can, and perhaps should, be hired based on their existing skills and knowledge because they can be immediately productive contributors to the organization's success.
- People have wide-ranging differences in how much of the five dominant personality traits they have.
- Personality traits have an influence on how people perform their jobs.
- Because personality traits are very difficult to change, it is important to select individuals with the right personality.

Part Two

The Seven Principles of Treating People Right

Chapter Four

Attract and Keep the Right People

TREAT PEOPLE RIGHT PRINCIPLE #1

Organizations must create a value proposition that defines the type of workplace they want to be so that they can attract and retain the right people.

Winning the "war for talent" is a serious never ending challenge for organizations. In today's world, the competition to hire and keep the best people is intense and sometimes even fierce. Work is getting more complex at a time when there is a shortage of skilled workers. With the death of loyalty, keeping talent is becoming an expensive and time-consuming process for many organizations, since they are forced to recruit their employees many times over.

Hiring and retaining high-performing individuals is not a matter that can be left to chance or happenstance. It needs to be based on intelligent strategies and implemented through effective practices that identify the right people, attract them, and retain them. How to develop these strategies and what practices to use are the major emphases of this chapter.

The competition for talent also has powerful implications for individuals. With the increased importance of human capital to organizations, people have a far greater potential to have more fulfilling and meaningful lives in the careers they choose. They are in a better bargaining position in terms of how they are managed and rewarded and what they do on a day-to-day basis. They also have the chance to earn a higher rate of return on the human capital they bring to a job. At the end of this chapter, I will highlight the implications that the competition for talent has for people building and managing their careers.

Creating a Value Proposition

An effective strategy for finding and keeping talent begins with creating a *value proposition*. In my view, organizations need to fashion a compelling platform that clearly establishes who they are, what they want, and what they can offer. This is truly the beginning of treating people right, because it establishes the initial set of practices to ensure that the organization employs people who are aligned with its values and goals.

In fact, think of the value proposition as a corollary of the *mission statement* that many organizations write to define their purpose in the world relative to their investors, customers, and employees. The value proposition supports the mission statement by focusing on what the organization offers in order to attract and retain the people needed to achieve the high-performance culture that allows it to succeed and to create a virtuous spiral.

I have several important guidelines and suggestions about how organizations can create an effective value proposition.

Align the Value Proposition to Your Strategy

First and foremost, the value proposition must be designed to fit tightly with your business strategy. Its purpose is to attract, motivate, and retain employees, but not just anyone. It needs to focus on enticing people who have the skills, knowledge, competencies, and personality to perform well and who can be motivated by the practices and programs your organization offers.

In terms of the Diamond Model, the value proposition must take into account the organizational design elements, capabilities, and competencies you need and the various environmental issues that might affect your ability to attract and retain the right people. An in-depth analysis of these factors needs to be made in order to define the basic planks of a proposition that will attract and retain the right people.

Southwest Airlines has done a particularly good job of aligning its value proposition with its strategy. Given that the company wants its customers to associate Southwest with freedom, fun, and flexibility, it aims to attract people who are sociable, if not zany, and who are willing to go the extra mile to provide a great travel experience for their customers. The company's advertisements frequently feature the friendly behavior and humorous antics of its employees, such as singing or telling jokes on flights. Southwest's business strategy also emphasizes the fast turnaround of their planes and consistent, dependable service, so the company also makes sure its employees are willing to work hard and are flexible about the work they do. Its value proposition has turned Southwest's people into a hard-to-copy competitive advantage and has been a big part of the company's ability to develop and maintain a virtuous spiral.

Technology firms such as Applied Materials, Intel, Microsoft, Cisco, and Sun Microsystems also offer value propositions that fit their strategies. These firms emphasize the opportunity to work on challenging technology issues with expert coworkers, along with, of course, the chance to accumulate a substantial amount of money if the business is successful. Their value propositions are particularly attractive to individuals who are interested in information technology, have strong technology knowledge, and are motivated by financial incentives.

As a result of their value propositions, these companies have been able to attract and retain world-class workforces that have allowed them to create virtuous spirals. All of these organizations had low turnover rates even during the dot-com boom of the late 1990s, at least in part because their employees enjoyed the benefits of being part of a virtuous spiral.

Design Rewards to Attract and Retain Employees

The second key issue in creating a value proposition is making sure it includes a reward system that attracts and keeps the right people. Given that individuals are motivated by and work for rewards that matter to them, the reward system must contain a mix of rewards that the workforce will value and respond to.

Naturally, what and how much your organization can offer depends on the type of business it is in, its financial resources, its size, and a variety of other factors. Organizations today need to be creative in developing a wide range of rewards to meet the diverse needs of their employees. As we discussed in Chapter Three, organizations can create both extrinsic and intrinsic rewards to attract and motivate people. What is important is that the rewards your organization offers be tailored to the people you are trying to attract and keep.

When you design a reward system, keep in mind two caveats. First, many organizations make the mistake of devising benefits that are good at attracting employees but fail to motivate them to perform. For example, if an organization's value proposition ties rewards and promotions to seniority, it may attract and retain the type of people who want a steady long-term relationship with your company, but it is not likely to motivate a large number of them to perform well. Most employees will conclude that all they need to do is show up to get raises and promotions. In order to motivate performance, a value proposition must include rewards for performance that pull people toward high performance.

Second, a value proposition must not just attract and motivate people; it must also keep them. You want to avoid hiring "walking floppy disks"—employees who enter your organization, get an expensive download of training and information, and then leave for a competitor.

On the other hand, you may not want to encourage people to stay with your organization for their entire career or, for that matter, for more than a short period of time. Because of the environmental changes that organizations must respond to, they increasingly need to employ people for short periods of time and to make frequent changes in the number and type of people who work for them.

For this reason, you need to consider the issue of retention right from the start, at the attraction phase, because that's when employees develop perceptions and expectations about working for your organization. The attitudes they form when reading your job postings, interviewing, and working during their first few months can ultimately have a significant impact on their feelings of job satisfaction and equity, which can in turn affect their interest in staying.

Admittedly, developing a reward system that succeeds in keeping people for the "right" period of time is challenging today. The traditional approach was the loyalty contract but it is obsolete for a number of very good reasons.

From the organizational point of view, using loyalty contracts to retain people locks your company into a long-term commitment that often becomes unproductive. You essentially create a handcuff that makes it very difficult for employees to leave. People know they need only to continue to show up to keep their job and increase their vacation days and retirement benefits.

Loyalty contracts also make change difficult. Change often requires that the organization hire other people with the new skills needed to develop new core competencies and new organizational capabilities. Or it can require that the organization motivate current employees to change their behavior, develop new skills, and adopt new technologies and new strategic directions. But the loyalty contract does not motivate employees to improve their knowledge, skills, and competencies, nor does it encourage them to embrace organizational change.

The loyalty contract is equally dysfunctional for many individuals. It limits their chances to develop and grow within their company because with stability there are few job openings. And it often hinders their ability to move to other corporations, particularly when many organizations are unwilling or unable to bring in "new blood."

Assuming that the loyalty contract is disappearing or already dead in your organization, you need to substitute a reward system that motivates retention in meaningful, productive ways. Research I have done in many organizations indicates that people are willing to accept a value proposition that stresses continued employment based on performance and having the right skill set for the organization's business strategy if they are rewarded for performance and skill development. Chapter Nine discusses reward systems in detail and provides you with the conceptual framework and many specific practices to help design a reward system that will accomplish this and create a virtuous spiral.

Design Multiple Value Propositions

In aligning value propositions with business strategies, it is important to consider having multiple value propositions. Organizations today must attract and keep a diverse and flexible workforce. For example, their talent may need to include a "core" of the highest-performing, most valuable employees, along with a group of high-performing solid contributors, as well as a group of short-term employees. As a result, they may need several value propositions in order to attract and retain individuals whose interests and needs vary greatly. Let me specifically address two of the groups here.

Core Employees

Core employees are the ones who are considered crucial long-term employees of the organization. The number of core employees needed in an organization varies greatly, depending on its business, technology requirements, and other factors. For example, in long-term investment businesses such as natural resources, there is usually a need for a large number of core employees, while in rapidly changing businesses such as high technology, a smaller number of core workers may be sufficient.

Core staffing needs most often exist in two key areas. First, you need people who have the necessary expertise to ensure that you meet your core competency and organizational capability needs. Failure is almost a certainty if the talent to develop and maintain them is lacking. Second, you need people who are effective leaders as part of your core staff.

In terms of retention, your value proposition for core employees must include rewards that will build their commitment to the organization. This typically means that the core members must be offered extensive development opportunities and usually a stake in the organization through stock ownership. Clearly, without these incentives, employees with key expertise will likely leave, taking with them core knowledge and important intellectual capital. Their departure can also result in the loss of important working relationships and information channels that may be critical to your capabilities and core competencies.

However, let me add that you don't want to go overboard in rewarding core employees. If you focus too much on pleasing core employees while ignoring others, you can end up creating a dysfunctional caste system. One way to prevent this from happening is to have mobility between the two groups. Noncore employees who have the potential and want to join the core need to know what they can do to meet *objective* criteria—such as skills, knowledge, competencies, and performance standards—that will move them into it.

Finally, keep in mind that individuals who fail to live up to the performance and competency standards required of the core employee group should be dropped from it. Being a core employee should be neither a birthright nor a permanent status for employees. It needs to be subject to performance, skills, and knowledge requirements as well as to the strategy of the corporation.

Short-Term Employees

Organizations need to make increasing use of short-term employees, such as temps and contract workers. This makes sense because of ebbs and flows in their business or because the nature of their work requires special skill sets for a limited period of time. Depending on the extent to which your organization needs such short-term workers, it may need to develop a separate value proposition that fits them.

For example, you can often attract short-term employees by offering a value proposition that emphasizes flexibility in work hours or work location. Many short-termers also respond favorably to the idea that they can gain enhanced employability by spending time at an organization that provides them with new skills and knowledge. Another option is to offer short-termers assistance in job hunting or writing their résumé once they are no longer needed. Last but not least, cash compensation packages often work well because they offer a valued reward and don't involve a long-term commitment.

Weigh Costs and Benefits

In developing a value proposition, treating people right doesn't mean rewarding them with everything they want. You need to weigh the cost of rewards against the benefits in motivation and retention they create. Organizations can go too far to satisfy employees in an effort to become an "employer of choice." Particularly since *Fortune* magazine and other publications have begun identifying companies as employers of choice and best places to work, I have seen some organizations have become too concerned about appearing to offer high levels of rewards.

On one hand, you need to have an attractive enough mix of rewards to retain the people on whom you have already expended effort in terms of recruitment and training. In today's world, you cannot afford to continuously lose valuable talent.

On the other hand, creating a country club type of environment, where virtually everything is offered to employees simply because they show up year after year, can be even more expensive than turnover. Your rewards must motivate people to excel and motivate those who excel to stay. This is the foundation of the virtuous spiral, in which both sides win and create success for each other.

One answer to the cost-benefit dilemma is to make at least some of your rewards contingent on individual performance and organizational success. This is most easily done with financial rewards. The use of stock plans and other contingent financial incentives makes it possible to tie significant amounts of money to people's performance and to the success of the firm. Keep in mind, though, that using money as a motivator works only if you have people who value it—and are willing to live with the reality of having some of their income at risk.

Another way to balance costs and benefits is to build a reward system that includes significant nonfinancial rewards whose costs are minimal but whose benefits are potentially high. For example, your value proposition can emphasize the opportunity to engage in interesting work, to learn new skills, or to work with cutting-edge technology. Many people are attracted by such nonfinancial intrinsic rewards.

Organizations can also emphasize social or spiritual outcomes. An important part of an organization's value proposition can be that the organization's work will make a difference in the quality of people's lives. Amazon.com has as part of its value proposition the opportunity to "have fun" and "change the world." Medtronic emphasizes making people's lives better.

From a motivational point of view, intrinsic and spiritual rewards can create high levels of involvement in the workforce. Many people want to do work that has an important impact on people's lives. This can help you attract people who believe in your organization's mission and who are interested in working hard to help you fulfill it.

Keep in mind that nonfinancial rewards are not equally appealing to everyone, but their motivational power can be very strong for those who value them. The most serious challenge in emphasizing these types of rewards in a value proposition is in motivation and retention. In order to be continually motivated to perform well and stay with your organization, people need to see that what they are doing is furthering the mission they signed on for. They will not stay if your organization does not live up to the intrinsic rewards promised and is not altering the world in the ways they imagined when they first joined.

Avoid Copying

Given that every organization has its own strategy and that its people are motivated by different rewards, a value proposition must be custom-tailored to an organization's specific performance culture. There is little benefit from basing your value proposition on what others do; this is in fact often a negative. The most important measure of your proposition's success is that it fulfills your organization's specific business strategy, not that it resembles or imitates others.

Several years ago, I conducted a CEO workshop in the Silicon Valley. The executives in the workshop were debating an issue related to their value propositions. The topic was whether or not to create a "family-friendly environment" in which individuals could have a job that balanced work and family.

One group of CEOs talked supportively about this. These CEOs related how their companies gave employees access to day care, take-home meals, concierge services, telecommuting, and flexible work hours. They swore that this approach proved to be a powerful magnet in attracting employees for them, and they talked about how it had facilitated retention in many cases.

But the other group of CEOs argued with equal conviction that they did not want a balanced-lifestyle environment. In their firms, they wanted a "24/7" environment that attracted people obsessed with work. They even teased the other executives by thanking them for creating family-friendly environments that attracted just the people their high-intensity companies did not want.

Which group is right? Both are. There is room in the world for both balanced-lifestyle and 24/7 organizations. Some organizations need a majority or even the totality of their workforce to be obsessed with work; they cannot afford to give employees options that allow them to assign nonwork activities an equal or a higher priority than work.

Many other organizations can operate effectively—perhaps more effectively—when the majority of their employees have a balanced life between work and nonwork. By offering this value proposition, these organizations attract a larger number of employees, keep their turnover low, and prevent the kind of burnout that may occur in high-workload organizations.

SAS Institute, the software company, is an example of an organization whose balanced-lifestyle value proposition fits its business strategy, though it runs counter to other companies in the software industry. SAS offers a comprehensive set of benefits to attract and retain individuals who have families and want to maintain balanced lifestyles. Unlike many other software firms, SAS does not value long hours of work, nor does it offer high levels of incentive pay.

The SAS value proposition has worked well for the company, especially in minimizing turnover. Maintaining long-term employees is a key factor for SAS, in part because its software products need updating and in part because long-term customer relationships are crucial to the company's competitive advantage.

Be Sure You Can Deliver

Whatever value proposition you create, you must be able to deliver on it. Failure to deliver on your promises will most likely result in high levels of dissatisfaction, which will inevitably lead to excessive turnover, adversarial union relationships, and a host of other dysfunctional outcomes.

Many dot-coms promised much more than they delivered. Once employees realized this, they left in droves. The result: dot-com after dot-com went into a death spiral. Less dramatic everyday examples include organizations promising a chance to make a difference and interesting, challenging work but assigning new employees to routine, repetitive tasks. Another common example involves training and development. Organizations often promise employees the chance to develop, but when push comes to shove, their training takes a back seat to getting the work done.

Assess Your Value Proposition Regularly

My final guideline in regard to creating effective value propositions is that you must regularly assess how effective your proposition is. You need to focus on four groups of people: potential and actual job applicants and current and former employees.

Potential job applicants. Clearly, it is important to know if your proposition is succeeding in attracting the right job applicants. Are these individuals forming an accurate perception of your value proposition? Is it attractive to them? You can measure this in several ways, such as conducting focus groups or phone surveys targeted to people who could be your future employees.

Actual job applicants. This group can provide useful data about how accurately your value proposition is communicated and perceived. You might ask applicants where they heard about your company and the job, and their responses will clearly help you assess your communication approaches. You can also ask questions about which rewards attracted them to your organization and how your company compares to other employers who compete in the same labor market. As with any marketing research, such information allows you to compare brands, image, and consumer behavior.

Current employees. Feedback from your current employees is vital in gathering data about your value proposition. You want to know if what they perceive your organization to be offering satisfies their wants and desires. As we discussed when examining the psychology of motivation, satisfaction information is a good predictor of future retention among your employees. A decrease in job satisfaction usually leads to increases in turnover.

I recommend that when performing surveys of employees, you should collect data more often than once a year. Limiting yourself to an annual cycle means it is often too late to take effective action if you find evidence of serious satisfaction problems developing. Given the importance of employee satisfaction, it should be measured in ways that mimic the frequency of data collection that goes on for financial and operational results.

Surveys are increasingly easy to administer with the growth of company intranets. It is now practical to distribute short surveys to all employees or to a random sample of employees on a monthly basis. Indeed, some organizations are even doing it on a weekly basis and providing managers with constant feedback on what's happening in their work groups.

However, be careful that you don't commit "survey overload." When people believe they are being watched over too intensely, they may come to resent the surveys and fail to provide answers or even intentionally misrepresent their feelings. This is particularly likely to occur when the results of surveys are not acted on.

Former employees. It can be very informative to ask former employees what they think of your organization and its value proposition. Ask them as they are leaving and then again six months to a year after they have left. Often their answers change over time because they have had time to reflect and they are usually more willing to be honest in their answers. They will also have had new work experiences that allow them to evaluate your organization with a different perspective than they had at the time they left.

Overall, there is no substitute for gathering data about how your organization's value proposition is perceived in the world. You can use these data to enhance your organization's value proposition, tune its reward programs, and ensure that it has the quality of talent it needs. Ultimately, these data can help your organization stay ahead of the game. The world is no longer static; as people change and as business changes, your organization's value proposition needs to be assessed and updated.

My last piece of advice about assessing your organization's value proposition is to keep in mind that the objective is not to listen to what *everyone* thinks about it. Your primary focus should be on listening to high-potential employees and your highest-performing employees. You want to pay special attention to how these two groups perceive your organization's value proposition and how attractive they feel it is.

Best Practices to Attract and Retain

Creating a value proposition is the first step in attracting and retaining the right employees. It is a foundation on which organizations can build policies, procedures, and structure to attract and retain the right employees.

To assist in this process, I have assembled a set of "best practices" that can help many organizations improve their capacity to find and keep talent. I selected these practices based on years of research and study of top-performing organizations. Each has been shown to produce measurable benefits that contribute to treating people right and launching a virtuous spiral.

I believe that these best practices can be transferred or adapted to most organizations, regardless of the business or industry.

Turning the Value Proposition into a Brand

Creating a value proposition is an important first step all organizations should take, but "branding" it is a very useful next step, especially if your organization needs to attract large numbers of job candidates. Just as with a product, branding your proposition means that you intentionally aim to create a strong, unique image that distinguishes your organization from others. Branding essentially crystallizes an organization's value proposition so that people have no doubt what they will gain as a result of working for it. Branding can be quite instrumental in adding zing and momentum to your organization's ability to attract top-notch talent.

Many organizations have built strong brand images as employers. Think of IBM, McKinsey, Microsoft, Amazon.com, the FBI, and even the U.S. Marine Corps. Recently, a number of other organizations have developed brands in order to be included in various books and published lists of "best places to work."

Cisco Systems is one organization with a strong brand image, one that emphasizes its leading-edge commitment to technology. One way Cisco communicates this is by requiring that all job candidates apply via its Web site. This clearly indicates to all potential employees that Cisco is a Web-enabled company. Although Cisco's brand may not appeal to everyone, it attracts the type of employees the organization seeks.

The development of a strong brand calls for intelligent thinking and planning. Like formulating a good marketing campaign, you have to take conscious, well-thought-out steps. You need to create a clear, positive image of your organization and then design an effective publicity and advertising program so that the public becomes aware of your brand. Your organization must be willing to risk openly declaring its value proposition, or at least a meaningful portion of it, so that even its competitors know what it is.

Branding a value proposition can be expensive. Southwest Airlines ran ads during a recent Super Bowl game largely aimed at attracting employees. The ads touted the freedom, flexibility, and enjoyment people can receive from working for the company. With this multimillion-dollar investment in advertising during the Super Bowl, Southwest succeeded in issuing a powerful statement about the importance of its employees. In my view, anyone interested in working for an airline who saw that ad got a clear understanding of the benefits of working for Southwest. Of course, the advertising also did a great job of publicizing to Southwest's customers the quality of the service they can expect to receive when flying with Southwest.

If your organization decides to brand its value proposition, it is important that you maintain a clear and consistent message during any and all recruiting. This includes college job fairs, internships, open houses, career days, and other venues. Whether it is your employees stomping for recruits on your behalf, materials you are publishing, or an Internet site, everyone and everything must deliver the same brand message to the public.

"Signature Extras"

Another best practice to boost your value proposition is to include in it truly unique benefits—*signature extras,* as they are called—that distinguish your company in the marketplace of employers. Today, more and more organizations are offering a variety of creative signature extras, such as a choice of forty-two different drinks and coffees "on the house," Friday pizza and beer blasts, season tickets to sports events, round-the-clock food service, sabbaticals, and flexible work schedules. At the corporate headquarters of Monster, for example, work hours are completely flexible as long as employees work forty hours each week. Employees can also declare themselves "vegetables for a day." This entitles them to leave work when they are having a bad day!

Signature extras are an effective way for organizations to establish themselves as desirable employers, often at a relatively low cost.

If chosen well, they can add an aura to your organization as an exciting company to work for, one that is willing to do things differently, take some risks, and be an attention getter. And if done with some smart PR planning, they can also help you obtain free press coverage and publicity for your branding efforts that might otherwise have cost a great deal.

Extras can help both individuals and organizations when they facilitate employees' personal lives while they work so that they can focus on their jobs. For example, one company regularly brings dental service to its parking lot in a mobile dental unit. Others offer take-out dry cleaning services, and an increasing number of companies have on-site day care for the children of working parents. Another common extra is signing employees up to a special on-line portal on the Internet where they can go shopping at a discount as members of a buying club sponsored by the company.

From an organizational point of view, the smartest extras are those that not only give people something they value but also educate them and help them improve their knowledge and skills. A good example is providing employees with free or low-cost computers and Internet access from their homes, as Delta Airlines has done. Supplying home computers can be especially valuable in companies where the Internet is an integral part of an employee's work. Clearly, the greater the ease and comfort employees have with using computers, the more productive they can be if their job calls for Internet-based work, customer service, or communication among employees via e-mail.

One of the most intriguing signature extras I have encountered is provided by a technology company in Silicon Valley that gives stock options to its employees' spouses. I asked the CEO of the company why he instituted this unusual benefit, and he told me that he wanted to thank the spouses for the sacrifices they made to help the company succeed. He added that because his employees often work 24/7 schedules, the spouses had to give up family holidays and weekends.

The CEO said he also understood that he needed to help the spouses understand the stock options. He therefore conducted open houses and educational programs on weekends to let the spouses know what was going on in the company and why the stock was a good investment. A slight smile then came over his face as he added that he has found that since the spouses have owned stock, they have been much happier about having their mates work 24/7 schedules. Indeed, he suggested that in some cases, the spouses were even encouraging their mates to work harder so that the stock would go up in value! I guess you could say he had found his own way to create a virtuous spiral.

Signature extras can produce excellent results in attracting employees when added to a company's value proposition. But there is a danger to consider. In some cases, they can attract people to an organization for the wrong reasons, and they may misguide people about an organization's overall value proposition. Ultimately, you need to find a good balance by offering important and unique rewards that help your organization attract and retain the right people.

Individualized Deals

In the spirit of avoiding a one-size-fits-all value proposition, an increasing number of organizations are allowing employees to customize or individualize their working relationships and benefits. I completely agree with this practice and in fact have long believed that individualization offers many advantages. In 1972, I wrote an article stressing how organizations can gain from individualizing various elements of the employment relationship. I argued that given the vast differences that exist in what people want, the most powerful way to attract and retain good employees is to give them a great deal of choice about their working conditions. In 2000, I updated this article with my colleague David Finegold.[1] Both my articles stress that organizations can give their employees choices with respect to when, where, and how they work as well as how they are rewarded and how their careers develop. In other words, multiple paths to virtuous career spirals are possible if organizations individualize their practices.

The problem with individualization has been that until recently, customizing employment relationships was very difficult from a record-keeping point of view. Tracking individual employees' choices in a large organization with hundreds or tens of thousands on the payroll was literally impossible.

Fortunately, that situation has now changed, giving a new boost to individualization and making it a good practice to implement. Today, it is very easy to customize the relationship between your organization and its employees through the use of Web-based human resource systems, called eHR systems. The technology is both abundant, offered by a wide assortment of software firms, and well developed, with most systems easily able to handle the complexities of mass customization of the employment relationship.

Cisco Systems and Sun Microsystems are among the companies that have done excellent jobs in using eHR systems to individualize work relationships. Using the company's eHR system, employees can change their benefit coverage to reflect changes in their personal situations or simply changes in their preferences. They can choose from a variety of benefits, including different kinds of health insurance and retirement plans.

Many employees can also choose where they work from. Because Sun Microsystems and Cisco are so Web-enabled, employees can relatively easily work from home or from a variety of company locations simply by signing on to the Internet. Many of the large consulting firms, such as McKinsey and Booz Allen Hamilton, have similar systems and have specifically set aside hotel office space for employees to use in a variety of their locations.

Keep in mind that the use of eHR systems requires assessing how much individualization is desirable in your organization. On one hand, many system designers are inclined to standardize processes and practices when they develop eHR systems because it makes it much easier to create the software. I highly recommend that you avoid this tendency when it comes to how employees are rewarded and how they work. In most cases, the payoff from individualizing is far greater in attracting and retaining people than any savings you accrue from standardizing work practices and rewards. What can be standardized are the choice process and the choices that are available.

On the other hand, I also caution you not to overdo individualization. If you allow every employee to have his or her own deal, you risk creating a hodgepodge workforce of people who have little in common. Too much individualization can destroy an organization's ability to develop a sense of community and a common mission or vision among its employees. You need to think carefully about where individualization can help your value proposition and where it might harm it.

One example of the need to limit individualization is in letting employees select when and where to work. Individualization might dictate that you let people have complete freedom of choice concerning their work hours and their location. However, if you do this, you can end up reducing or eliminating the strong bonds people form by being together. This social contact has been shown to be pivotal in creating well-functioning teams and projects. It fosters the sharing of knowledge and the exchange of ideas, as well as people's commitment to their team or group. Without at least some social contact, you can ultimately hurt your ability to create new products and speed them to market.

Using Technology to Cast a Wide Recruiting Net

Even when you have an attractive value proposition, a strong brand, and great signature extras, getting a large number of strong applicants can prove difficult. This is especially true in times of low unemployment. Depending on your recruiting goals, you may need to "cast a wide net" to find people by using a wide variety of recruiting methods.

Keep in mind, however, that regardless of the recruitment method, if you are branding your value proposition, you need to be consistent in the message you deliver at all functions and recruiting events. This means making sure that all employees representing the company and all print materials promote the same value proposition.

The most common recruiting methods include open houses; summer internships, career days, and recruiting events at high school and college campuses; professional meetings; and national association meetings. Casting a wide net in today's world requires experimenting with a number of new recruitment tools. Internet-based systems, videoconferencing, and even advertising on national TV are increasingly becoming components of the recruitment process for many organizations.

In particular, the Internet has radically changed what organizations can and should do with respect to the recruiting process.

Firms such as Dell, IBM, and Hewlett-Packard have created powerful Web-based systems for recruiting and placement purposes. These companies make job information—openings, requirements, and benefits—readily available to people both inside and outside the organization.

Web sites also make retention easier because employees who want to stay with a company can easily find out about the internal opportunities available to them. In the past, many employees found it easier to find a new job in other companies than in their own, so they changed employers. With Web-based systems, this need no longer be true.

Some managers do complain that posting job openings on an internal Web system leads to a greater internal movement of people, along with the associated costs of replacing workers. I don't disagree, but in general, they have a substantial positive effect on external turnover, which, as I have noted, can be even more expensive than internal movement.

Some Web-based recruitment systems offer many advantages over traditional recruiting, such as brief tests that help applicants self-assess whether they are right for the job. They can also provide career guidance and help people avoid disappointment by applying for jobs for which they are not qualified or in which they would not thrive. They can also help inform potential applicants about your value proposition, what it will be like to work for your organization once they are hired, and what rewards are offered.

Dow Chemical does an excellent job of providing information to existing employees about job openings via the Web. The job announcement system allows Dow employees to apply for any announced job, regardless of its geographical location or placement in the company structure. All employees have access to the job opening information and can review the competencies associated with each position. If they believe they are good potential candidates, they can nominate themselves. This system has become the primary way that Dow fills jobs internally.

I particularly like the Dow system because it emphasizes competencies. An important part of treating people right is effectively managing human capital by identifying the competencies needed to perform tasks and tying those to the development opportunities that exist within a company. In the case of selection and placement, a good understanding of what competencies are needed can be very helpful in determining whether employees are strong candidates for a particular position.

Web-based systems make it especially easy for the internal movement of employees to be dynamic and interactive. Current employees can provide profiles of their background, interests, and skills, which are then stored in the system. When jobs open, the characteristics of the job can be matched to the database of profiles, allowing the technology to make a first determination about whether there might be a good fit. Push technology can then be used to inform the individual of the job opening. This has the obvious advantage of providing current employees with a strong assurance that your organization wants them to stay, values their skills and experience, and will help them develop their virtuous career spirals.

Web-based systems can also meet the staffing challenges of managers who must fill open jobs. They can use the technology to search the profiles of skills and competencies and identify any employee who fits a particular job opening. This is a quick and efficient way for the people doing the staffing to quickly obtain a list of qualified internal candidates.

Let me address one important issue about using this technology properly. Creating a valid database that allows for the type of automated searching just described requires two data sets:

1. The characteristics of individual employees specifying their skills, knowledge, competencies, and career aspirations
2. The characteristics of the jobs, identifying the skills, knowledge, and competencies an employee needs to possess in order to do the job

Creating these data sets is not an easy task and in most cases, is best done by your human resource organization. Ideally, the HR organization should develop a set of skill descriptions and competencies that can be applied to each individual and to each job. Certifying individuals on these skills and competencies can be done through tests or through peer and supervisor evaluation. Capital One, the large financial services firm, has found it useful to rely on a well-developed competency model to guide the selection, staffing, and appraisal process. Each job at Capital One has a competency profile, and individuals are assessed against it when they apply for a job and during periodic performance appraisals.

If your organization seeks a type of talent that is rare, it can be worth the added expense to recruit through a search firm. Increasingly, the best of these firms have their own profile-matching Web-based systems that will help you find the person who has the key skills and work performance characteristics you need. By searching through their information base, a good recruitment specialist can easily find for you that "special accountant" who can do cost accounting, will relocate to Russia, and works well in a multitasking team environment.

Employee Referrals

You may be surprised to find employee referrals included among the best practices to attract talent, but they are. In fact, referrals have become an increasingly important part of many companies' recruitment strategies.

Encouraging your employees to make hiring referrals has significant advantages. Employee referrals help build your brand and promulgate your value proposition. When potential applicants receive a testimonial from an employee, it usually carries more credibility than other recruitment techniques. In addition, referrals often result in getting very good applicants, because the recommending employees have done a certain amount of prescreening of job candidates. In general, employees don't want to bring in people who are likely to be poor performers or difficult to deal with; they would rather attract people who have good skills and work values.

I have some warnings, though, about using employee referrals in your recruitment process, particularly when you encourage them with rewards such as cash. Rewards can decrease the effectiveness of referrals. They may push employees to paint an inaccurate picture of your value proposition just to get their friends to apply. Rewards may also reduce the normal tendency to prescreen potential applicants. Instead of thinking critically about whether their friends will make good employees, they may be driven simply to get credit for a successful referral. Further, they may even coach their referral on how to "beat" the selection process.

Overall, referrals are a good idea. Logic and research both suggest that they are an inexpensive and effective way to recruit good employees. There is also reason to believe that employees who are recruited in this way are more likely to stay with the company because they have friends and quickly become part of a social network.

Scouting Talent

Scouting talent is becoming increasingly necessary in many businesses. Financial service firms, technology firms, and many other organizations where knowledge and human capital are critical to success cannot afford to simply wait and see who applies for jobs. They need to aggressively pursue individuals who have the expertise needed and who represent a good fit for the organization.

I have seen some very effective scouting programs in technology firms. They typically start with an all-out effort to identify the best individuals in the world in their key technical areas. The firms compile their lists from talking to university researchers, checking patents, checking the employment rolls of other companies, and attending professional meetings to see who is presenting papers. After this intense and broad search, the companies typically develop a "hot list" of individuals who are of world-class stature and are potential recruits. (They also use the same process for less established individuals in the field and for graduate and undergraduate students.) Once the firm establishes its list, it begins a selective recruitment process targeting the individuals who appear to be a particularly good fit.

If the steps I have described for scouting and recruiting sound a bit like what goes on in professional sports, it should not be surprising. Professional sports teams' success depends almost entirely on their human capital, and increasingly, the same can be said for many businesses. As I have been stressing, human capital often makes the difference between success and failure in many businesses and therefore deserves to get the same degree of attention that the greatest sports teams (the Yankees and the Lakers!) devote to it.

Rerecruiting the Best

In the past, many organizations have not recruited former employees, believing that people should have only one shot at working for them. Although this ultimatum may at one time have deterred some people from leaving, it is not necessarily a good practice today.

People leave companies for a variety of reasons, so a much better practice is to part amicably and to keep in touch with former employees at least in part for the purpose of rerecruitment. In many ways, former employees often make the best future employees because they have already had a realistic preview of the work situation and of the organization. They are already trained and tested as to whether they can do the work of the organization. If, indeed, they were outstanding performers when they worked for the organization, there is a tremendous advantage to rehiring them.

For example, during the 1990s, many people departed large organizations to join dot-coms and other start-ups. When the dot-coms failed, some companies took an "I told you so" attitude and refused to rehire their "disloyal" former employees. However, a number of companies took advantage of the sudden availability of their old colleagues and rehired the best. I interviewed a number of these individuals after they returned, and it was quite clear that they are now much less likely to leave their existing employer in the future. In many cases, there is evidence that they are even better employees as a result of having worked in the dot-com world. They learned new ways to operate and grew as a result of the challenges they faced, and they had a greater appreciation of the advantages of working for their former employer.

The lesson is clear: it is to your advantage to treat valued employees who leave as potential future employees. You should do everything possible to ensure that they leave with a favorable image of your company and keep track of them once they have joined their new employer. When and if the time is right, an effort should be made to rerecruit them.

A good practice is to have an automatic schedule for contacting former employees to see if they have an interest in returning. Of course, this practice should be limited to individuals who were very effective during their employment.

Moving the Work to the Workforce

The new realities of global commerce sometimes make moving the work to the workforce a particularly good idea when it comes to finding the right people. Especially when unemployment is relatively low or particular skills scarce, getting a large pool of applicants for low-paying jobs and skilled jobs may prove difficult. The answer may simply be to move the work to a location where a better applicant pool exists. Many organizations have done this by moving unskilled work to low-wage countries, and today the same approach can be used for skilled jobs. For example, there are very good software engineers in Russia, Israel, India, and other countries.

Many U.S. firms are now using Indian labor to staff call centers. Employees are hired in India, trained in American culture and accents, and in many cases prove effective in relating to U.S. customers who want "personalized local service." Although the training costs are high to teach an Indian national to answer calls for a U.S.-based organization (particularly if the employee has to chitchat with a customer about the weather or how the Yankees are doing), the extra costs are easily offset by the lower wages and the existence of a large applicant pool.

Acquiring Companies and Human Capital

As the value of talent and the difficulty of acquiring it increases, more organizations are using corporate acquisitions to obtain high-performing people. Until recently, acquiring a company just to garner its people was not high on the list of reasons for mergers and acquisitions. A company's human capital was simply not seen as important enough to warrant the complexities and cost of an acquisition; it was easier to hire the people away than to buy the entire company.

But now, acquiring corporations to obtain the skills of their employees is gaining credibility. Many companies find that this is often a quick and relatively easy way to get a large quantity of valuable talent that has worked together for a period of time and has capabilities and core competencies.

Cisco Systems and other technology firms have used acquisitions as a way to build their talent and add to their core competencies. Sysco, the food services company, has used it to acquire human capital in markets it wants to enter.

The challenge in using acquisitions as a way to collect talent is retention, particularly when the people acquired have an equity position in the acquired company. If the terms of the acquisition make them wealthy, there is a danger they will take the wealth and leave the company. For this reason, if you decide to acquire, be sure the deal is structured in ways that lock the desired employees and managers in to working for you. This can be done by delaying the payout of the stock or cash that comes to the equity holders and by making them valued and satisfied members of your organization.

Cisco has done an especially smart job in this regard. In its acquisitions, it tends to acquire firms with no more than a few hundred employees, making it easier to assimilate the acquired people into the firm swiftly. Cisco has a team that specifically focuses on the cultural integration process and makes it clear that the acquired staff are now Cisco employees, entitled to Cisco's excellent benefits and HR practices. This strategy has allowed Cisco to avoid losing most of the top talent it has acquired.

Realistic Job Previews

Realistic job previews are nothing more or less than giving potential employees an accurate portrayal of your organization during the hiring process. The goal is to let applicants know precisely what will be expected of them if they join your organization and what rewards you will offer.

You can create a realistic job preview using many different techniques, from showing videos to applicants to having them interview with all their potential coworkers to requiring them to do an internship or be hired on a temporary basis. I will present these techniques in greater detail in Chapter Five when I discuss the actual hiring process.

With respect to attraction, realistic job previews are a best practice for one important reason: they act as a sort of self-selection process, helping both the organization and the applicants decide if there is a good fit. The more your organization can clearly demonstrate what performance is expected and what rewards are available, the better information your applicants will have to determine if they can commit themselves to your organization. Particularly in times of low unemployment, people will not take jobs that do not seem to them to be a good fit.

Let me give you an example. I studied one company that considered itself very cost-conscious. To make sure that prospective employees understood this aspect of its culture, the company always put job applicants up in an inexpensive hotel when they came to interview with the company. Not surprisingly, this caused the loss of quite a few applicants, but at least the company knew that these people would probably not have fit into the organization anyway.

Employment Contracts

The discussion of best practices for finding and keeping talent is incomplete without examining the issue of employment contracts. Until the 1980s, most large, successful companies enticed managers and professionals to work for them through the use of a tacit or explicit loyalty contract. As mentioned earlier, the loyalty contract essentially guaranteed a great career, retirement benefits, and other perks, with little risk of being terminated. But this type of contract has become much less common and will likely become extinct among large corporations in the not too distant future. A recent survey I did of large U.S. corporations found that only 16 percent said they place a strong emphasis on loyalty, and only 5 percent said they reward seniority.[2]

So what are companies doing today to replace the loyalty contract? About 25 percent of the companies in the United States have adopted a practice I like: a written formal statement of their employment contract that states what they have to offer as an employer and what they expect from their employees.

I believe that most organizations should have employment contracts because they are extremely effective in establishing the relationship between the organization and its employees. I especially like the contract used by Allstate Insurance Company (see Exhibit 4.1) and consider it a best practice. Allstate's contract stresses the mutual commitment shared by the individual and the organization. It identifies both the responsibilities that the organization has to its employees and what they are expected to contribute to Allstate.

Exhibit 4.1. Allstate Employability Contract.

You should expect Allstate to:

1. Offer work that is meaningful and challenging.
2. Promote an environment that encourages open and constructive dialogue.
3. Recognize you for your accomplishments.
4. Provide competitive pay and rewards based on your performance.
5. Advise you on your performance through regular feedback.
6. Create learning opportunities through education and job assignments.
7. Support you in defining career goals.
8. Provide you with information and resources to perform successfully.
9. Promote an environment that is inclusive and free from bias.
10. Foster dignity and respect in all interactions.
11. Establish an environment that promotes a balance of work and personal life.

Allstate expects you to:

1. Perform at levels that significantly increase our ability to outperform the competition.
2. Take on assignments critical to meeting business objectives.
3. Continually develop needed skills.
4. Willingly listen to and act upon feedback.
5. Demonstrate a high level of commitment to achieving company goals.
6. Exhibit no bias in interactions with colleagues and customers.
7. Behave consistently with Allstate's ethical standards.
8. Take personal responsibility for each transaction with our customers and for fostering their trust.
9. Continually improve processes to address customers' needs.

Source: Courtesy of Allstate Insurance Company.

Notice that the contract does not promise job security, only the opportunity to obtain certain rewards and to develop skills and knowledge.

Written contracts like Allstate's have many advantages. They aid in the recruitment process by reinforcing an organization's value proposition and thus contributing to a realistic job preview. And after people are hired, written contracts establish the ground rules for performance and rewards and serve as a touchstone for the organization and the individual throughout their entire relationship.

Most important, my research shows that employment contracts can be a significant enabler of an organization's ability to change. Among the organizations I have studied, those that contractually link skill development with continued employment—and rewards with performance—handle change more effectively than others.[3]

In a sense, you might say that good contracts create "mobile" human capital; people who realize that they must continue to learn, develop, and perform to maintain their positions and careers. Today, organizations need mobile capital. Getting stuck with obsolete human capital is just as big a negative as getting stuck with outdated equipment and materials. And whereas you can readily buy new equipment, often you can't easily buy talented human capital. Instead, organizations need to create a culture that emphasizes that its people must continue to learn and grow as the organization and environment change.

An important corollary to our discussion of contracts is the fact that increasingly, organizations will need to have not a single contract but several in order to handle the diversity of its employment relationships. Historically, most organizations have had two tacit employment contracts, both dysfunctional: one was for managerial and professional employees, the other for nonexempt or hourly employees. The former was the loyalty contract, quietly ensuring job security and various special benefits and perquisites such as company cars, executive dining rooms, and training and development programs, while the latter featured union membership, layoffs, pay by the hour, strictly defined job descriptions, and seniority-driven reward systems.

What should replace them? I believe core employees should be covered by an Allstate-type contract. Noncore employees should have ones that feature rewards for performance and as-needed employment. Having a clear contract for noncore employees can enable you to hire people with particular skills to whom you do not want to make a long-term commitment. Such employment relationships allow you to fill short-term work assignments and to respond to rapid changes in your business.

If your organization begins using multiple employment contracts, be sure that the language of each contract is absolutely clear. The noncore contract must prevent people from developing unrealistic expectations about their chances for long-term employment and for growth and training while they are on the job. Microsoft and several other companies have gotten into difficulties because of just this issue. They used temporary employees extensively, and the lack of clear contracts opened them to lawsuits because the employees believed that they would eventually be treated as regular employees. A clearly written employment contract can avoid this problem and increase the chance that people who take noncore jobs fully understand their relationship with the organization.

Holding Managers Accountable

The behavior of managers is a particularly critical determinant of whether individuals will be satisfied with their jobs and therefore remain with an organization. Managers directly affect the satisfaction of people who work for them. It is one of the most important interpersonal relationships that most people have at work. Further, managers have considerable influence over the financial rewards, development opportunities, and promotion opportunities that individuals receive.

In all too many organizations, managers are assessed only on the basis of how effectively they manage their financial capital and physical resources. They are not measured on how they manage their human capital. This is changing, however. Increasingly, well-managed companies evaluate managers on how well they retain and develop their human capital.

How can your organization evaluate managers on their human capital management and hold them accountable? The answer is relatively simple. You can monitor the satisfaction level of employees in a particular part of the company and get a good indication of how well they are being managed. You can also look at turnover rates and make a judgment as to how effectively managers are performing. It is particularly important to monitor the turnover rates among core employees and individuals who are critical to the core competencies and organizational capabilities of the organization. Losing a core employee is very costly for an organization and therefore needs to be assessed.

Finally, it is important to measure how much the employees who work for a particular manager are developing their skills and knowledge. Good indicators of this are whether employees are moving to more complex, higher-level jobs and whether they are attending training programs.

Holding managers accountable for the satisfaction of their employees and for the retention and development of key human capital is a best practice that more and more organizations are adopting. For example, Sysco Corporation sets satisfaction targets for all its business units. This sends a clear message to managers: you need to pay attention to the development and satisfaction of your key employees and to be sure that they have the kind of opportunities to develop that will keep them wanting to work for you.

Implications for Individuals

The implications and benefits of the increasing focus of organizations on acquiring and retaining human capital can have significant benefits for individuals. So let me indicate what you can learn from and do about the principles and practices set forth in this chapter.

The first lesson is that you can better position yourself as an employee or potential employee by learning about the value propositions organizations offer. If you are considering joining a company, try to find out about its value proposition and what it offers you. If you are currently employed, the more you understand your organization's value proposition, the better position you will be in to know what is expected of you and what rewards you can earn.

As I said earlier, some companies make their value proposition very well known, through extensive branding efforts that make it quite easy for you to learn what the company says it offers. Other organizations don't publicize their value propositions. Often this is because they don't have a clear sense of what it is. As a potential or present employee, this should be of concern to you.

If an organization's value proposition is attractive to you, you should also do research aimed at determining whether it lives up to its commitment. One relatively easy action to take is to visit an Internet chat room that focuses on the organization of your interest. Chat rooms often have considerable background data available and can give you a reasonable idea of what the current issues are in that organization, what the feelings are among employees, and what problems, if any, the company has.

You can also check to see if a corporation is listed on any of the lists of best places to work. If it is, this is clearly a positive sign. If it isn't, it doesn't necessarily mean that the organization is not a good employer; it may simply indicate that the company maintains a low profile or that it has chosen not to enter the competition for these lists.

Any interview you have at a company is also an occasion to assess its value proposition, especially if the company uses realistic job previews that enable you to talk directly to potential coworkers. These people are perhaps your most credible source of information about the organization's value proposition and if the company truly fulfills it. If meeting existing employees is not part of the normal selection process of the organization, it should be a warning signal about what it is like to work in that organization.

I also recommend that you ask organizations you are considering joining for the results of any attitude surveys they have done. If the answer is that the company doesn't do surveys or that it has done them but doesn't want to share them with you, that should also be a warning sign. In general, organizations that don't want to share data and be open with applicants are not good employers. It often is an indicator that the organization is managed in a very traditional bureaucratic way and that as a result there is a good reason for them not to be open to providing a valid sense of what it is like to work there.

There are a number of questions you can ask if you are concerned about the ethical condition of a potential employer. Given the recent history of some major corporations, I hardly need to emphasize that you should be concerned about a company's leadership and ethics.

What should you look for in this regard? A good place to start is by asking whether there is a code of ethics, and if there is one, how widely it is distributed and how it is enforced. A good indication of whether an organization's top executives really want to know what is going on is whether there is a formal "secure and safe" channel for employees to report unethical and illegal behavior, as well as inappropriate behavior by members of management. Finally, it can be useful to ask whether ethics training is given to employees as part of their introduction to the company. It can also be telling to find out if there are examples in the company's history of how it has responded to any ethical problems that have occurred and how whistle-blowers have been treated.

Finally, you can learn a lot by checking on the financial condition of prospective employers, since their ability to deliver on their value proposition is subject to their performance and their financial condition. Find out what financial analysts say about the company, if it is publicly held, and visit its Web site to review any financial data offered to investors. Perhaps you can talk to employees who work for competitors or research the industry as a whole to gather data about your prospective employer's financial condition and business strategy. A wise job candidate needs to understand the economics of the organization's business and the direction that it may take with respect to both its business strategy and its technology.

Creating Your Own Value Proposition

The concept of value propositions can actually be useful to you in a second way, one that is perhaps even more important. Just as organizations can gain clarity about their employment needs by developing a clear value proposition, you can benefit from creating one of your own. The same is true for branding.

Developing your value proposition can help you create a more highly defined sense of who you are and what you are seeking in an employment situation. Given that most people are unaware of their needs and the types of challenges that motivate them, it can be well worth your time to write out your personal Diamond Model—listing your strategy, capabilities, competencies, and the environment in which you perform well. This exercise can then serve as the impetus for allowing you to create a meaningful value proposition about what type of "human capital" you are and what brand you can create in the job market.

Another action to develop and support your value proposition is to take psychological tests or engage in objective assessment activities that provide you with feedback about your skills and knowledge. A wide variety of well-developed tests are available and offered by counselors, placement firms, and career-oriented Web sites. When answered honestly, these tests can provide you with valuable feedback and recommendations about the types of job and work environments that suit your personality.

The Web sites of some of the leading executive search firms increasingly contain assessment tools that you can use to determine whether you fit particular job openings and to assess your strengths, weaknesses, and career orientations. For example, Futurestep, a middle management Web site maintained by Korn/Ferry International, provides multiple assessment instruments, and applicants are provided feedback and potential job fits.

Doing your own value proposition may also help you better understand the rewards that motivate you. Too many people choose jobs without thinking deeply about the mix of rewards that will motivate them to excel and develop a virtuous career spiral. If you find an organization that offers the rewards that meet your needs, you will be challenged to perform well and to seek further growth and development in your career.

Once you have created your value proposition, you can employ some of the same practices that were recommended for organizations to find and attract the right people. Obviously, the personal version of casting a wide net is easily done today using any of the many Internet sites that allow you to search for job opportunities and upload your résumé for companies to view. Your wide net should also include job fairs, which are becoming increasingly popular, and referrals from your friends.

Many people might look askance at the idea of accepting an internship or a temporary assignment. But the implication of this chapter is that if your career is important enough to you, these options, which provide a realistic job preview, can help ensure that you find the right fit in any job you accept. So before committing to a career, keep yourself open to being hired on a temporary basis until you are confident that the fit is right. Or you can apply for multiple jobs, to give yourself more choice before selecting a single organization.

In essence, your value proposition should enable you to optimize the return on your human capital. As a credible, high-performing individual, you need to ask yourself whether the situations you are considering fit your needs in a way that will ultimately satisfy and motivate you to excel.

Changing Jobs

The movement of companies away from loyalty contracts means that you have a lot more options. You can change jobs every few years without being branded as disloyal or difficult. Today, moving to new jobs is so commonplace that it is often regarded as a sign of smart career management.

If you are dissatisfied with your current job and are thinking about changing jobs, there are two additional pieces of advice I have to offer. The first is, don't decrease your performance. If you do, you will harm yourself more than you will harm your organization. You run the risk of getting a reputation as a poor performer, which can make it difficult to get another job and prevent you from being rehired if you quit and then at a later time want to return.

Second, before you take another job, be sure to research your potential employer carefully. There is a tendency for situations you don't know well to look better than they really are.

Once you have decided to change jobs, there is one last issue to consider if you are currently employed: be sure to carefully manage your exit from your existing organization. Give your employer adequate notice, and be sure to leave in a way that doesn't burn your bridges behind you. Not only are you likely to need a reference from your former employer, but the time may come when you would once again like to work for the company.

How do you leave gracefully? Among the factors to consider are the amount of notification you give and your willingness to train and provide information to the person who is going to replace you. Finally, when explaining why you are leaving, it is better to talk about the positive things that have attracted you to another employer rather than to be negative about your current situation.

Chapter Five

Hire the Right People

TREAT PEOPLE RIGHT PRINCIPLE #2

Organizations must hire people who fit with their values, core competencies, and strategic goals.

People can rarely be forced to fit into an organization after they are hired. This makes hiring the right employees absolutely essential. As much as humanly possible, you need to select applicants who will fit into your culture and perform effectively—and who will ultimately contribute to your organization's virtuous spiral.

What Leads to Good Hiring Decisions

Hiring requires a disciplined process and clear practices that thoroughly assess the competencies, skills, knowledge, personality, and needs of the people you consider hiring. Through the hiring process, you need to be able to determine how well a candidate will fit the current and future needs of your organization. Fit can be quite complex and difficult to determine, so you need to use specific and objective criteria that are based on the kinds of work your organization offers and the kinds of skills, knowledge, competencies, and personality that people need to possess to perform that work effectively.

The hiring process represents the first critical point in the relationship between an organization and its employees. But keep in mind that this is often not the last time you will be making job placement decisions concerning your employees.

Today, as organizations continuously seek to fill newly created jobs and eliminate old ones, many current employees will seek out new opportunities, and you will need to decide whether to move them up or laterally to a new job. As time goes on, further changes in the skill needs of your organization are also likely to create situations where you will have to decide which employees to retain and which to terminate.

Effective decisions about whom to retain and whom to terminate are critical in upgrading the quality of your workforce and being sure that it has the skills to execute the core competencies and capabilities your organization needs.

The selection process is particularly important because it is a clear decision point. As such, it is very important that you test the major principles and practices that your organization uses to guide its selection and placement decisions against the ones that are recommended in this chapter.

Convey the Importance of Hiring

All too often organizations use a hiring process that solely emphasizes selecting the best individual. But the hiring process needs to be more than just an effort to hire the best people. It needs to introduce them to your organization in a way that gives them a realistic expectation of what work will be like and places them in an environment that helps them make a good decision as to whether the organization represents a good fit for them.

A careful selection process can be critical to giving individuals the view that they are valued by the organization, that the organization is a desirable place to work, and that it cares about its human capital. It can help give new hires the impression that they are fortunate to be working for the organization. People tend to value membership in organizations that have high entrance standards and carefully assess all potential members. This is an important phenomenon and one that organizations need to put front and center as they design their selection processes.

Southwest Airlines interviews twenty-five applicants for every one they hire. They can do this because they have a clearly established, attractive brand as an employer. It allows the company to hire people who are potentially a great fit and helps convince new hires that they are truly special and fortunate to get a job with Southwest.

Microsoft puts every new employee through an intensive multiple-day interview process. Job candidates talk to people from different parts of the organization and are asked very difficult interview questions. No one who survives the process has any doubt that Microsoft takes hiring seriously.

Use Objective Data

In my view, organizations need to increasingly use objective data in the hiring process. Many available assessment tools can be brought into play here, from personality tests to knowledge exams to realistic job previews and work samples.

There is no magic formula concerning how much and what kind of data you need from people to determine whether or not they will be a good fit with your organization. But a useful generalization is that you need to determine if the applicant has all of the following:

- The skills and knowledge you require
- The competencies required to learn new skills and adjust to new tasks
- The interpersonal skills to deal with coworkers and customers
- The motivation to perform well

In my view, data about these issues are best obtained from multiple sources. Interviews are not enough, nor are tests or background checks; instead, you need to use all of them, as well as any other sources of data on how job candidates have performed in the past.

Don't Neglect Background and Ethics

A good rule of thumb in hiring decisions is that past behavior is the best predictor of future behavior. For this reason, don't neglect checking on an individual's past history, through both reference checks and résumé validation.

As surprising as it may seem, nearly 35 percent of all job applicants put false data on their résumés and job applications. This is true for even high-profile individuals, so don't assume that integrity can be questionable only up to a certain level of executive.

For example, Al Dunlop, who became known as "Chainsaw Al" because of his downsizing of Scott Paper and his destruction of Sunbeam Corporation, circulated a falsified résumé for years. To make his background look better, he modified his employment history so that it excluded a stint he had as a CEO of a small company that ended up in bankruptcy. Surprisingly, this omission was discovered only after his failure at Sunbeam Corporation.

A stranger example of résumé falsification is the case of Al Martin, a major league baseball player who played for the Seattle Mariners and several other major league teams. He included in his biography the claim that he played college football for the University of Southern California. He even talked to his teammates about plays that he made during his football career. It all sounded good, but Martin never played football at USC; in fact, he never attended USC at all. Then there is the case of the Pulitzer Prize—winning professor who claimed to have been active in the Vietnam War. He even lectured in his class about his exploits. The problem was that during his military career, he never went overseas. When the truth came out, his university suspended him.

The moral is, be diligent in checking an applicant's background. You don't want to end up in the situation of hiring someone, only later to discover evidence of ethical lapses or poor judgment in the past.

Involve the People Who Will Work with the New Hire

In most cases, it is beneficial to involve the people who will be working with the new hire in the selection process. There are at least two reasons for this. First, they are familiar with the work situation, so they can ask and answer relevant questions and bring an informed perspective to the hiring process. Second, their commitment to helping the individual be successful once in the organization is partly determined by whether they have endorsed the hire.

This second point is often overlooked but is an important factor to consider. People will often make an extra effort to see that someone is successful when they have been asked for their opinion on whether to hire the applicant. This is particularly true in group and team situations. When team members have an active role in interviewing and hiring, they will work hard to ensure the success of the individual who is hired.

However, if you involve people in the selection process, be sure that they are fully trained in the legal and organizational issues involved. Managers and others who are going to be involved in recruitment and selection need to know about testing, interviewing, behavior-based selection interview processes, and what questions cannot be asked.

Failure to train interviewers and managers involved in selection and placement processes can lead to disaster. It can result not only in bad hiring decisions but also in significant legal liabilities caused by behaviors that violate regulations with respect to discrimination and the rights of applicants. It can also result in new hires having unrealistic expectations.

Validate Your Selection Results

It is very important that your organization validate its selection process on a regular basis. I am not talking about simply tracking the success rate of individuals who are hired. Validation efforts need to determine the accuracy of the different parts of your organization's selection process in predicting the performance of individuals once they have joined the organization.

There are literally thousands of studies on the selection practices used in companies. These studies consistently show that many widely used practices, such as simple personality tests and unstructured interviews, are not valid predictors of how effective an employee will be. Some of these practices may be fine in serving another purpose, such as contributing to a realistic job preview or increasing the commitment of employees to helping the individual succeed, but they are not valid predictors of whether someone will actually be successful.

Every selection process must have at least some tests or processes that have been validated, and these need to be the major factors in determining who is hired. Ignoring this point can open you to numerous legal and ethical problems. You owe it to yourself and the applicants to use validated selection processes. To do otherwise is to invite trouble. Hiring the wrong individual has high organizational and social costs because it typically leads to poor performance, premature turnover, and weakened organizations.

Apply the Same Selection Process to Career Moves

I recommend that the same principles I have enumerated to guide the selection of new hires be used in the placement of current employees in new positions. They need to be given a realistic preview of the nature of the job and what the work will be like. They need to be assessed in terms of whether they can do the work. And the individuals with whom they will work need to have input into whether they are given the job or not.

Often the placement processes in organizations are relatively informal, relying on networking to choose candidates. As a result, placement decisions are often seen as unfair and arbitrary. In most cases, the systems are in fact dysfunctional because they do not create a culture that continuously emphasizes the importance of managing human capital well.

Although it is more time-consuming and in some ways more bureaucratic, it is typically far better to go through a public process in order to fill a vacant position. This is true even though the intention is to fill it with someone who already works for the organization. You should make a public announcement that the opening exists, that there is an opportunity for individuals to apply, and that there will be a formal process to select the best-qualified individual.

It is only by conducting a thorough, formal process that the best placement decisions can be made and that people can feel that they have opportunities within the organization to develop and advance their careers. This practice can also help organizations better understand the career aspirations of their employees and help them assess the knowledge, skills, and competencies of their workforce.

Provide Continuous Feedback

To support treating people right, creating a good fit between individuals and organizations needs to be a continuous process. It must start with a selection process that is well developed and carefully done and must continue throughout the employee's entire history with an organization. Rather than being an event-driven process, it needs to be an ongoing process. By this I mean, rather than being something that occurs only when a job opening occurs and individuals are screened for that opening, it needs to be an ongoing process in which individuals are given the opportunity to take on new tasks, assignments, and work roles.

The process should involve making public the opportunities that exist internally, notifying people of their opportunities, and giving them feedback on how they are progressing in their skill and knowledge development. GE, Honeywell, and a number of other companies have taken steps to formalize career development feedback to individuals. They do an annual talent review that looks at the development of all their key employees. In the case of GE, the CEO looks at the top two thousand managers in the corporation. The outcome of this review is a decision to develop some employees and to terminate those whose skills are not developing or do not suit the direction in which the corporation is heading.

Eliminating individuals who no longer fit the strategic direction of the business is a realistic part of maintaining a virtuous spiral in an organization. It is, perhaps, the most important step an organization can take to indicate that the continued employment of its employees depends on their performance and skills. To prevent the implementation of this policy from being dysfunctional, decision making has to be handled extremely well. As we will discuss in later chapters, it needs to involve a valid assessment of the person's performance and skills, feedback to the individual, and an opportunity to improve their skills and performance when there is a problem.

Best Practices in Hiring and Placement

In my research, I have found a variety of selection and placement practices that support a good fit between individuals and organizations. This is an area where rapid change is occurring in what organizations actually do. The increasing importance of human capital is motivating organizations to try new approaches and to make sure that they are using the best possible practices. I will highlight some of the most powerful practices organizations are using and analyze the implications of their use in terms of treating people right.

Realistic Job Previews

We talked about realistic job previews in Chapter Four, noting how they help organizations impart their value propositions to applicants. As you recall, the goal of a realistic job preview is to make sure the applicant knows precisely what the job entails, what is expected, and what rewards are offered. But realistic job previews can be much more than that. They can be an opportunity to verify that the applicant can perform the job in the way that you want.

In fact, one of the best practices in conducting realistic previews is to have applicants actually do the work or produce a work sample.

One company I worked with in the customer service sector simulates for applicants some typical customer service encounters that occur. They use real customers with the applicants, and then ask the customers whether they would like to be served by the job applicant in the future.

Southwest Airlines bases its hiring decisions on a realistic preview. It has job applicants tell jokes and make announcements in front of a group of employees. This is intended to simulate the kinds of situations found aboard airplanes and as such serves the needs of both the company and the applicants. It gives the organization considerable information about how the applicants will perform while giving them a good sense of the type of work that they will be expected to handle.

Some companies ask that applicants do an internship—a very effective way to give them a chance to experience the work while giving the organization a chance to assess the candidate. Particularly if the internship lasts several months, both the individual and the organization can get a good feeling for how well the person fits into the culture.

Other companies hire applicants as temporary employees to ensure that they have firsthand experience on the job before agreeing to hire them. One manufacturing firm I studied had a significant turnover problem in one of its plants. Although the facility was clean and safe, the work was very repetitive, and a large number of new employees, having an unrealistic idea of their what their jobs would be like, were disappointed once they started and soon left. To implement a realistic job preview, the company opted to hire all applicants only as temporary workers for at least four weeks. After this trial period, those who were good performers were given the opportunity to become full-time employees, and the others were released. The people who stayed usually turned out to be excellent long-term employees.

Another application of realistic job previews is to begin to socialize and educate people into your organization's culture. This can be accomplished in many ways. One simple technique is to have job applicants interview with most or all of the people they will work with. Comprehensive interviews can provide applicants with a good sense of the social and cultural atmosphere they will encounter.

To provide a preview, some organizations such as Ford Motor Company and Cummins Engines show applicants a video that presents views of people doing the actual work. Let me interject a small caution about this, though. Your video can be as forthright as you want it to be, but you may want to use some discretion. Years ago, Ford produced a video called *Don't Color It like Disneyland* that portrayed their jobs so honestly that no applicant could doubt the boring nature of Ford's assembly line work. The cold directness of the video helped reduce turnover, because people knew from the start what to do expect, but Ford decided to cease using it because it left such a negative image of the company.

Realistic job previews should also be used for job changes that involve your current employees. Though these employees already work for you, the same benefits can be gained by asking them to go through a realistic job preview.

For example, FedEx uses a realistic preview situation to select first-level supervisors from its employees. When employees say they are interested in being promoted to this level, they are asked to come to a workshop, designed to have candidates participate in a number of simulations of the kind of interpersonal situations that first-line supervisors face. FedEx offers this workshop only on weekends, specifically to emphasize to the candidates that being a supervisor involves a significant time commitment over and above being a nonmanagement employee. Demanding a weekend of time is thus a way to initially screen applicants with respect to their commitment to being successful as a first-line supervisor.

Realistic job previews cannot always be done because in some cases people need training or certification before they can do the work required. But when they can be done, they are clearly a win-win proposition. They help avoid wrong hires, and they provide applicants with enough information to decide if the work situation will meet their needs. In my view, they also are extremely important from the point of view of treating people right, in that they support informed choice and help people become more thoughtful decision makers in managing their careers.

Matching the Interview Process with the Job

Unstructured interviews that are simply general discussions rarely provide data that improve selection decisions. However, interviews with targeted questions can provide valid data and can help facilitate the selection decision, especially if the interview process focuses on the behaviors you need the person to excel in.

For example, if you are looking for someone to fulfill an entrepreneurial role in your organization, you want to know whether the applicant has demonstrated entrepreneurial behavior in the past. You can find this out only by asking specific questions in interviews about past experiences, entrepreneurial efforts, and so on. The same is true if you are looking to hire someone who can work effectively in teams. Questions concerning the roles applicants have played in teams in the past, examples of successful teams they have been on, and the like, can be critical in determining whether candidates have shown propensity in the past to work effectively in a team environment.

General Electric is a good example of a company that uses carefully structured interviews to select managers. Interviewers ask key questions about applicants' past behavior in order to determine whether they have a history of demonstrating leadership. For example, candidates for a managerial job are asked what positions they have had in the past that required them to be leaders. Follow-up questions then focus on how they got things done, what their leadership style was, and what results were produced.

Microsoft adds an interesting twist to the interviewing process: it has at least one "outsider," a person who will not work with the applicant, meet and assess the applicant. Microsoft does this to avoid too much of a "groupthink" phenomenon in the hiring process and to obtain a broader perspective on who gets hired. Part of the rationale is to avoid developing pockets of divergent cultures because different parts of the organization engage in their own hiring and selection activities.

Testing

In today's world, organizations must constantly meet the challenge of jobs that have a changing portfolio of tasks and assignments, and they must constantly make decisions about fitting employees to tasks and tasks to employees. This means that it is increasingly important to hire people with an eye toward how well they fit the organization's need for change, particularly in regard to their ability and willingness to learn new skills.

This is where psychological testing is a best practice worthy of adoption in most organizations. Testing can indicate, for example, the underlying competencies and personalities of people and thus be a good predictor of someone's ability to learn specific knowledge and skills. Where people are being hired for their potential, it makes a great deal of sense to assess their ability to learn.

It also makes sense, in many situations, to use tests to assess an individual's personality, which, as we said earlier, is relatively fixed by the time a person enters the workforce. A test that assesses personality can be a predictor of how the person will react to changes in the work environment and to learning opportunities.

Although they can be useful, personality tests have an important limitation. Some people do not provide accurate data when completing tests. They often provide the answers they think the company wants to hear. That is why it is very important to compare any data that come from tests with data from interviews and other assessments of personality that might be available. For example, test data can be compared to interview reports about how people have made their career choices, as well as the kinds of activities they prefer.

Tailoring the Selection Process to the Employment Contract

When organizations have the need for different types of employees—for example, contrast those who are needed for immediately applicable technical skills and knowledge with those who are hired with development in mind—it becomes important to tailor the selection process to the hiring situation.

The selection process for those who are hired for their particular technical expertise and operational excellence will usually need to focus on their present skills and their motivation to apply those skills to a specific project. You especially want to assess whether it is possible to develop *commitment* among these employees, by which I do not mean loyalty to the organization but rather commitment to performing well on an already identified task, under existing working conditions.

As for long-term developmental hires, obviously, your selection process needs to be extensive, rigorous, and in-depth. What matters most in selecting them is an evaluation not so much of a set of specific skills as of their underlying competencies, working style, personality, willingness to learn, long-term career aspirations, and preferences with respect to rewards. It is also particularly important to look at their fit with the culture of your organization.

Web-Based Tracking Systems

In recent years, technology has come to the rescue to improve many aspects of the hiring process. One excellent innovation is Internet-based systems that track job applicants during the selection process. As people go from interview to interview, the interviewers can access the system to record their impressions, as well as to raise additional questions that future interviewers should follow up on as the candidate circulates.

Microsoft has an excellent Web-enabled interviewing process. As part of a carefully structured interview, interviewers ask a number of questions to test an applicant's ability to think. After each interview, the interviewer enters key issues on the appropriate Web site, suggesting follow-up questions that should be asked by the next interviewer. This creates a dynamic process that is both structured and cumulative, since it is informed by previous answers. The result is a selection experience that Microsoft feels is very effective at both hiring the right people and giving applicants an honest sense of what working at Microsoft is like.

Evaluating Your Selection and Placement System

Consistently evaluating the effectiveness of your selection and placement system is a best practice that I highly recommend. I am referring to actions that go beyond validating its predictive accuracy. As I mentioned earlier, this is important, but more needs to be done. You need to collect survey data regarding the satisfaction of employees with the hiring process on a regular and systematic basis. Dow Chemical, for example, does this in assessing its internal job-posting system. Employees are regularly asked about whether they feel the system is meeting their needs.

It can also be useful to look at how outside job candidates view the entire hiring process of the organization. Find out what impression they get about your company and whether they feel they were treated fairly in the process. Gather this information from people who joined the company as well as those who did not.

Overall, the selection and placement systems of your organization are so important to your human capital management that you cannot afford not to continually assess and improve them.

Managing Layoffs and Downsizing

Reductions in staff are high-risk actions for organizations. When carelessly and indiscriminately managed, layoffs and downsizings can ruin your brand, damage your culture in ways that make the people who remain less productive, result in the loss of significant knowledge and social capital, and be major triggers of death spirals. In many ways, how you handle layoffs can be even more crucial to your reputation for treating people right than initial hiring decisions.

The truth is, many companies simply overreact to downturns in their business. A growing body of evidence says that organizations tend to eliminate too many people in times of economic distress, incurring long-term costs that are often far greater than the short-term savings. These costs include losing people who are not easily rehired when the economic downturn is over; losing people who carry some of your organizational capabilities and core competencies; losing your social capital, which is found in the relationships and implicit knowledge that former employees have; and causing existing employees to lose faith in your company and its management, resulting in turnover among the remaining employees when the labor market improves.

Clearly, it would be foolish to argue against all staff reductions. Sometimes layoffs and downsizings are necessary for a variety of good reasons: your strategy changes, a restructuring is needed to bring in different skills, or an economic downturn forces the need for cost reductions. Sometimes building a new core competency can be accomplished only by recruiting new employees.

But there are significant advantages to not downsizing or doing only a little of it. For example, in an economic downturn, you may be able to grab market share or even gain a dominant position over competitors who overreduce their staff. This is particularly true if your competitors lose their ability to service their customers well or if they are in a poor position to recover when the downturn is over. You can also use a period of downturn to develop new products or to improve your employees' skills and knowledge, either of which can boost you over competitors and launch or support a virtuous spiral.

In my view, staff reductions should be used only as a last resort, after weighing the many other less disruptive options you may have to reduce labor costs, including these:

- Voluntary leaves/terminations
- Shorter working hours
- Pay reductions
- Delayed start dates for new hires
- Cutting back on the use of temporary employees
- Shortened workweeks
- Reduced bonus and variable pay amounts
- Reduced benefits and extras

If involuntary reductions in staff are necessary, I also believe it is critical that senior management make a strong case for them as the only practical alternative under the business conditions. It is important that management and employees have a good understanding of the nature of the business, the economic condition of the industry, and the status of the organization so that everyone comprehends why the reductions are needed. When the business case is compelling, reductions may slow down your virtuous spiral, but they don't have to end it.

Downsizing must be handled in ways that fully support your value proposition and your brand. For example, in deciding whom to lay off, many companies follow the traditional method of basing layoffs on seniority, but this does not really fit the demands of today's business environment. It often means that some of your best employees will be lost, and as a result, your organization's ability to perform will be diminished.

Reductions in staff are nearly always more effective when based on performance and ability, assuming you have good performance measures on which to decide. This means that you need to be sure to have done your homework to obtain high-quality data on the performance of your people through regular performance appraisals. Making performance-based staff reductions on the basis on poor or inadequate performance data is perhaps the worst step you can take; it damages your credibility and fosters mistrust among the remaining employees. It can also result in the wrong individuals being laid off; it may even lead to lawsuits.

In addition, once you decide to lay off an employee, be sure to assess whether the person is someone you may want to ask to rejoin the organization at a later date. Particularly in the case of a business cycle downturn, you can benefit by rerecruiting laid-off employees, so it is important to make sure that good performers leave the organization with positive feelings. You can foster goodwill in a number of ways, including a good severance package, offering placement services, and career counseling.

Some of the best practices I have seen in managing layoffs occurred in technology firms during the 2001 technology downturn. For example, Cisco paid employees part of their salaries if they went to work for volunteer organizations or contributed their time to public service. Other organizations paid tuition for laid-off employees so that they could improve their knowledge and be ready to reenter the organization at a later date with better skills and a positive attitude toward the company. Charles Schwab offered a

$7,500 "hire-back" bonus to anyone rehired within eighteen months. And at Microsoft and a host of other technology companies, the best employees were offered incentives to stay.

It is hardly surprising that these companies created these practices, given the importance of human capital to them and the difficulties they had recruiting and retaining it in the 1990s. Their response to the downturn is perhaps an indicator that more organizations in the future will be centered on human capital and will deal with future economic downturns in the spirit of treating people right.

On the other hand, not all firms dealt effectively with the downturn. Some firms overreacted to it and reduced their labor force too extensively. Many even showed less concern for their employees than they had in the past, perhaps reflecting the death of the loyalty contract in their firms. Because they overreacted, they lost credibility as employers and as a result will likely have difficulty in responding when the markets for their businesses turn around.

Implications for Individuals

The recommendations in this chapter for how organizations need to approach their selection and placement process have powerful implications for all individuals. The more that organizations adopt these hiring procedures and best practices, the more you can benefit by finding satisfying and rewarding jobs.

But in order to benefit, you must be an effective manager of your job search and career. The overarching message to learn here is that as valuable human capital you have increased importance to organizations.

However, to capitalize on your capital, as it were, you must develop a strong sense of your knowledge and skills and of what you find rewarding about work. As I suggested in Chapter Four, the first step of this process is to fashion your own value proposition.

Your ability to gather data on yourself is an increasingly important element in successful career management. One way to do this is to not be shy about applying for jobs, both internal and external; and to use the selection process to learn something about the options that are available to you, as well as about your personal strengths, interests, and competencies. If the opportunity presents itself, negotiate with prospective employers for complete feedback on the results of any tests they ask you to take. This includes psychological tests, assessment center processes, or any other experiences they have where data have been gathered about you that can give you insight into your own needs, desires, and competencies. In fact, it makes sense for you to target positions that are likely to give you direct feedback about your abilities.

As an active manager of your own career, check employment postings on your company's Web site on a regular basis. In addition, look outside your organization to see what is available. It is impossible to be a good self-manager without actively gathering information about the various opportunities that exist for you.

Learn to exercise discipline in accepting jobs. Avoid putting yourself in situations that do not have a high likelihood of meeting your needs or in which you risk performing less than successfully. This can happen if you present an image of yourself that is not realistic. For the selection and placement process to work well, you need to be candid in your self-description and accurate in the information you give organizations.

An organization's selection process usually yields important information about its culture and concern for its human capital. Be especially cautious of any organization that doesn't take the selection process seriously and fails to gather good data from job applicants. That reflects a serious lack of attention to the importance of human capital to the organization, a lack that might come back to haunt you should you decide to work there.

A long hiring process—which can be frustrating at times—may actually be a good sign. That often means the company values its people and wants to take its time—à la Microsoft—in choosing new hires. Microsoft takes several weeks and requires intensive time commitments from potential applicants, but its process is well designed and results in selecting good employees, who then are sure they want to work there.

Of course, the process can become too long and too bureaucratic, and you want to avoid organizations that keep you on hold indefinitely. For example, some government agencies, such as the Los Angeles Police Department, are infamous for taking six months to a year to process a job applicant. This is clearly the type of situation to flee from.

If you are applying for a position and are offered an employment contract or are in a position to ask for one, don't hesitate to pay a great deal of attention to the contract's termination clause. In the past, the idea of an applicant discussing a termination agreement was considered counterproductive, if not insulting. Many executives interpreted this to mean that an applicant lacked confidence and was not committed to staying with the organization a long time.

Today, however, senior executives almost always have employment contracts that include termination clauses. Indeed, they often get extremely generous payments when they leave the organization (ten of millions of dollars in the case of key executives who have left Disney and Mattel, to mention just two examples), even if they leave because of poor performance. Obviously, most employees cannot realistically expect to get a generous severance package if they are let go as a result of performance or downsizing.

But if you are in high demand, you may well be able to at least get an employment contract that calls for weeks or months of pay as part of the severance package. You may also be able to negotiate for the immediate vesting of your stock options and a continuation of your benefits.

At the very least, you should ask about specific policies regarding severance benefits when you join an organization. (You should also research as much as possible the history of how reductions in staff have been handled, particularly with respect to severance pay and unvested options.) In short, the day has come when you absolutely must pay serious attention to your exit strategy and take it into consideration when deciding which job to choose and the kind of deal you can make.

Finally, it is now time to recognize that your "job" is likely to be a regularly changing set of duties and responsibilities rather than a fixed set of tasks. Historically, many companies have had job descriptions that adequately captured what people were expected to do for a considerable period of time. But with today's rapid pace of change in business strategies, organizational design, and technology, it is unrealistic to continue thinking that today's jobs can be set in stone.

Instead, you should think of your job as likely having opportunities to take on new tasks and assignments on a regular basis. Each change represents a chance to learn a new skill and perhaps some-thing about yourself. Rather than resisting new assignments and change, I suggest that you embrace them, eagerly agreeing to par-ticipate in new activities and to learn new areas of expertise.

The fact is, there is little security in today's business environ-ment. It is critical that you clearly realize that the only security you have in this chaotic business world consists of your skills, your knowledge, and your track record. So take full advantage of all the learning and growing opportunities any new environment offers you. As I tell my M.B.A. students, take the best job you are offered, learn everything you can, work hard while you are there—and be prepared to leave.

Chapter Six

Develop People Right

TREAT PEOPLE RIGHT PRINCIPLE #3

Organizations must continuously train employees to do their jobs and offer them opportunities to grow and develop.

People enjoy learning—there's no doubt about it—and it touches on an important treat people right principle for both organizations and people: the value of continuous, ongoing training and development in creating a virtuous spiral.

Learning is an intrinsically satisfying and rewarding experience. Most people enjoy opportunities to learn, develop, and experience new things. Learning is especially useful when it comes to careers. It allows people to develop new skills and knowledge that raise their ability to perform and excel. It increases their market value and helps them compete for more rewarding and challenging jobs.

Why Train and Develop

Learning is a winning proposition for organizations too. Companies need skilled employees in order to develop their organizational capabilities and core competencies. Increasing the skills of employees is fundamental to sustaining a virtuous spiral. Many research studies have shown that an investment in skill and knowledge development can lead to significantly improved job performance. Overall, organizations can gain by making wise commitments to training their employees.

Given the potential benefits, it is surprising that many organizations have not made larger investments in developing their people. One probable reason is that for much of the twentieth century, many jobs were structured so that they could be done by people who didn't have much in the way of skills or knowledge. Under the old "scientific management philosophy," work was intentionally designed to reduce the need for skilled employees and avoid the costs of training. It was thought to be far cheaper to create easy-to-do jobs than to train and retain skilled employees.

Today, this approach no longer works. An ever-increasing amount of work is inherently complex, requiring people with advanced levels of skill and knowledge. Most organizations need people with a high degree of knowledge and a variety of skills, especially in technology and expert service businesses. They simply cannot make do with an unskilled workforce.

That said, we need to consider when and how organizations should train their employees. To answer this question, I have identified some essential principles to guide companies in designing development programs that support a virtuous spiral.

Adopt a New Stance Toward Training

In the past, when organizations did training, it was based on looking at existing jobs and analyzing the skills people needed to do them. A person's job and perhaps career path largely dictated the kinds of skills and knowledge the person needed to learn. Training and development were consequently focused on preparing people to do their current jobs and possibly their next ones.

This approach to training worked well for many years, largely because organizations knew or could easily predict what jobs would be like. This allowed them to develop the programs needed to train employees for the jobs they would have in the future.

Today's business environment is radically different from those simple times. Many business organizations in the twenty-first century don't know what jobs they will need to fill in the coming year or two, much less the coming decades. The challenges of global competition, the rapid growth of knowledge, and the constant changes of technology have made it almost impossible to reasonably predict what jobs will exist and what skills employees will need down the road.

One might even say that as a whole, the idea of individuals having a single career is obsolete. People no longer will have careers that involve working for only one or two organizations or in just one or two areas of expertise or knowledge. Organizations today are likely to need to develop new core competencies and capabilities at least every decade, so the concept of permanent areas of expertise no longer applies for them either.

Does this mean that companies should not invest in the development of their people? I don't think so, but it does suggest that organizations need to take a very different approach toward training. This approach is founded on two premises.

The first is that organizations are simply no longer in a position to make most decisions about what their people should learn and how they can be best positioned for employment in the future. If organizations want to retain their people and support their development, about the best they can do is to provide them with information about what is happening within their walls, what their business strategy is, and what kind of technical areas and core competencies they anticipate they will need in the future. Yes, there may be some instances when organizations also should provide people with financial and technical support if they are learning essential skills the company knows it will require, but in general, organizations can no longer take responsibility for the long-term development of their people.

That first premise gives rise to the second premise. In this new world, people need to be—and are, whether they like it or not—responsible for making their own decisions about what they learn and how they develop their careers. Organizations may provide them with information about what new skills are likely to be needed in the future and perhaps a chance to learn those skills, but for the most part, people must make their own choices about what skills to develop and how to develop them. They are now responsible for their own employability. This increases the risk for people, since they may judge incorrectly and find themselves poorly positioned to remain employees of their current organization or, for that matter, most organizations. No matter how anxiety-producing it may be for them, the reality is that it is now up to employees to make more and more decisions about their careers.

In my view, this career self-management approach will increasingly become the model on which organizations and people fashion employment relationships. It is a critical part of what I referred to in Chapter Five as "mobile human capital." It may not sound like a way to create a virtuous spiral, but it is. Here's why.

We have now entered an era in which the reality is that careers must be flexible and changeable. People need to move from job to job and from organization to organization to pursue their careers, and organizations can afford to keep people only for the time during which their skills are useful. People need to make significant changes to their skill set several times during their lifetime, simply because many skills will become obsolete and need to be replaced by new ones.

Meanwhile, organizations cannot continue to employ people simply because they are loyal. They need people whose skills and abilities fit their ever-changing strategies. Mobility has become more than a new buzzword; it is the new reality. Given this reality, organizations need to do what they can to support their employees being employable, but they should not promise something they cannot deliver—a career.

Decide Whether to Buy or Develop Talent

Organizations always have had to decide whether to buy or develop their talent. Each choice has pros and cons.

Buying talent—hiring experienced people—allows organizations to change more quickly because they can bring in the skills they need at a moment's notice. However, buying talent leads to relatively higher labor costs because it costs more to attract already skilled people. Buying talent also tends to create less loyal employees, who are able and willing to move to other organizations that offer higher pay and better opportunities.

Developing employees to handle new business challenges and new technologies results in longer-term, more loyal employees. It also gives organizations more control over their training, ensuring that people learn to do things in ways that precisely fit the organization's needs. However, training requires an investment of time and money. It is also a slow approach to changing a company's core competencies.

The radical changes in today's business environment are altering the old pros and cons of the buy-versus-develop decision in many ways. One critical factor is that most organizations now need to travel light. They have little room for redundancy in resources, particularly human capital. The downsizings of the early 1990s and the early 2000s have created organizations with little slack. With relentless pressure to constantly improve shareholder value, it is unlikely that organizations in the future will ever again develop a great amount of slack.

The effects of this on the development side of the buy-versus-develop equation are significant. Although organizations may want to train and develop their people, it is likely that any training they undertake will have to be clearly oriented toward solving immediate problems, rather than long-term career development. Organizations can no longer afford to train people in exchange for loyalty. Their most pressing goals will dictate the type of training they need to offer.

The one exception here may be management and leadership skills. These skills always seem to be in short supply, and how people are led is a key source of competitive advantage. An organization needs to have a core group of leaders who set the leadership culture of the organization by modeling how the organization wants its people to be led. I am convinced that this can be best done by developing leaders, not buying them.

Even when an organization wants to develop its employees, the rapid pace of today's business world may rule it out. All it takes is one competitor to develop or implement a new technology to make an organization realize that it simply doesn't have time to retrain an existing workforce. It will lose its competitive edge unless it hires people who already have the skills it needs today. Thus hiring talent may be the only way some organizations can survive in the future.

On the other hand, in some cases, organizations may simply not be able to find the talent they need because there are few people, if any, in the labor market who have the necessary skills. This is particularly likely to happen to organizations that are technology leaders, like Intel and Applied Materials. When this happens, some organizations may have no choice but to train and develop their existing employees to support a virtuous spiral relationship with their workforce.

In the end, I believe that most large organizations will need to be good at both buying and training people in order to keep pace with change. They will need to be able to size up the situation quickly and respond accordingly—buying talent when quick change is needed and developing it when time and costs allow.

Whichever approach to skill acquisition an organization takes, I believe it must be stated in the employment contract. An organization's approach to skill development very much shapes the way people look at their work situation and needs to be made clear at the time people join the organization. Employees need to be told who is responsible for their careers, what support they can expect, and how the organization thinks about the development of their careers.

Use Just-in-Time Training

Even organizations that favor buying talent and skills need to use targeted "just-in-time" training. This type of training is undertaken with little advance warning and is focused on content that the organization suddenly realizes its people need to do their current jobs.

In today's world, just-in-time training is often needed for new hires as part of their onboarding process, as well as for current employees, who may need to update their skills when a new approach to technology, customer service, budgets, or some other management system affects the area in which they work.

The advantage of just-in-time training is that it actually fits well with the way adults learn best. Adults tend to learn best when they need to solve a problem and when the training they receive addresses a specific issue on which they need to work.

Provide General Training

I do not want to dismiss completely the idea of companies providing general education because this type of training has certain potential payoffs worth considering. First and foremost, general training can ultimately increase employee performance. Teaching people basic thinking, problem solving, and other skills often makes them better equipped to do their jobs and to acquire other skills relevant to the work they do.

A commitment to general training can be part of an organization's brand as an employer and can be used to persuade people that the company has a commitment to its employees. This, in turn, can lead to having employees who are more satisfied in their jobs and hence more likely to remain with the company. Training can thus be seen as a significant benefit of being employed by the company and as a result act as an effective recruiting and retention device.

Investing in your employees' general development can also have a significant impact on the culture of your organization. It is a tangible way to indicate to employees that the organization values its human capital and that it wants to foster education and development.

The downside of providing general education to employees is that you effectively enhance their value to other employers. Some people in your organization who want to progress in their careers may feel more empowered to leave, thanks to the education you have given them. In general, people usually do not leave while they are still enjoying the opportunity to take courses and improve their skills. However, once they have acquired these skills, they may very well decide that they can better utilize them and earn more as a result of working elsewhere. And since loyalty is dead, they leave.

Best Practices to Develop Human Capital

Organizations can take many types of actions to develop their people. Of course, the most common are traditional approaches involving formal training programs. Evidence indicates that the amount of formal training by companies is increasing. My research shows a steady upswing since 1987.[1] In particular, many companies have made great efforts to improve the information technology skills of their people through the use of formal training.

One of the most interesting training actions of many U.S. corporations is the creation of "corporate universities" that effectively consolidate the various training programs within an organization. More than a thousand corporations report that they have a university. Many of these are virtual universities that rely on outside vendors and have no faculty or buildings, but they demonstrate a solid commitment on behalf of the corporation to providing training and skill development. Depending on the degree of choice given to people, on-line universities may also be consistent with the approach of allowing people to shape their own careers and learning.

But simply offering courses is no longer enough. In many cases, organizations need to find new and unique training methods that go beyond offering courses to truly make a difference in developing their human capital. Here are a number of interesting and innovative best practices I have found among the corporations I have researched.

Training as Part of the Onboarding Process

The first few days of a new hire's employment deserve special consideration. People's initial experiences are critical in forming their long-term attitudes and beliefs. For this reason, this period needs to be especially well managed and structured.

Some organizations devote the first few days or even weeks of a new employee's time to an onboarding course that provides new hires with information about the organization and prepares them to begin performing immediately. At Capital One, for example, every employee goes through a four-day onboarding course that explains the basic business of the company and its values and at the same time assesses his or her skills and competencies. The program is closely tied to the company's competency model, which is used throughout employees' careers as a way of guiding their development and learning.

Another interesting approach to onboarding is the use of the Internet before new hires even start their job. For example, Cisco asks new employees to go on-line to read much of the basic information about the company before they even show up for their first day of work. The company Web site teaches new hires about how Cisco is organized and structured, and it provides details on the company's benefits programs and allows new hires to sign up for the coverages of their choice. In this way, much of the traditional paperwork drudgery and information overload around benefits and employment policies is dispensed with, allowing people to become productive right from their first day of work.

If you decide to create onboarding training, consider these tips. First, avoid making your program too long. Excessive training turns employees off and overloads them with information. I typically recommend no more than a weeklong initial training program and then perhaps a refresher session after a month or so. A few weeks of actual work experience are typically very useful in helping people see what further training they may need. Doing the work for a while also tends to make people more receptive to spending additional time in a formal training program.

The second tip concerns the absolute need to demonstrate to new hires the importance your organization places on its people. In a number of companies I have worked with, the CEO or COO participates in every training program for new employees, talking about the organization's beliefs, values, and management style. This is a powerful way to convey to new hires that their employment relationship with the company is valued.

Firsthand Experience

Experience is often a far better teacher than classroom or formal training activities, especially when it comes to leadership and management development. Study after study has shown that managers are more likely to learn when they are given a challenging job assignment that forces them to deal with new situations. These kinds of experiences can stimulate people to learn new skills and test out new behaviors.

This link between experience and development has important implications. Organizations that are highly committed to the development of their employees must carefully consider the value of experience when making staffing decisions. As openings appear, it is sometimes wiser to select people who can benefit from a challenging experience. This might mean bypassing an experienced person who can easily do the job but would not learn a great deal from taking the position.

This is not to say that you should throw people into a challenging work assignment without support. You can take many supportive actions to help them, such as providing a mentor or coach to guide them through the most difficult junctures. (Mentoring is discussed in more detail later in this chapter.) Alternatively, you can devise a training program, held before or during the work assignment, to facilitate learning and create a faster learning curve.

Rewards for Learning

Rewards are a great motivator that can inspire people to learn. Developing a skill-based pay system that rewards employees for learning new skills applicable to their jobs can motivate them to learn more quickly. Rewarding specific learning also helps retain workers, in that rewards show people that the organization is committed to their development and also raises their compensation level so that they are less likely to be attracted to another job.

Rewarding general non-job-related learning is somewhat more controversial. If it fits an organization's overall approach to management, however, it may be a good practice.

United Technologies Corporation has a program that follows this line of thinking. The company rewards people for completing college courses and college degrees, even if they are not directly applicable to the employee's work at United Technologies. Rewards include paid tuition, time off to study, and stock in United Technologies once the degree is completed.

In my view, two rationales justify rewarding general skill development. First, offering a significant reward for completing a degree can be an effective approach to retention. At the very minimum, people will stay with your company until they complete their degree—and often longer out of feelings that the company helped them and they should pay it back.

Second, supporting general learning can reinforce a learning culture throughout the organization. This is especially important in technology companies that need a workforce whose skills and abilities need constant updating. United Technologies, for example, profits from the halo effect created by rewarding employees who earn degrees for general skill development; their learning tends to create a companywide culture that values and appreciates learning in all its forms.

Admittedly, many organizations do not accept the arguments in favor of general learning. For example, SAS Institute, the software firm mentioned earlier as one of the best places to work, takes a narrow approach to development, rewarding people only for learning skills directly applicable to SAS work. SAS does not reward getting an M.B.A., for example, which it regards as a mobility degree and not a commitment degree, because the company is concerned about posteducation turnover. This policy is consistent with the company's employment contract, which is based on a long-term, almost paternalistic relationship with employees.

A Learning Culture

Clearly, creating a learning culture is, in my view, an essential element of treating people right and launching a virtuous spiral. The practices just reviewed—rewarding learning, making time available to take courses, paying tuition, providing people with challenges—are just a few of the ways that organizations can promote a widespread learning culture throughout the corporate environment.

Another important way to encourage learning and foster development is to enable people to experiment and try new things. Some companies that have been innovative in this area include Intel, W. L. Gore, and 3M. These organizations have taken such actions as creating a special budget to support new ventures and giving people time to learn and experiment with new ideas and new projects. They then reward people whose experiments and efforts are successful.

If your organization embarks on creating this type of learning culture, it is important not to become blind to the value of failures. Many organizations do an excellent job at analyzing and rewarding success, but far fewer allow people to learn from unsuccessful efforts, and even fewer reward failures. These too must be part of a learning culture. In fact, often more can be learned from failure than from success.

In my view, a vital aspect of a learning culture is conducting postmortems whenever there has been a failure. Tremendous value can be gained from asking questions like "Should this project have ever been started?" and "What should we do next time, given the problems that developed with this effort?" Learning cannot happen in organizations that blindly punish failure. At the very least, it is better to take no action when "good failures" occur, and in some cases, it even makes sense to reward failure.

Admittedly, the most difficult thing to do in creating an innovative learning culture that allows experimentation is to manage risk. Enron, for one, failed in this critical area. It developed an innovative culture that encouraged risk taking and new ventures but failed to effectively manage risk.

To manage risk in experimentation, you need parameters that limit the amount of exposure your organization has when freedom to try something new is given. One way is to set budget limitations on the amount that can be spent on experiments. Another is to create critical milestones that must be met when new efforts begin. At each milestone, a careful review of the project needs to be done to determine if unforeseen problems have developed and whether the project is worth continuing. Finally, it is critical to monitor whether the new venture fits within the organization's mission and whether business is done in a manner that is consistent with the organization's ethical standards.

A Managed Exchange of Knowledge

Managing knowledge is a major challenge—perhaps the biggest challenge—for organizations in today's world. Under the loyalty contract, it was easy to preserve social and intellectual capital because people who made discoveries or developed new knowledge typically stayed with the organization and acted as a type of corporate memory. This made transferring corporate memory to new employees when older employees retired a very simple matter. Given that the timing of retirements was well known, it was easy to plan for succession and to train new employees in the knowledge that needed to be passed down. Most retiring employees were also quite willing to mentor their replacements.

Today, the situation is dramatically different. Most employees have a transitory or at best an uncertain employability relationship with their organizations. They are often disinterested in training other people because it makes them look less valuable and more expendable. These days, you cannot predict when people will leave, taking key intellectual property with them.

There is no simple solution to this knowledge management challenge, but you can take some precautions. One increasingly effective solution is to create an Internet-based knowledge management system that stores the organization's knowledge and facilitates its movement among people.

A good Web-based knowledge management system requires certain design elements. First, you need to appoint a chief learning officer or knowledge management officer for the organization, whose job is to champion the system and make it highly visible in your organization. Second, you need an easy-to-use software system that allows people to input their knowledge easily and access content from others.

Finally, research shows that it is important to reward people for sharing their knowledge and developing new information. Without rewards, people have little incentive to spend time entering their knowledge into the system. Rewards also help people overcome their fear that if they share their knowledge, they may lose a certain amount of power and leverage in their relationship with the organization.

Rewarding Managers

Managers don't always work to develop their employees, for many reasons. They may fear that training their people results in losing their best employees to other jobs. They may worry that training takes their people away from the work at hand, causing a negative effect on their performance. Finally, they may simply feel threatened that a more highly trained employee might overshadow or replace them.

To counteract these fears and concerns and prevent them from destroying a learning culture or negating the potential benefits of training, organizations need to have policies and practices that acknowledge and reward managers for developing their people. This means evaluating managers based in part on their performance as developers and "exporters" of high-performing people and rewarding them more highly than managers who do not develop their people. It is far better to have managers who lose employees to better jobs because they develop their people than to have managers who drive employees from the firm because they won't develop their people.

Measuring Human Capital Development

If you are going to reward people for developing talent, you need a measurement system that accurately captures the condition and location of the talent. Without this, it is hard to administer a fair reward system that motivates managers to train and develop others.

There are two additional very important benefits to measuring and tracking employee development. First, considerable evidence indicates that investors care about the condition of an organization's human capital. The more the investment community thinks you know about your people, the more confident investors will be that you can achieve your business goals. Second, good information about people's capabilities is useful for strategic planning and for determining the allocation of human resources. The more you can measure your human capital, the smarter you can be about your strategy, capabilities, competencies, and environment (the elements of the Diamond Model, you will recall).

How can you design a system that tracks your human capital? The old method, as we discussed in the beginning of this book, was to put human capital on the balance sheet by assigning an asset value to each individual. But this approach has never been popular because it suffers from a fatal flaw: How can you put a dollar value on people's skills and abilities?

A much better approach is to measure such hard factors as the satisfaction level of your employees, absenteeism, training hours, skill certifications, and turnover rates. Many of these factors can be tracked by the human resource function; others can be assessed through employee surveys.

The development of company intranets makes it possible to go beyond simply recording data on satisfaction and turnover to assessing and posting each member's skill set and competencies. This is now being done in many consulting firms, who use tests and job performance reviews to measure the skills of their consultants. Positively knowing their consultants' skills has proven to be extremely useful in staffing jobs, planning for new projects, and bidding on new work.

One sticky issue in developing skill profiles is the question of who should keep them up to date. Should it be the individual worker, the supervisor, or a third party, such as someone in human resources? In my view, the best approach is to allow people to initiate updates on their own skill profile but to require a sign-off by either a direct supervisor or a subject matter expert. In this way, you institute controls on "skill verification" and avoid the potential for résumé inflation. Unfortunately, when résumés are publicly available on the Web, some people will falsify their qualifications in order to "look good." Controls lead to a fairer process of placement when people are applying for jobs and those in the organization who are reviewing the applications actually have no firsthand knowledge of the applicant.

Competency Systems

Many organizations are adopting competency systems as the basis for the assessment of their human capital. Competency systems can help tremendously in understanding your organization's human capital. They can also be a useful predictor of what your people need to learn while serving as the basis for determining rewards.

The challenge in developing useful competency systems is to be sure that everyone agrees about what the needed competencies are and how to measure them. In some companies, competency consists of very general abilities like problem solving, leadership, and communication. In others, it refers to specific skills and relates to the ability to perform particular tasks or apply a particular business model.

In the most successful systems, key competencies are identified by top management and defined in terms of specific skills and behaviors. Specific competency profiles are then developed for each role in the company, and the technical skills and knowledge needed are identified. These are shared throughout the organization, and people are evaluated on how well they have mastered the competencies. If employees want to move to another position in the company, they are told what training programs and other development experiences are available to help them target the competencies they need in order to get new jobs and follow the career path they wish to pursue.

Web-Based Training

Information technology is revolutionizing the way learning experiences can be managed and delivered. For example, your organization's intranet can include a list of all the learning options your organization offers. This gives people a clear sense of what learning is available to them. More sophisticated systems can even give brief tests on-line to see if workers qualify to take a course or program and provide them feedback on their current level of skill development. Employees can sign up for courses over the Web, substantially reducing the paperwork that so many training departments currently have.

The most exciting and interesting use of technology for training purposes is without question the delivery of skill training over the Web. The technology in this area is advancing rapidly, allowing more and more people to have interactive training sessions delivered to them virtually anywhere in the world. Dell, Sun Microsystems, Cisco, and Hewlett-Packard are among the companies that offer substantial amounts of Web-based training. Some training is delivered in the format of a standard course with a fixed meeting time and an interactive course instructor. Other courses are delivered on demand around the clock.

Just-in-time training is one of the best uses of the Web and company intranets. Learning modules that people can access when they face the need for a particular set of skills are especially valuable. For example, a supervisor who needs to do a performance appraisal for a particularly difficult individual at Cisco or Intel can access a brief tutorial on performance appraisals in preparation for the activity. Similarly, a supervisor who needs to discipline an employee can obtain a brief tutorial on how to do it.

As noted earlier, this type of just-in-time training fits well with what is known about adult learning. Adults learn best when they receive information about a problem that they are grappling with at the time. Creating learning modules that can be used in important but common situations is a particularly good application of Web-based education for employees.

Certain kinds of content material are clearly better delivered over the Web than others. Procedural content is well suited to the

Web; the delivery of process-oriented content may not be quite as effective with Web-based training systems. Nonetheless, Internet-based educational systems are quite cost-effective and may prove to be useful for many kinds of process training. They can at least alert people to what the key issues are in analyzing problems, dealing with interpersonal issues, leading groups, and so forth.

Web Access

Given that a tremendous amount of information can be obtained from the Internet, it is hard to argue against giving all employees access to the Internet for knowledge acquisition purposes. Research shows that Web access is a common feature of most companies' knowledge management systems.[2] Employees are typically allowed to search for information and ask experts for their opinions.

Of course, there is the danger that Internet access can be abused; we all have heard stories of employees who spend more time at their favorite sports Web site or checking their stock market investments than they do taking advantage of the learning opportunities available on the Web.

Nevertheless, the risk is worth taking, given the benefits of open Internet access. The kinds of information and knowledge available on the Internet can potentially aid both individuals and the organization. Even nonwork use of Web technology can help people grow, learn, and become more facile in using the Web, an outcome that can help them be more effective if they perform their regular work using the Internet.

Career Centers

As organizations move away from providing clear career paths for people, it becomes more important that they provide substitutes for the guidance they formerly gave. One of the best ways to do this is through career centers.

Companies such as Hewlett-Packard and Cisco have established excellent career centers to help people analyze and plan their careers. These centers provide counseling, as well as a tremendous amount of information about the availability of jobs both within and outside the company.

In addition to providing information, career centers are an ideal location to give employees access to assessment technology. Tests of all kinds can help people understand where they are in terms of their interests, skills, and abilities, allowing them to realistically evaluate their best career choices.

If you implement such a career center, it is wise to hire skilled counselors as contract employees or bring in a consulting firm, rather than having counselors who are regular employees. This reduces the potential conflict of interest in having one set of employees counseling others. Similarly, assessment testing is best managed by consulting organizations that specialize in doing psychological testing and running assessment centers. These firms can often give people feedback on how they compare to the overall workforce in terms of their interests, skills, and abilities.

As the use of company intranets grows, it is increasingly possible to implement virtual career centers. You can put considerable amounts of assessment technology and career information on a career Web site to give people personal tutoring, advice, and feedback without their ever having to contact another individual. Deloitte Touche Tohmatsu has done this and reports that it has gotten a very positive response from its employees.

An intranet-based development system also fits nicely with the increasing use of 360-degree feedback appraisals. In these appraisals, people are asked to nominate others who can give them feedback about their performance. The nominees receive e-mails asking them to assess the individual seeking feedback; their replies are then fed back to the individual to provide a sense of how others see his or her work performance and skills.

Pratt & Whitney, the aircraft engine division of United Technologies, has developed a particularly impressive Web-based approach to helping employees develop their skills. It includes regular updates on what skills the organization thinks it will need in the future and what skills are becoming obsolete. It even includes push-technology that alerts employees who are in danger of becoming obsolete. Finally, it serves as a resource for employees who want to learn new skills. It lists all training and degree programs available to employees and the names and addresses of employees who can act as resources in key learning areas. Employees don't have to follow the advice they get from this system, but they cannot accuse Pratt & Whitney of failing to provide the information they need to make informed career decisions.

Mandatory Training Days

Several leading companies in human capital management, including Motorola, have implemented policies that require people to attend a certain number of training programs each year. These companies also evaluate managers annually based in part on whether their reports actually participate in the required amount of training. This is a powerful way to create a climate of learning and demonstrates a strong organizational commitment to creating a learning culture. This practice can be used as an alternative or a supplement to programs that reward the completion of training and learning experiences.

However, despite its potential benefits, the idea of mandating a certain number of days of learning might be viewed as bureaucratic in some circles. In my view, it is often an appropriate way to help organizations kick-start their first efforts to focus on human capital development. But after a few years of mandated training, organizations should shift to a different model, such as determining each worker's training needs based on a formal career planning session that takes place between the individual and his or her manager. This method allows for reasonable commitments to training according to the career direction of the individual and the tasks that he or she is likely to be assigned, rather than being dictated by a corporate policy.

This is not to discount the fact that sometimes organizations may need to require everybody to take a particular training program. For example, if your organization adopts new standardized procedures on Internet use or accounting, it may make sense to require everyone to attend a specific training course.

Mentoring Programs

Mentoring relationships are common in organizations, often arising spontaneously when an older, more experienced organizational member supports the growth and development of a junior employee. Considerable research suggests that this type of *informal* mentoring relationship contributes greatly to development because it provides people with wisdom, personal advice, and in some cases, direct skill training.[3] It tends to increase job performance, job satisfaction, salary level, and organizational commitment.

Because of the success of informal mentoring relationships, some organizations have implemented formal mentoring programs. In these programs, experienced workers are assigned to mentor the inexperienced. These programs are usually established in the hope that they will lead to the same results as informal mentoring. Though there is no current estimate on how many major companies have such formal mentoring programs, as many as one-third may have them.

However, the research on formal mentoring suggests that while it often leads to some of the positive benefits of informal mentoring, it tends to have a number of negatives outcomes associated with it. The negatives run all the way from mentors being threatened by their mentees to mentors and mentees simply not liking each other and feeling that they were forced into a "shotgun marriage." Such evidence provides support for the argument that mentees often appreciate informal mentors more than formal ones.

What conclusion can we draw about mentoring programs? My reading of the literature on mentoring suggests that it is worthwhile to have a formal program, as long as certain cautions are respected. First, obtain support from top management; encouragement from the top confirms that the organization endorses mentoring as part of its learning culture. Second, be sure to involve employees in developing the program. Obtain their opinions as to the structure and operation of the program, the length of time needed, and the criteria to be used to assess the success or failure of a particular relationship.

Next, provide training for mentors. Although people may have the right work experience needed to teach inexperienced workers, they may not have the people skills needed to make mentoring go smoothly. Live or Web-based training can assist in laying out the ground rules for dealing with mentees.

Finally, do not mandate mentoring partnerships. Formally designated relationships risk creating poor matches and hence producing more negatives than positives. Voluntary partnerships are preferred, although they are clearly harder to create. This is where intranet-based assistance can be quite helpful. You can use intranet programs to match profiles of mentors and mentees and even use push technology to suggest particular mentors for particular mentees.

Coaches

Coaches to facilitate the development of leadership and other skills are increasingly popular, particularly for senior managers. Companies typically bring in coaches from the outside so that they can develop a confidential relationship with the person being coached. The coaches offer job-relevant thoughts, advice, and learning opportunities

So far, little research has been done on coaching. Not much is known, for example, about how prevalent coaches are, how effective coaching is, what characteristics create a successful coaching relationship, or what qualifications are needed for someone to be a good coach.

My guess, and it is only a guess, is that in some situations, coaches can contribute significantly to the development of leadership capabilities in some people. They have the advantage of being personalized and available when needed. However, I am also quite sure that many coaching efforts end in failure.

The fact is, coaches have many obstacles to overcome. Because they are outsiders, they often do not understand the organizational context that their client operates in. Thus they are limited to suggesting behaviors, without an in-depth understanding of the situation the client is in. More important, they do not control any of the rewards and structures that influence leadership behavior. Leadership behaviors are strongly shaped by the environment, rewards, and the actions of others; thus major changes in behavior often require changes that the coach cannot control.

Nevertheless, it is certainly possible that through ongoing discussions and feedback, coaches can help potential leaders understand how their behavior affects people and also find new behavior options. Some coaches—particularly those who have a doctorate in psychology—may also be able to help executives understand the underlying causes of their behavior and perhaps deal with their flaws at a much deeper level.

Implications for Individuals

The implications of this chapter for individuals can be captured by two basic conclusions: there is great value in working for a development-oriented organization, and you need to manage your own development if you want to grow your skills and expertise. Let's examine each of these separately.

First, there is no doubt that you can profit greatly if you are part of an organization that has a commitment to developing its human capital. Organizations that have a learning culture can provide you with skills and knowledge that make you more mobile and more valuable. They can put you into mentoring relationships that provide direct contact with a highly skilled, experienced individual who will transfer everything he or she knows to you to prepare you for a great future with the company. Above all, they can give you the opportunity to enjoy a wide variety of learning experiences that will make you a more skilled employee and a more valuable one.

Given the choice, the advantages of working for a development-oriented organization mean that you should always choose to work for one, other things being equal. How can you tell whether an organization is committed to developing people? It isn't hard; the signs are usually everywhere. Look at its training facilities; check the courses it offers; talk to employees; ask for a commitment that you will be trained.

Unfortunately, the discussion about the value of working for an organization that develops its employees pretty much stops here. It is important, but it is not enough. As we said, most organizations will no longer to be able to train you extensively or prepare you for the multiple careers you may have in your lifetime. They will no longer make altruistic or paternalistic decisions about what you should learn and how you should apply what you learn. The second implication of this chapter is therefore far more significant: your development is up to you. In the future, you will need to make your own decisions about your development. You need to become a consumer of knowledge about development and the manager of your own human capital.

As stated in earlier chapters, you need to think of yourself as a product or brand that has a certain value and cachet in the market. You can alter and develop your brand through investments and learning. Having a strong brand and a high human capital value is ultimately the most secure position for you to be in—and the most potentially rewarding to you. In the era of mobile human capital and employability contracts, job security does not come from your organization; it can only come from your having the kinds of skills and knowledge that organizations need in order to be effective.

Given the incentives for organizations to buy rather than build talent and their orientation toward just-in-time learning, you cannot rely on training programs offered by organizations to develop you in a way that makes you attractive to other employers. In fact, some organizations may not even develop you in ways that allow you to enjoy a long-term career with them.

You need to attend classes and seek out a variety of development experiences that build your competencies, skills, and abilities. These can be formal classes or social activities, such as churches and clubs that you are engaged in outside the workplace. You need to make choices about learning that contribute to your brand and help you establish and create the opportunity for a virtuous spiral career with your present employer or else with another organization.

You need to carefully assess your skills and continue to add to them. One implication of this is that you should choose your employer based in part on the kinds of learning experiences that the company can provide you and in part on how the company can help build your brand. This orientation can help you decide whether to take a position in a new organization or whether to take a particular training or development opportunity offered by your current organization.

You also need to proactively lobby for access to certain kinds of training and learning experiences in your organization. You should not be shy about asking to go to a course, obtain access to the Internet for learning, take on new work and responsibilities, or take advantage of whatever is the best vehicle for you to learn the kind of knowledge and skills that you value and think will enhance your brand. You should look at each task assignment and learning opportunity through a lens that analyzes it from the perspective of enhancing your market value.

Keep in mind that simply learning and developing skills may not be enough. It is wise to find situations that establish proof of your learning and skill enhancement. Ask questions like: "Does this give me marketable skills that I can document?" "Is there any way what I have learned can be documented so that others will recognize that I have done something significant and have certain skills and knowledge?" When possible, find courses and programs that certify your work, such as through professional licensing programs, professional associations that grant certifications, or simply course credits given by a university that can be documented through transcripts. Certifications can be particularly useful if you are not a core long-term employee of an organization.

Certification may be a necessity if you are in a competitive labor market. As more people vie for jobs, having a credential that establishes your immediate ability to perform in a particular area can tilt the selection process in your favor. You simply become more valuable in the labor market.

In short, effective career management means achieving independence from a single organization. This requires an investment in yourself that may not be made by your existing employer.

In addition, begin recognizing that you are likely to have multiple careers. Failure to learn new skills in today's environment inevitably means lower rewards, particularly extrinsic rewards, and ultimately the loss of job and position.

At this point, you may be wondering if you should ever trust the development of your career to an organization. After all, there are still organizations that talk about a loyalty commitment, offer a loyalty type of contract, and claim that they look after their people. Frankly, such organizations may be well intentioned, but if history has taught one lesson, it is that no organization can guarantee the career employment of an individual.

A few years ago, the strongest loyalty contracts were those offered by IBM and AT&T. Yet both organizations have engaged in significant layoffs, disrupting the careers and lives of thousands who worked for them. When IBM and AT&T made their commitments, they were extremely stable and well-intentioned organizations; it seemed inconceivable that they would not be able to live up to their commitments—and yet they did not.

If such venerable institutions couldn't make good on their commitments to employment stability, it is likely that no organization can say with certainty that it will live up to a long-term employment commitment. The world is simply changing too rapidly and too unpredictably for this to be a realistic position for organizations to take.

The implication is clear—regardless of what an organization says, be ready to leave. Work hard while you're there, enjoy what you do, but be prepared to leave.

Perhaps the best way of summarizing the implications of this chapter for your career is to emphasize again that you have a tremendous amount to gain from your growing importance to organizations. But you will develop a virtuous career spiral only if you make good decisions in managing your career. You need to make decisions about what training, learning experiences, and jobs you will take within a framework that questions whether it will lead to your developing the kinds of skills and knowledge that can be certified, transferred, and in demand in the future marketplace for human capital.

Chapter Seven

| Design Work Right

TREAT PEOPLE RIGHT PRINCIPLE #4

Organizations must design work so that it is meaningful for people and provides them with feedback, responsibility, and autonomy.

Did you know that job design greatly influences employee motivation, satisfaction, and performance and ultimately has a powerful influence on organizational effectiveness? This is absolutely true.

How Job Design Affects Performance

A great deal of research evidence shows that when jobs are designed to contain high levels of involvement and challenge, the result is high levels of intrinsic motivation and satisfaction.[1] Offering involving and challenging jobs also helps attract outstanding employees and makes them want to stay. Ultimately, great jobs lead to commitment and high performance, which in turn lead to organizational effectiveness and a virtuous spiral.

Of course, designing interesting and challenging work is not easy. Organizations need to understand the factors that determine what makes work involving, challenging, and rewarding for people, as well as the criteria involved in actually designing jobs with these characteristics. I have spent many years researching these issues and have developed the following analysis and recommendations to serve as your guidelines.

Avoid Simplified Jobs

Let me begin by discussing first why so many jobs are not motivating or challenging. Much of the problem can be traced to the scientific management movement, which was the dominant approach to work design during much of the twentieth century. This movement called for standardized, specialized, simplified, and where possible, machine-paced jobs—all in the name of efficiency, productivity, and low labor costs. People were expected to add little value beyond their manual labor, and thus they could be easily hired, trained, and replaced when needed. To keep people working hard, two carrots were used: financial incentives and the threat of being fired.

Although rarely stated explicitly, a key assumption behind the scientific management movement was that in return for a job, people should be willing to behave like machines for eight hours a day. There was no reason, and hence no attempt, to create work that people would find motivating, satisfying, or involving; it simply wasn't a consideration. The classic image of a dull, boring, and repetitive job on an assembly line is the poster child of the scientific management movement.

Not surprisingly, the scientific management approach to work design has been shown to be highly flawed. Its use in most large organizations for decades caused low intrinsic motivation on the part of employees, high rates of turnover and absenteeism, and a strong inclination to solve workplace problems through unionization. In response to their mind-numbing repetitive jobs, employees frequently engaged in counterproductive behaviors, such as shoddy-quality work and even sabotage. Poor quality and productivity, along with constant labor-management disputes, were problems that frequently plagued U.S. car makers and for that matter most other U.S. manufacturers for decades. It was these problems that opened the door to foreign competitors.

The severe problems associated with the scientific management approach to job design began sounding alarm bells among organizational researchers as early as the 1950s. Many academics began to think about and study how work could be made more involving and challenging. The objective became to see if work could be designed in such a way that people would be both motivated and satisfied by it. Researchers tried to discover how jobs can be designed to support ever-increasing levels of satisfaction, motivation, and performance. This research has resulted in a number of important findings about how work should be designed. Indeed, these findings indicate that when jobs are correctly designed, a virtuous spiral results.

Design "Enriched" Jobs

The first set of job design guidelines arises out of the research into what is called "job enrichment." This research analyzed the nature of jobs and found that when certain identifiable job characteristics exist, people who desire personal development and intrinsic rewards can be both motivated and satisfied by their work.

In particular, my research work, performed with J. Richard Hackman, led to the identification of the critical characteristics of enriched jobs.[2] For work to be motivating, three psychological conditions must be present in workers' minds:

1. The experience of meaningfulness
2. The experience of responsibility for outcomes
3. Feedback or knowledge of results

When all three of these conditions are present in the minds of employees, the work itself can be both motivating and satisfying. However, if any one of these conditions is not present, research suggests that people will not be motivated because they will not experience a connection—or line of sight, as we have called it—between feeling good and performing well.

The connection between each of these factors and performing well is perhaps most obvious in the case of feedback: without feedback on their performance, how can employees know they have performed well and feel good about their work? They can't, and as a result, the motivation to perform well is absent.

The same logic applies to the other two conditions. Without responsibility, it is hard for people to feel good about their performance because they don't "own" it. Similarly, without a meaningful task, people do not feel that they have done something worthwhile, and so they don't experience a positive feeling, even if they perform well.

The research results become slightly more complicated at this point, but they are well worth understanding. For each of the three conditions to exist in the minds of employees, jobs must be designed with certain characteristics. Each of the three conditions has its own set of necessary job characteristics, as follows:

Meaningfulness. There are three characteristics of job design needed to create meaningfulness in work. They are whether the work involves doing a *whole* or *complete* piece of work, whether it involves doing a *significant* task, and the degree to which the work requires the use of *valued* skills. As you might guess, since these three characteristics are somewhat difficult to define, a certain amount of subjectivity exists in determining whether they are truly present. The challenge in creating this condition is therefore understanding that what might appear to be a meaningful task to one person may not be seen as meaningful by another and to match people to the tasks they find meaningful.

Responsibility. One single defining characteristic must be present for the condition of responsibility to exist—autonomy. Autonomy occurs when people feel they can determine their own work methods and procedures and operate without close supervision. Autonomy is what allows people to take responsibility for how well they perform. When freedom and choice are not present, people feel that someone else is controlling them so much that they literally disown the results of their own behavior.

Feedback. Employees can receive feedback through the procedures and processes that organizations set up to channel performance information to them. The best performance management systems, for example, create a variety of formal procedures that allow people to get meaningful feedback from their managers, peers, and customers (called 360-degree feedback, which we will discuss more later). But employees can also experience feedback when they see the finished products they participated in building and by having an opportunity to observe customers using their products. Another form of feedback occurs when organizations provide people with hard information about their effect on the company's performance, such as quality, cost, and sales volume numbers. In this way, people see precisely how much they contribute to the organization's success.

When jobs are designed with these three conditions in mind, the result is what is called an "enriched job." In fact, the job enrichment approach to work design has proven to be extremely useful to many organizations. Many companies have redesigned their work to create enriched jobs for their employees. My research suggests that over 90 percent of large U.S. firms have made some effort to enrich their jobs.[3] My research also shows that job enrichment efforts have had tangible bottom-line results in terms of reduced absenteeism, higher performance levels, and greater employee satisfaction. In short, I find that enriched jobs have helped create a number of win-win virtuous spiral situations.

Sometimes enriching jobs is not all that easy. In particular, I have found that most corporate enrichment efforts initially focus on only the two conditions of meaningfulness and feedback. Companies frequently give employees greater involvement in producing a whole product or service and upgrade the amount of feedback they receive, especially from their customers. The third condition—giving people more autonomy—is less frequently created, and as a result, many job enrichment efforts fail. Fortunately, autonomy is slowly becoming more common, often because it means having fewer managers. This, of course, can result in a significant cost savings.

Not all jobs can be easily enriched. Enriched white-collar sales and service jobs are far more common than enriched production jobs. It is hard to modify jobs in manufacturing plants, since job redesign may involve moving equipment around or eliminating assembly lines. Sales and service jobs also do not involve the complexities of material handling that are found in manufacturing. It is absolutely impossible for a single individual to build an entire truck or an airplane, whereas a sales job can usually be redesigned to handle the entire customer transaction.

This point brings up a second good reason why job enrichment makes sense in sales and service situations. The research on quality of service shows that customers often prefer dealing with one specific person during their transaction and even want to develop a relationship with that person, rather than being passed around among many people to complete their business.[4] This finding is spurring organizations to increasingly redesign sales and service jobs so that a single employee deals with a service transaction from beginning to end.

Design Effective Work Teams

Many work situations call for people to work in teams, especially in today's world where work is complex, and interdependent teams are becoming a widely used work structure. So how do you go about enriching the work of teams?

Not surprisingly, research has shown that the same types of conditions that need to exist for people to be motivated and satisfied with solo work also need to be present for teams to be motivated and satisfied. The team as a whole needs to feel that it has a meaningful piece of work to do, is responsible for the outcome of its work, and gets feedback about the results of its work.

Also not surprisingly, these conditions apply regardless of the type of team used. While many kinds of teams are possible, three types seem to be the most prevalent today. First are problem-solving teams, which typically focus on quality and process improvements. Next are self-managed work teams, which actually produce products and services. Third are project teams, which take on special activities such as new product development or special one-of-a-kind production efforts. A fourth type of team, the virtual team, in which the members meet and communicate via technology rather than in-person, is becoming common.

Weigh Individual Jobs Against Teams

If both individually enriched jobs and team-based work can provide satisfying and motivating work for people, is it better to design work to be done by individuals or teams? This is the right question, but unfortunately, not one for which there is a simple answer. There are, however, several useful research findings that can serve as guidelines and cautions about the pros and cons of each type of work design.

The first important tip is that teams, particularly high-performance, self-managed teams, are very difficult to build and maintain. They are, so to speak, the Ferraris of work design—impressive-looking and high-performing but costly in terms of development and maintenance. Because many high-performance teams take on assignments that were previously done by managers and specialists (for example, supervision and scheduling), they need to contain highly skilled people, and the members must know how to work together effectively. Teams can also lead to very high replacement costs. If someone leaves the team, it is often hard to find a replacement who can fill the particular niche or skill vacated. And even when someone is found, it can be difficult and time-consuming to integrate the new person into the team.

Given these factors, the most logical conclusion is that sometimes the Ferrari approach just isn't worth it. If a single person can do the work, it is usually better to design individually enriched jobs to handle the tasks than it is to build a team.

On the other hand, creating individually enriched jobs is not always possible. In some situations, the flow of work simply does not allow a single person to do an entire piece of work alone, given the costs, complexity, knowledge, and time demands of the work. This is particularly true when the output of the work consists of complicated knowledge products or when the products or services require the expertise of people working together at the intersection of multiple disciplines.

For example, one person cannot possibly design, develop, and manufacture a new car in today's world. The same goes for developing or building computers, software products, and providing complex financial services. Even the development of a particular subsystem or part of a car, computer, software product, or financial service can rarely be done by a single individual. It simply takes too much expertise and often needs to be done too quickly.

In the past, the traditional solution to the challenge of designing and producing complex products has been to break up the tasks into small parts and assign each piece to an individual. But this solution creates specialized, often repetitive jobs that require close supervision and extensive management coordination. As a result, this solution doesn't work very well because the resulting jobs are neither motivating nor satisfying. As many organizations have discovered, the only way to motivate employees in these types of jobs is through financial rewards and close supervision.

Clearly, the best alternative for the design and manufacture of complex products and services is a team. For this type of work, teams that share responsibility for performance are the preferred and perhaps the only effective work design.

Every analysis of when to use teams or individually enriched jobs needs to consider one additional factor that cannot be forgotten—the people involved. We cannot neglect that people differ in their desire to work in teams. Some people love working on their own and cannot work any other way. Putting them on a team serves not to increase but to lower satisfaction. Teamwork may even frustrate them to the point that they quit.

Here are two solutions to prevent assigning the wrong people to teams. First, if your organization relies greatly on teams, give people a realistic job preview when hiring them. In most cases, someone who does not enjoy working in teams will decide not to join a team-based work organization. Second, identify people who prefer individual work by using tests and behavior-focused interviews that ask about the choices they have made in the past concerning work design.

Teams can be very effective where the work demands it and people can be found who enjoy working with others. When these two conditions are met, the use of teams can be a positive experience from both the individual's and the organization's point of view, but they are not for everyone or for every situation.

Consider Alternatives to Enriched Work

Enriching the work of individuals and teams should be done whenever possible to support a virtuous spiral, but there is also a reality that must be faced—not all repetitive work can be eliminated, nor can all jobs be individually enriched or assigned to high-performance work teams. A number of jobs in retailing, food processing, garment manufacturing, and a host of other industries entail relatively simple-to-make products or services that just do not lend themselves to job enrichment. High-speed meat and poultry processing is a good example of the type of work that is hard to either enrich or turn over to a machine.

Ironically, some jobs in information technology can be harshly repetitive. For years, data entry was a great offender until optical scanning came along. Today the call centers that support many retail and Web businesses often involve highly repetitive, boring, unchallenging work that does not easily lend itself to automation and in most cases cannot be enriched.

So what can be done when boring, repetitive work cannot be changed? Often the only alternative is to find people who are willing to do this kind of work. This may be entirely possible—as long as certain incentives are included to keep people motivated to perform and stay in the job despite the poor work design. Since there is no way to make the work intrinsically satisfying and rewarding, companies need to hire accordingly and then to offer good working conditions and high extrinsic rewards. These situations require practices like flexible hours, part-time work, generous fringe benefits, child care, skilled supervision, and bonus pay.

Alternatively, a viable choice for organizations that cannot staff repetitive and simplified work is to outsource. In some situations, the best way to get the work done is to farm it out to other organizations that are better at staffing and managing this type of work and are willing to provide the necessary extrinsic rewards for structured, simplified, repetitive task performance. This may mean outsourcing the work to countries where income levels are lower and where finding people willing and available to do this kind of work is not a problem.

Many U.S. manufacturing firms in electronics, clothing, and toys have moved much of their work out of the United States. They have either moved their manufacturing operations to Asia or Mexico or have contracted with outside companies operating in those countries. For example, Selectron has grown rapidly as a result of being effective at operating low-cost electronics manufacturing plants producing electronics products for Hewlett-Packard, Apple, and a host of other firms.

Design Jobs for Change

Job enrichment is easy when the work that needs to be done is relatively stable. If people can be said to "hold jobs," and organizations can write job descriptions and make relatively permanent assignments of responsibility, designing enriched jobs is easily done and highly recommended. The same goes for work teams. If teams have relatively permanent membership with an assigned set of duties, accountabilities, and responsibility, such as in many manufacturing and service situations, designing the team's work for enrichment is easy and should be done.

However, today's jobs often aren't fixed and involve more than one kind of task. Many knowledge workers in today's new economy organizations have a continuously changing set of activities that they must perform. People today often work on several teams, as well as on their own individual assignments.

It is artificial and unrealistic to think of designing a fixed enriched job, given that for many people it is almost impossible to even define their job. Among their changing portfolio of tasks to perform, some tasks may be quite enrichable, while others will always be boring and repetitive. Some tasks may be highly team-oriented and challenging, while others may require individual work that is not particularly meaningful.

What, then, can be done to enrich "dynamic" changeable jobs? You must look at the combination of work activities and weigh whether people have, on average, interesting, challenging work to do. The balance must tip in the direction of enriched work. The three factors that make work motivating and rewarding are still applicable for this type of job. People in dynamic jobs still need to have meaningful work, autonomy, and feedback. Among all their different assignments, their work still needs to fall predominantly in the category of enriched work. A good benchmark is 80 percent: if 80 percent of the tasks a person is asked to do are enriched, it is a good job.

The key is therefore to examine task design, rather than job design. People need to be involved most of the time in challenging team assignments or enriched individual work assignments that are motivating. This is true whether the person is considered a core, long-term employee of the organization or a short-term employee who is brought in to contribute particular expertise for a limited period of time.

Design Enriched Virtual Work

Job design for remote work and virtual collaboration is yet another challenge that needs to be addressed. As more and more people work from multiple locations, connecting via the Internet or other telecommunications devices, rather than in a single location, designing challenging, interesting, and motivating work gets even more complicated and important. Here's why.

First, remote-based people are often very autonomous. They may be scattered in a variety of locations, including telecommuting from home, satellite offices, and part-time offices. For example, Sun Microsystems has established satellite offices for people who prefer to work closer to their homes than the main office. A number of consulting firms have set up office space for traveling consultants to use so that people can have a place in which to work when they are on projects away from their home office. Some workers and consultants have no permanent office or work location—they simply work wherever they are needed.

Second, work is often very abstract, performed by people involved in knowledge-intensive professions such as consulting and research. Such abstract work also often requires people to work on virtual teams, using telecommunications and the Internet to communicate, and their results are not always tangible and easily measurable but rather take the form of recommendations and reports.

What do these factors suggest about job design? The first implication is that any task assignment that involves virtual work needs to be intrinsically motivating enough so that people will perform the work effectively on their own. With people spread apart or mobile, managing them is difficult. Traditional supervisory roles based on observation and command-and-control behavior simply won't work, so the task assignments themselves need to provide direction and motivation for employees.

The second implication is that the design of work must find ways to keep employees psychologically attached to the organization. In the absence of a physical workspace and the social relationships that develop in a central office, people may have few links to their company. They become prime candidates for indifferent work performance and turnover. As a result, their work design must be sufficiently challenging, motivating, and satisfying that they not only want to perform well but also want to remain with the organization as long as they are needed.

Best Practices for Work Design

I believe that it is increasingly possible to design work that is good for both people and organizations. As more work is focused on the exchange of knowledge, and the evolution of information technology increasingly enables jobs to be more meaningful, challenging, and impactful, it will be far easier to create positive work experiences for people. It also has the potential to improve work processes and increase organizational performance.

This will not happen by chance, however. It requires that organizations purposively design work that is both motivating and satisfying. It also requires that organizations use modern technology to support the kinds of work relationships and job structures that are attractive to people and that provide meaningful work experiences.

Organizations already employ many excellent practices to make their jobs motivating and satisfying, but they can do much more to make work right for people. Although the practices discussed here are not applicable in every situation, they are generally useful, and you should consider them whenever work is designed in your organization.

Feedback and Performance Measures

Given the importance of feedback in keeping people motivated, it is particularly important that if you are in a managerial position you make sure that the people who work for you receive valid feedback about their performance. There are a number of ways to provide high-quality feedback.

First, whenever there are direct customers at the receiving end of an individual's job performance, you can collect data from the customers and give it directly to the employee. For example, you can share customer satisfaction surveys, statistics on revenue produced, reports on the profitability of transactions, and a host of other indicators that the person has directly influenced.

Many of the leading hotel chains have adopted a good feedback practice. They post customer satisfaction scores on a hotel-by-hotel basis for all of their employees to see. Some have also added a recognition feature that rewards the highest-scoring hotels.

One of the most interesting feedback practices I have seen was used by a high-tech manufacturing firm that I consulted with a few years back. Each production team in the company had its own phone number, which was stamped on every product shipped from the plant. Any customer who had a problem with the product could then call the manufacturing team. This created a direct feedback mechanism to the production team about the quality of its work. If there was a problem with an item the team made, the team was responsible for helping the customer by phone. If that did not solve the problem, the customer could ship the product back to the production team, which immediately sent out a replacement. This practice also helped each team improve its production methods because members could identify production problems by analyzing the returned items.

Another way to ensure that employees receive feedback is to have regular formal performance reviews. By "regular," I mean at least every year, without exception, and in rapidly changing organizations, it may mean every six months or even every quarter. Reviews should be based on goals that are established beforehand and on objective performance data. In addition, the reviews should be comprehensive, by which I mean that they need to include information from peers, customers, and the relevant financial and operational records of the company that reflect performance. This type of comprehensive feedback, often called a "balanced scorecard approach," makes for meaningful feedback that lets people and teams know how well they performed the tasks assigned to them.

In addition to formal feedback, my view is that the best managers also provide their employees with regular ongoing feedback. Regular feedback is important for two reasons. First, it provides just-in-time correction of performance problems and recognition rewards that motivate performance. Second, it means that when the formal review occurs, there are no surprises, no "you never told me" moments.

Mini-Enterprises

If you are in a large corporation, one of the best ways to provide people with enriched jobs is to create small teams or groups of employees who have complete operational and financial responsibility for a set of customers or products. Called mini-enterprises, these units are a very effective way to give people a grasp of, and responsibility for, an entire business process, as well as ongoing feedback on their performance.

McDonald's and Jack in the Box use this approach in their restaurants. Each restaurant has bottom-line responsibility and receives regular feedback about its profitability. Each one also receives regular customer satisfaction data so that it has information about how well it is performing as a business unit. Similarly, the success of W. L. Gore, 3M, Sysco, and many other multidivision businesses is also partly due to their skillful use of mini-enterprises.

A word of caution is needed here, though. A successful mini-enterprise approach can potentially create problems for large organizations, as Hewlett-Packard learned. For decades, HP consistently created separate divisions for each of its new products. Each unit received a series of measures that accurately reported the performance of its business. Although these individual enterprises had to do things the HP way, they owned their own products or services and their own customers. Their ownership was reinforced by a bonus plan that rewarded them for the success of their enterprise.

The heads of the business units felt like they were running their own small businesses. They were able to develop a high level of commitment to success among their employees, leading to a strong sense of ownership for the business results. In effect, they created their own virtuous spirals in their business units.

There was no doubt that these mini-enterprises were a success at HP. However, this success created a problem when in the late 1990s, senior management at HP decided to modify the company's business strategy away from the mini-enterprises to a "one face to the customer" approach. Management believed that the new strategy would improve HP's ability to sell multiple products to its major customers such as Ford and General Motors. Unfortunately, the independent divisions throughout HP liked their autonomy so much that they resisted senior management's efforts to create the more integrated approach to product and service offerings. Even after HP acquired Compaq in 2002, it continued to struggle with the challenge of integrating its divisions.

The moral is that major organizational change is difficult to execute when people are asked to alter a strategy that has succeeded to the point of creating a virtuous spiral. As will be discussed in the Epilogue, often it takes demonstrating clearly to employees that the virtuous spiral that has carried them forward for a considerable period of time is no longer working and that a major change is needed to keep the spiral moving upward.

Moving Decision-Making Power Downward

As I noted earlier, one of the three conditions that must be in place in order to have motivating and satisfying jobs is that people need to feel responsible for their work. And since the key ingredient of responsibility is autonomy, people need to have the power to make the decisions that influence the success of their performance.

Employees without power are seldom motivated to high performance. A common feeling among employees who lack decision-making authority is that they are automatons carrying out somebody else's plan. If they succeed, they don't get the credit, and if they fail, they get blamed because they failed to correctly execute somebody else's directions. Ultimately, the more organizations can design jobs to give employees autonomy, the more those employees will take ownership of their actions and strive for success.

Mary Kay Cosmetics and Tupperware provide good examples of how autonomy can help grow a company and establish a virtuous spiral. In both companies, individual customer sales and service representatives basically run their own small businesses. They buy products from the manufacturing arm of Mary Kay and Tupperware and sell them directly to their own set of customers. Customers tell them what they want and don't want. The representatives have tremendous power to decide how to handle their sales activities. The organization structure is clearly designed to enrich their individual jobs by making them highly autonomous and responsible.

Giving Teams Power

Autonomy is important in creating effective teams, though how much autonomy and authority teams should be given depends on the type of team and its specific situation. A good rule of thumb is, the less supervision there is, the more autonomy teams have. For example, work teams in high-performance organizations usually operate without a great deal of direct supervision. There are no frontline supervisors, only middle managers who supervise multiple teams.

Problem-solving teams may be the most problematic when it comes to determining how much decision-making authority to grant them. Most organizations restrict problem-solving teams to recommending changes in work practices, rather than giving them the full authority to approve and implement their changes. This limited ability to create change is often why problem-solving teams do not survive long in many organizations. People see them as a waste of time and lose interest in joining them.

I have seen two practices that can offset the lack of authority in problem-solving teams. The first is to give them a clear charter about the kinds of recommendations the organization seeks from them and which ones might be acceptable. The second is to designate a specific executive who is responsible for reacting to their suggestions and empowered to implement them. You can also give the team some true authority by setting aside budget money that it can use to develop and implement its ideas.

The well-known General Electric "workout process" has problem-solving teams present their recommendations to a senior manager, who immediately makes a decision. This ensures that the teams get quick feedback and that their recommendations have a reasonable chance of being favorably received and quickly acted on.

Before moving on, let me clarify one additional point about teams and their decision-making authority. Newly formed work teams of any kind should not be given a great deal of autonomy. This is because work teams are almost always ineffective at making decisions in their earliest months, especially about such tough issues as work assignments and pay. It is far wiser to let work teams build up their decision-making capabilities over a period of time. It can often take a year or more of working together for a team to gain the ability to make a wide range of tough decisions effectively.

The truth is, most teams require a great deal of time to reach their performance potential. They need a substantial up-front investment in training, learning, and technical support. It can take months, if not years, before a team functions well enough to become truly self-managing. Unless you can allow a team to stay together for a substantial period of time, designing it for self-management may not be cost-effective because of the start-up costs involved to take a team to the self-management stage.

Some of the most effective work teams I have studied were in a Kansas-based TRW plant that supplied the oil industry. After five years, these teams had completely matured and were able to run themselves very effectively. Their ultimate test came when the oil business fell so sharply that TRW faced layoffs. Management asked the teams to recommend which of their members should be laid off. Instead of using criteria related to seniority, the teams decided to look at the value of the team members to the organization and to lay off those who were judged to be least valuable. These were tough decisions that could only be handled by a team capable of a high level of self-management. They required balancing personal issues with the future effectiveness of an organization that was enjoying a virtuous spiral.

Ultimately, the best conclusion we can reach about how much autonomy and what kind of authority people need is that situations differ greatly. One thing is clear, however: once decision-making authority is granted, management must avoid second-guessing and micromanaging. If you are in a leadership position and end up reviewing most decisions, your employees will inevitably feel a lack of responsibility. This is what destroys motivation, satisfaction, and performance.

"Whole" Jobs

Another rule of thumb is that the more "breadth" a job has, the more motivating and satisfying it is. Jobs that consist of only single steps or are just part of the process that leads to the final product or service are inevitably neither motivating nor satisfying.

Although it may be impossible to completely eliminate single-step or piecemeal jobs, there are ways to enrich them, at least partially. One solution is to combine as much as possible the smaller steps of a work process and assign responsibility for all of them to either a single person or a team. This gives the tasks the breadth of an enriched job. It has the potential side benefit of encouraging learning, because people need to develop all the skills needed to handle all of the tasks. Obviously, the number of tasks that can be combined is a function of your specific production or service process.

Even when it is impossible to combine tasks in such a way that a single person or team has ownership of the entire process, such as when there needs to be a physical separation between machines, it may still be possible to enrich the work by rotating people among the individual tasks. This gives employees a much greater sense that they are part of a larger work team responsible for the entire product or service. Many Procter & Gamble plants, which are largely process production operations, combine tasks and assign them to self-managing teams with cross-trained members who rotate from task to task. The result is employees who understand and care about the performance of their plants.

Another solution to stand-alone tasks is to electronically connect people doing one task with the employees who are performing other phases of the work. Using the Internet or an intranet, a chain of isolated people working on individual parts of a customer service or design activity can become a well-connected virtual team. Team members can either simultaneously or sequentially work on different phases of the project, such as an engineering drawing or a financial plan for a client, and thus truly participate in the creation of the whole service or product.

A third approach to enriching stand-alone jobs is to alter the physical layout of your workplace to colocate work groups. Instead of putting people together based on similar activities, you position people together based on the same or similar products, services, or customers. For example, in the manufacturing world, the traditional approach to organizing factories is to cluster together people who work on similar kinds of machines. But a much better approach in many cases is to group people who are working on the same product, even though it may require putting different machines in the same area. The advantage of this repositioning is that it creates a series of product-focused cells, with each cell producing an entire product and thereby experiencing the satisfaction of seeing it produced and knowing the cell's role in producing it.

This same thinking can be used in many service industries. For example, in the mortgage department of banks, people can be grouped according to the mortgages they are working on, rather than the step in the process they handle. This encourages a group of people to feel accountable for a particular set of customers and the delivery of mortgage services to that group, rather than people who feel responsible for just one step in a long mortgage creation or service process.

Chrysler, before it was acquired by Daimler-Benz, implemented colocation teams with great success. In its product development facility, Chrysler put together people who were working on the same car designs and also formed them into cross-functional teams to facilitate the integration of different parts of the design process. This strategy was in direct contrast to the earlier method of having people and groups work separately on their own part of the car. The old method typically led to a long and difficult integration process in which any conflicting design issues, which were frequent, had to be reconciled by the organization's rather extensive hierarchy.

An important result of colocating people working on the same product and putting them into teams with decision-making authority is often a faster design process. People and teams are simply positioned to communicate more easily, allowing them to review, negotiate, and decide more quickly among the different design features under consideration.

Information Technology for Tracking Work

Given that today's employees often do many types of work, from solo tasks to teams and from simple to complex, and that what they do is constantly changing, job descriptions often cannot do justice to pinpointing people's responsibilities and accountabilities. Simply stated, job descriptions are quickly becoming obsolete, along with the fixed jobs they describe.

Nevertheless, this doesn't mean that people should not and cannot be accountable for their tasks and performance. Managers still need to stay informed about what people are accountable for, especially in this era of global competition and rapid change.

Information technology can help organizations and managers meet the need to stay up-to-date with what and how their employees are performing. Company intranets can be used to enable people to record, easily and quickly, the appropriate information about their task assignments, including such items as deliverables, timetables, and percentage of time allocated to different projects.

On-line records have several advantages. Employees can update them frequently from anywhere. They are available to anyone—supervisors, peers, teammates—who needs to know what projects and tasks others are working on. And they can become part of the organization's feedback process, supplying the data needed for formal and informal performance appraisals.

FedEx and many other organizations use company intranets for this purpose. They have their people update their descriptions at least every quarter and then use these as the basis for measuring their performance.

The one caution about using information technology is that creating and updating dynamic task assignments on a regular basis takes considerable discipline and effort. Employees need to carve out regular time to maintain their records. But when traditional job descriptions go by the wayside, this type of record keeping is necessary. It can help both managers and workers gain an overview of the total portfolio of activities in which they and others are involved. Ultimately, it can also contribute to making sure that people have a meaningful, motivating, and satisfying set of work assignments.

Implications for Individuals

The changing nature of work and jobs is both good news and bad news. The good news is that the more organizations offer challenging and interesting work, the more opportunities will exist for you to learn and experience intrinsic satisfaction from the work you do, allowing you to build your own virtuous career spiral. With luck, skill, and planning, you can conceivably spend your entire working life in jobs that are both motivating and satisfying. And if there is further good news, it is that you will have increasing options available to you regarding what tasks you work on, whether you work alone or on a team, and where you work.

But with such increasingly available options, the bad news is that it will be up to you to manage not just your career but also, to a large extent, the design of your job. To do this, you need to develop a good understanding of the conditions that allow you to perform well and what types of projects and tasks you find satisfying. You need to see your job as a constantly shifting portfolio of tasks you are asked to perform. Like a good poker player, you therefore need to know when to stand pat and when to take new cards or, in the case of work, new tasks. You need to be sure that the new tasks you take on fit your skills and your needs for interesting work, high pay, skill development, and whatever other rewards are important to you.

Over and above managing the various aspects of your job, you face three specific challenges in the world of dynamic and changing jobs: receiving credit for your good work, generating a clear career direction, and developing your personal brand.

For the first challenge, if you are prone to taking on multiple tasks and multiple assignments, you run the risk of spreading your efforts over so many different activities that you not only become overworked but also fail to receive credit for what you achieve. In essence, you run the risk of making yourself visible to a number of people but having the entirety of your work not truly visible to anyone. The obvious antidote is to be sure that you constantly update a description of all your activities and that you make an effort to keep it visible to key people in your organization.

Keep in mind also that at times it may be advisable to limit the number of projects and work assignments in which you are involved. You can get overcommitted and end up on multiple task teams or in too many problem-solving groups, which, when combined with your "regular" work activities, can result in an overload situation, poor performance, and low satisfaction.

A virtual or flexible work situation can have a number of positive ramifications. These types of work assignments can help you balance your family and work roles better. They can free up time that you might otherwise have wasted in travel and commuting.

But there are also dangers for people who live in the world of virtual work. If you telecommute from home or have no company-provided work location, you can miss out on establishing social connectedness with others in your organization.

Social contacts and relationships are very important in establishing your presence in the organization, as well as in staying informed about what is going on. If you don't go regularly to your company's location, you may miss opportunities to bid on assignments and resources such as budget increases and equipment because you are not aware of them or are late hearing about them. Further, others may fail to see that you are an important contributing member of the organization. This can ultimately influence whether or not you get promotions, raises, and development opportunities.

There is no simple way to avoid the problem of being isolated and cut off from your organization once you join the virtual work world. However, there are some actions you can take to counteract the negatives. For example, you can maintain regular social contact with people who are critical to your success in the organization and with those who are generally knowledgeable about the goings-on inside the company. You can do this by going to your company work location at least one day per week. In addition, you can schedule meetings and social events with people who are well connected and informed.

You can also take advantage of the Internet to keep informed about what is going on in your organization. Visit chat rooms, establish e-mail relationships with people in the organization, and do other things to keep yourself visible within the company.

The challenges in creating a career direction and developing your personal brand are similar. There is a real danger that people who do multiple tasks will be seen as good contributors but as not having a core marketable expertise. This is not necessarily a problem if you plan to stay with an organization for a long period of time and your job is secure, but it may have a definite impact on your employability and may be a major problem if you intend to or have to move around. In essence, you may lack a brand that establishes you as a highly marketable individual because you don't have skills or sets of skills that are easily identified by other organizations seeking employees.

But there are things you can do to develop a clear career direction and brand even though you are working on multiple tasks. One, of course, is to be very selective in the tasks you work on. When you can, turn down tasks that don't fit the identity you seek to develop as part of your brand. If you must accept unrelated tasks, be sure to maintain at least some tasks that are central to your brand. You also need to be very sure that you develop credentials to support your particular brand and career direction. As mentioned in the chapter on development, you need to seek out professional certifications, courses, and training that document how you have kept your skills and knowledge current.

In addition to the implications for your virtuous career spiral that I have discussed, if you are in a management job, you need to consider your impact on others. Indeed, it is impossible to emphasize how much influence you have on the degree to which your subordinates have enriched jobs. The tasks you assign to people have a large impact on the meaningfulness of their jobs.

Perhaps less obvious, but equally powerful, is your impact on responsibility and feedback. If you micromanage by watching and directing everything people do, you will destroy their feelings of responsibility.

You are also a very important source of feedback. What you say and how you react, whether you intend it to be or not, is experienced as feedback by the people who work for you. You need to pay attention to the messages that people are receiving and be sure that they are reinforcing the behaviors you want to see.

To conclude these implications, let me summarize by saying that, as valuable human capital, keep in mind at all times that you always have the option of finding an organization that offers you motivating and satisfying work. Research supports the fact that organizations are increasingly enriching jobs, giving employees access to the Internet and company intranets, and using many different kinds of teams. This represents a tremendous increase in the number of opportunities available to you to find or create work that fits your needs and motivates you to excel.

In the future, you are likely to have more chances to shape many aspects of your work. You need to be proactive, constantly looking for new ways to organize and manage your work. You should develop at least some expertise in work design so that you can suggest ways to your organization for your job to be improved or enriched. If your organization refuses to consider your suggestions, it may well be time for you to look elsewhere for employment. An organization that doesn't respond to your desire for more responsibility, feedback, and challenging work is not one that will tend to treat people right or be successful in creating a virtuous spiral.

Chapter Eight

| Establish the Right Goals

TREAT PEOPLE RIGHT PRINCIPLE #5

Organizations must develop and adhere to a specific organizational mission, with strategies, goals, and values that employees can understand, support, and believe in.

Performance goals are a powerful source of higher and higher levels of organizational performance and employee satisfaction. They are at the very core of what a virtuous spiral is all about. Not only are goals a powerful motivator of behavior, but people who accomplish goals develop deep feelings of intrinsic satisfaction. They tend to strive for higher performance and to form stronger commitments to their organization's goals, furthering the momentum of the virtuous spiral.

Impact of Goals

How can organizations tap into the power of goals to motivate their people? What are the characteristics of goals that lead people to being committed to achieving them? What kinds of goals lead to virtuous spirals?

Research has revealed a number of identifiable characteristics of goals that answer these important questions.[1] They include understanding the reasons for the goals, how well the goals are set and communicated to people, the degree to which people have a line of sight from their performance to the goals, and the feedback that people receive about the effectiveness of the organization in reaching its goals. I will explore these characteristics and then present a variety of practices that implement them.

Establish Meaningful Goals

It goes without saying that organizations differ enormously in their purposes and missions. Some organizations have spiritual purposes, others have business purposes, and some have both.

Organizations that have spiritual or noble purposes have the easiest time using goals as a way of motivating and retaining their employees. A wide range of people willingly volunteer to work for organizations, such as charities and religious organizations, whose purpose appeals to their values. Preventing disease, helping unfortunate people, teaching children, protecting animals, supporting a particular lifestyle or set of spiritual beliefs—these are all goals to which many people can become very committed. Spiritual organizations in particular attract people who enjoy helping others aspire to "higher" goals.[2]

But what about organizations with down-to-earth financial, business-oriented missions? Can they use goals in a powerful way?

Definitely yes—as long as the goals appeal to people in some meaningful fashion. Fortunately, organizations can make their business goals meaningful and appealing in a variety of ways.

One of the best ways is to mix both noble and social improvement goals in with the more mundane financial goals. Many organizations have this type of hybrid mission that can be characterized as "doing well by doing good." For example, many health care companies have as their mission something along the lines of improving the health of people while at the same time producing a reasonable rate of return for their shareholders.

Consider Johnson & Johnson, the global pharmaceutical and health care firm. For decades, Johnson & Johnson has done an admirable job of merging profitability with a dedication to improving health care. Beginning in the 1930s, the company developed a one-page credo that set out its commitment to improving health care and benefiting its customers. The credo is posted in all its facilities, and all employees are expected to know it. Management and employee training programs emphasize the credo to reinforce its prominence in the company. The credo even gained considerable public visibility during the Tylenol poisoning case in 1982. When tainted Tylenol tablets appeared in stores, Johnson & Johnson acted swiftly and voluntarily to remove them from the market. Executives made public statements stressing that given the company's credo, it always put its customers' well-being first and as a result had no choice but to remove all Tylenol from the market.

Another way some organizations make their goals motivating and appealing is to associate their business with noble causes, even if those causes are not directly related to their products and services. For example, Ben Cohen and Jerry Greenfield, the founders of Ben & Jerry's Ice Cream, proved themselves very skillful at building a successful company by integrating the two goals of making tasty ice cream and being a socially responsible company. Throughout their marketing campaigns and employee commitment program, the company focuses on their use of socially beneficial ingredients. They also include among their charitable practices donating a portion of their profits to environmental causes.

Patagonia, the clothing manufacturer, focuses on environmental concerns and goals to attract both employees and customers interested in preserving the earth while creating a profitable clothing company.

One of the most unusual mixtures of financial and business goals occurs at ServiceMaster, the large cleaning and maintenance company. It combines business and religious goals, and in a unique twist, it even puts the noble side ahead of the financial side in its communications. This is visible in the company's mission statement, which lists "to help people develop" and "to pursue excellence" ahead of "to grow profitably." ServiceMaster visibly translates its religious commitment into real life—with an eleven-foot statue of Jesus washing the feet of a disciple outside its headquarters in suburban Chicago and by hosting regular Bible study classes for employees. By focusing on spirituality in this way, ServiceMaster has created a higher purpose than if it only focused solely on business performance in what is clearly an unglamorous business.

Huntsman Chemical has a corporate mission that focuses on three goals: pay off corporate debt, be a responsible corporate citizen, and relieve human suffering. Its high-profile good works include sponsoring cancer research and supporting numerous charities. Jon Huntsman, the owner, believes that the commitment of the company to good works inspires its employees and increases their spirit of accomplishment.

But what about organizations that do not have a noble and higher-order mission or purpose? Can they still motivate people through goals?

Again, the answer is yes. The fact is, a very wide range of people can become quite excited about and committed to purely financial and operational performance goals. While it often helps to have a spiritual or noble purpose, it is not at all a necessary condition to using goals as a powerful and effective force to achieve individual and organizational results.

Use Business Performance Goals

As a matter of fact, companies can tap into a very powerful human trait to motivate people with purely financial goals: the competitive spirit. Many people are by nature tremendously competitive and love a good contest. They can become very motivated to perform simply by putting in front of them the immodest goal of winning—whether it's market share, operating profits, customer satisfaction, or growth. In fact, competitive goals are often much more effective in motivating people than establishing dry performance goals such as increasing earnings per share by a certain percentage.

The competitive spirit is actually quite effective when it is put into action. It also has two surprising properties. One is that the prize for winning does not need to be particularly significant or valuable in order to entice people to compete. I am constantly amazed at how easy it is to produce a highly motivated group of people simply by telling them that they are competing for a prize, any prize. This can be true even for incredibly unimportant tasks. People will actually overlook the negative aspects of a task if it offers an opportunity to beat a competitor.

The other surprising property of the competitive spirit is that it does not require an existing opponent or enemy. A competitor can be just about anyone, even people randomly selected within your own organization to be on a competing team. Given the right setting, people will work very hard to carry water balloons faster than another team, throw a Nerf ball at a target better than others, and so on, simply because they want to beat the opponent, whoever it is.

A competitor can even be a concept, such as being "the best" at something. People often take great pride in being part of the best organization in any number of fields of endeavor, even if the field does not have high social value like delivering medical care.

Ultimately, organizations without a noble purpose or association can make good use of the competitive spirit. They simply need to find or invent competitors and measure their performance against them to motivate their people. Whether it's winning a game or being number one or being ahead of a competitor or being world-class, having a competitive mission is often sufficient to attract, retain, and inspire people in ways that lead to a virtuous spiral.

Promote and Publicize Your Goals

Whether the goals are noble or purely financial, people cannot be motivated by them unless they are aware of them. Organizations must clearly declare their goals and make sure everyone knows what they are. One of the best ways to do this is to tie the goals to a mission statement that captures the overall purpose and direction of the organization in a few simple sentences.

In fact, I highly recommend that organizations have an "elevator speech" that quickly summarizes what their goals and mission are and why they are important. An elevator speech is simply a statement that anyone—whether a senior executive, middle manager, or mailroom clerk—can recite in the time it takes for an elevator to ascend from the ground floor to the upper floors of a high-rise building!

Creating mottoes and physical symbols or icons can also be a powerful way to communicate an organization's goals. Service-Master, for example, devised the motto "We Serve," which has a purposeful double meaning for this Christian cleaning company. Medtronic emphasizes that it develops devices that "save people's lives," while for decades General Electric has made its theme "We Bring Good Things to Life" into a well-known brand.

As for publicizing your goals, there are innumerable ways to let people know about them. These include all the typical methods of communicating information, such as speeches, video, print-based communications of all kinds, the company's home page or portal, and advertising. Whatever the method or methods, a key to success is repetition. As with any type of communication, it takes many impressions for people to absorb a message so that it becomes an accepted part of their attention.

Finally, it is also important in publicizing goals to provide regular feedback about how people and the organization are performing against the goals. Employees need to get frequent updates on where the organization stands in relation to its goals.

Use Competitive Data to Inspire

Providing data about your competitors is a key to making business performance goals a powerful motivator. Letting employees honestly know how they stack up against competitors serves to boost their competitive spirit. Even goals that are not necessarily highly appealing from a spiritual or nobility perspective often become exciting when they take on a competitive edge.

Look at the world of sports for an example of this. Fans become astonishingly committed to their team when the competition heats up. But if there were no scores to indicate winners and losers, many people would undoubtedly lose interest. There is simply no competitive excitement from a game that has no victor. It's the winning and losing that matters in a competition.

Your competitors do not have to be the best or top organization in your field or industry. They do have to be organizations that are similar to yours and worthy opponents. People can become awfully excited about winning an event even if their opponents are just "amateurs." The competitive spirit can thrive at the lowest levels of competition as well as at the highest.

In fact, in some cases, it is counterproductive to choose a world-class competitor because it sets the standard so high that people believe they can't possibly win. Research on achievement motivation indicates that people are most highly motivated by *moderately* difficult goals. Setting goals that are perceived to be unreachable may simply turn people off to competing.

It is best to select a visible competitive organization that provides your organization with a challenge that you can reasonably expect to win. A good plan is to start by choosing an organization that is only slightly better than yours, one that can indeed be overtaken if your organization improves. This provides a sufficient competition to launch a good game. Then once your initial competitor has been "defeated," you can keep your virtuous spiral going by looking for the next toughest competitor or competitors and using them as the new basis for comparison.

If no reasonable corporate competitor can be identified, an organization can compete against its past performance. It can adapt a continuous improvement approach and set higher and higher goals. This may not be quite as compelling as competing against a visible "bad guy" opponent, but it still can be motivating. It clearly appeals to people's achievement and development needs and can consequently help drive an organization's virtuous spiral.

Finally, everyone needs to understand the scoring system used in the game. It doesn't work to simply set up a list of goals, publicize them, and name your competitor. People need to understand how they are being scored and compared to their competitor, what measures are used to do the comparisons, and especially what they can do to influence the outcome of the competition. Setting financial targets, for example, is unlikely to excite people and motivate them if they do not know how the results are tabulated or recorded or what they can do to influence them.

This suggests that all employees need to be educated in the organization's business model and the type of scoring system used to determine success and failure. It is also very helpful if people have a piece of the financial action so that if the company wins, they win too. As will be discussed in Chapter Nine, financial rewards can have a very positive impact on achieving goals.

Establish a Clear Line of Sight

People are most likely to be committed to reaching goals when they can see a direct connection between their behavior and the results required. As noted earlier, this is called the "line of sight."

A clear line of sight is especially important if your organization's goals are not particularly noble or spiritual. A considerable amount of evidence suggests that people will work hard if they believe strongly in the mission and purpose of the organization, even when they know that their efforts have little impact on the overall results. For example, hospital and charity volunteers will do boring, menial tasks that are only weakly related to the overall success of the organization just because they believe wholeheartedly in its mission and purpose. Since this type of strong commitment is much less likely to exist in for-profit organizations whose goals are not especially noble, a clear line of sight is important in motivating people.

Let me take this point one step further. Wherever possible, people should see clearly how their individual or their team's work influences the entire organization. In other words, aim to create not just individual job involvement and commitment to team performance but a commitment to excellence in *organizational* performance.

But what if achieving a line of sight to organizational performance is difficult or impossible, as it often is in very large organizations that have many divisions and hundreds of thousands of employees? In these situations, the best approach is usually to create a line of sight in which people see how their job performance influences their particular mini-enterprise, organizational unit, or work area. But if possible, it is better and well worth the effort to try to create a line of sight to the entire organization.

Let me emphasize once again that ongoing feedback about your organization's performance and whether it is reaching its goals is critical to keeping motivation and a virtuous spiral alive. Just as in sports, people need to get frequent feedback about their performance. Without feedback, they fail to see the cause-and-effect relationship between their behavior and the organization's success. Without feedback, they do not experience the intrinsic rewards that come from achieving their goals. A lack of feedback can ultimately destroy your organization's attempt to motivate employees and sustain a virtuous spiral.

Best Practices for Establishing Commitment to Goals

Getting people to strongly commit to an organization's mission and goals can be a daunting task. Clearly, it will occur only if the organization has adopted specific practices dedicated to goal setting and goal achievement. In most cases, this is also not a matter of simply adopting one practice. An entire pattern of practices is required. Most or all of the practices that I present here need to be in place. These practices can be implemented by most organizations and can provide significant support for virtuous spirals.

Employee Involvement in Mission Statement Development

Mission statements are often developed in isolation by senior managers or outside consultants and then presented to and ultimately imposed on employees. No wonder employees misunderstand or, worse, ignore them.

A far more effective strategy is to involve employees in the creation of the mission statement. A good way to open up the process is through a "town meeting" in which everyone in the organization, or at least a representative sampling of employees, is invited to spend time crafting a draft of the mission statement. If necessary, later meetings with fewer people can be held to refine the statement.

The goals that grow out of the mission statement are also best set using an employee involvement process. The research literature on goal setting clearly shows that participation in setting goals increases people's commitment to the goals. In many companies, the town meeting process has resulted in mission statements that are broadly accepted and goals that are meaningful to people at all levels of the organization.

Rally Goals

A rally goal—a single metric or key accomplishment your organization is striving to reach—can be very powerful in motivating people to improve performance.

Two qualities are needed to create good rally goals. First, the goal must be set at a high enough level of difficulty that it requires people to "stretch" to reach it. If getting to the goal is too easy or happens too quickly, the rally goal becomes meaningless. Ideally, it should take considerable effort and time to reach so that it keeps people motivated. Second, the rally goal needs to improve the organization's long-term competitiveness. It does relatively little good to create a rally goal aimed at fixing short-term behaviors or increasing short-term results. (There are some exceptions to this. In a crisis, short-term rally goals, handled properly, can be quite useful.)

The power of rally goals, as well as their downside, is illustrated by an example from Continental Airlines. A few years ago, Continental created a rally goal when the CEO challenged the company's employees to turn it into one of the top four airlines in on-time departures. As an additional motivator, he promised a bonus if Continental reached it. The employees took the rally goal very seriously and accomplished the goal; they also received their bonuses.

Unfortunately, the rally goal failed to emphasize the importance of the total customer experience. What happened was that Continental's employees did a variety of counterproductive things in order to reach the rally goal and get their bonus. For example, they left baggage behind, stranded passengers in terminals, and failed to load full meal services so that they could get their planes away from gates on time.

Fortunately, Continental set up a new and considerably smarter rally goal of having the highest level of customer satisfaction in the industry. This new goal led to many fewer inappropriate behaviors and has proved to be more robust and effective.

My three favorite examples of organizations using rally goals to get amazing results are the NASA goal to land a man on the moon by the end of the 1960s, Pepsi's goal to beat Coke in the domestic market, and GE's goal for every one of its businesses to be number one or number two in its industry. Each of these rally goals had the effect of focusing the organization's people on the right kinds of performance and led them to success.

Surveys to Assess Goal Commitment

As we have discussed, employees must both understand your current business strategy and fully accept your goals in order for them to be good motivators of performance. So rather than rely on hallway comments and word-of-mouth rumors to assess whether employees are truly committed to the goals, a good practice is to conduct regular formal attitude surveys.

Dow Chemical Company does just this. Dow surveys its people by asking questions about what the employees understand the performance goals to be, what business model the company follows, who the competitors are, and what each employee can do to help the company achieve its goals. By regularly assessing workers' perceptions and attitudes, Dow also gets useful feedback on how well senior management has fulfilled its role as communicators of the business goals and objectives. The results of the surveys are also used to guide corrective action when the results show that employees have misunderstood a goal or don't understand the strategy.

Informal "pulse" surveys, consisting of just a few questions, can be a valuable tool for real-time measurement of the visibility and impact of goals. Pulse surveys can be quickly and easily done over an intranet and can be sent out every few months, at minimal cost. In addition to getting feedback, another advantage of pulse surveys is that they act as a gentle reminder to everyone of the organization's goals.

Motorola uses pulse surveys on a regular basis to assess employee commitment to goals. Motorola makes its surveys proactive by asking employees to provide feedback about certain actions the company is considering taking. The employee input from the surveys thus becomes a way to involve people in shaping Motorola's goals and practices, which in turn spurs increased commitment to the company's mission.

Highlighting Goals in the Hiring Process

Your organization's mission and goals should be an important part of your organization's brand as an employer. They should be out in front beginning with the selection process. The mission and goals should be promoted and publicized to all applicants as part of giving them a realistic preview of what working for your organization will be like. Knowing the mission and goals helps applicants decide for themselves if they fit your organization.

Being specific about your mission and goals in the selection process can also help your organization improve its ability to hire the right people. For example, if your organization's goals focus on winning a competition against another company or meeting a certain performance target, your selection interviewers know they should spend their time looking for people with a competitive bent and who have a history of high achievement. They need to focus on asking applicants questions about their past activities in sports or other types of competitive games to find candidates who appreciate competition and are excited by the chances your organization offers to win and score well against opponents.

Similarly, if your organization's basic mission is more spiritual, you will want to look for other characteristics. Clearly in this case, you want to focus the interview process on finding people who have previously worked or volunteered in organizations whose spiritual goals were similar to yours.

Whatever the case, it is very useful to have interviewers use behavioral interviewing questions that get candidates to speak about what they look for in an organization, what they have found particularly rewarding in their past work situations, and how they respond to different environments. Answers to these types of questions will help you determine if your mission and goals match what applicants can commit to.

Employee Portals

My surveys of Fortune 1000 companies show that many of them do not communicate their financial results to their employees.[3] These companies don't even send employees an annual report! Given this lack of information, it is not surprising that many employees give no evidence of being committed to seeing their organization perform well and don't get excited when there is good news. They don't even know about it.

The Internet can change this dramatically by facilitating the entire process of providing feedback to all employees in a way that educates and motivates them. As Bill Gates pointed out in his book *Business @ the Speed of Thought,* the Internet makes it possible to put your company's business on every employee's desk.

This is easily done today using an employee portal where the organization publicizes its mission statement, values, rally goals, long-term goals, and even up-to-the-minute financial news such as the current stock price. In the best of all worlds, the portal also provides as many operating and financial measures of performance as possible so that every employee gets a real-time picture of how the company is doing.

Cisco Corporation now has a virtual closing process that allows the company to have financial results at the end of each day and at the end of every financial period. It allows employees to get frequent and up-to-date feedback on the performance of the company and in some cases on their department or business unit.

Many large organizations may be tempted to develop a portal for each part of their business and allow only the employees in that division to see their own results. But in my view, it is better to allow all employees access to all results so that employees know not only how their own division or unit is doing but also how the overall organization is performing. Your portal should generate in employees the same type of feeling when they get performance information as they get watching their favorite sporting event or other competition—ongoing valid data that indicate who is winning and who is losing.

Board Membership

In U.S. corporations, employee representation on the board of directors is virtually nonexistent. This is not true in Europe, where one can find employee representatives on the boards of many organizations.

In my view, many factors argue for putting employees or their representatives on corporate boards. To begin, employees increasingly own stock in the companies they work for; as a result, they have an ownership stake in the issues that come before the directors.

Second, as indicated earlier, today's workers are valuable capital, representing a crucial resource for companies. Their voice should be heard and their needs taken into account in connection with many strategic decisions. Failure to do so runs the great risk of damaging or preventing a virtuous spiral relationship and triggering a death spiral.

Third, putting employees on the board makes a powerful statement that the organization truly values human capital and takes its responsibility to its employees seriously. Having employee board members effectively validates that the organization's goals have been established with a complete understanding of what employees can contribute to the organization and what they value. This can greatly improve goal acceptance and more strongly link the employees to the organization's goals and mission. In short, it can be very supportive of a virtuous spiral.

Finally, having employees on the board also serves a valuable role in creating respected voices that are well positioned to communicate the mission statement and goals to all other employees. Employee board members can often become very effective spokespeople to the rest of the workforce, helping them understand how they can influence goal accomplishment. In essence, it can go a long way toward improving the line of sight between employee performance and corporate performance.

Implications for Individuals

Recognizing how organizational mission statements and goals can affect you directly as an individual can be very useful in managing your career.

To begin with, the extent to which you find working for a particular organization satisfying and rewarding is likely to be strongly influenced by how closely its mission and goals match yours. Your own value orientation and personal bent—whether spiritual or competitive—needs to coincide with how the organization defines itself in order for you to find a good fit. Rarely does an organization change its basic mission or goals, so don't assume that you can change the nature of an organization just to create a situation where you will have your needs met.

This reinforces the idea that you need to carefully analyze the goals of any organization that you are considering joining. Finding a good fit is particularly important if you have a passion about making a difference in the world. If you are seeking a noble or spiritually oriented organization, you will not enjoy working for one that focuses on financial results and competitiveness.

Not only do you need to pay attention to an organization's mission statement and values, you also need to be especially sure that the organization actually lives up to them. All too often, organizations publicize a mission that seems and sounds attractive, but on close examination it is clear that the way the company operates diverges from it significantly. A deviation between mission and reality can create a particularly frustrating and disappointing situation for you.

It can be a challenge to find out whether an organization truly lives up to its mission statement and values, but here are several useful actions you can take to do some detective work of your own. First, talk to current and former employees. See if they can help you assess the correspondence between the organization's statements and its behavior. Ask them also about what the organization's performance appraisal system measures. Whatever the organization measures, that's what it gets—and in most cases, that's what it deems important. Also, visit various chat rooms and read what employees and customers say about the organization. Next, talk to the customers or clients of the organization and see if they believe the organization lives up to its mission and values.

Another good approach is to check with outside activists or groups that monitor the organization's social or ethical behaviors. For example, the Sierra Club rates organizations on their environmental behaviors, which might be a factor of interest to you. Many other organizations exist that maintain a variety of ratings on a wide range of companies.

Another issue relevant to mission and values is the organization's honesty and openness about its performance information. As I have noted, companies vary tremendously in how much and how frequently they keep employees informed about their performance. In my view, any organization that does not provide its employees with ongoing, current performance data is one you should be cautious about joining. You need this feedback to experience a sense of goal accomplishment and intrinsic satisfaction when you perform effectively and contribute to the organization's success.

Information and feedback are especially vital in the context of today's rapidly changing business world, in which you must increasingly be vigilant about managing your own career. Information about the business successes and failures of an organization is critical to your understanding and ability to decide such issues as whether or not to stay on a job, where to seek new employment, how to direct your skill development, and whether you can achieve a virtuous spiral by working there. Without good financial data and other metrics about your organization's performance, it can be very difficult for you to make intelligent career choices.

Finally, I also recommend that you evaluate the leadership of any organization you are considering joining. You can learn a considerable amount about how likely an organization is to live up to its mission statement by examining its leaders. Senior leadership, in particular, is crucial in determining the degree to which an organization behaves consistently with its mission statement and values. It is very reasonable for you to ask about the makeup of the senior management team and to obtain specific examples of decisions these managers have made.

You should also look at who is on the board of directors and how the members balance the needs of employees, customers, and financial investors. A board that is made up of CEOs and investors, for example, is very likely to focus the company on financial performance, not on a spiritual mission or human capital development.

Ultimately, you are most likely to feel highly committed to the goals of an organization only if you feel a sense of involvement in establishing them and determining how they will be reached. Look for organizations where you will have a chance to participate in setting goals and achieving them. In short, look for an organization that has such employee involvement practices as self-managing work teams and shared leadership.

Finally, if you are in a management job or are considering taking a management job, ask yourself how much you believe in the goals of the organization. If you don't believe in them enough so that you are comfortable basing your leadership behaviors on them, you probably shouldn't be working for the organization. Why? Simply because you will not enjoy a virtuous spiral of your own, and you may prevent your organization from achieving one.

| **Reward People Right**

Treat People Right Principle #6

Organizations must devise and implement reward systems that
reinforce their design, core values, and strategy.

Designing reward systems that are good for both organizations and
people is usually thought of as an impossible feat. A common view
is that reward systems are a zero-sum game: the more one side
wins, the more the other side loses.

My research shows, however, that it doesn't have to be this way.
In the spirit of the virtuous spiral, both sides can be winners. It is
entirely possible to design a reward system that motivates people
to excel and satisfies them while at the same time contributing to
organizational effectiveness.[1]

Motivation and Satisfaction

The key is to create a high-performance organization that generates
a large pool of rewards, particularly financial rewards, so that both
individuals and organizations can achieve a high level of return. Admittedly, this task is not easy, but it can be done. My belief is that a
well-designed reward system can create a large enough pool of
money and other extrinsic rewards to allow both financial investors
and human capital investors to have their needs met.

For a reward system to satisfy both employees and investors, it
must reward performance, but that is not enough. It must be aligned

with and reinforce the organization's design, strategy, and goals, as you will see in the concepts and practices presented in this chapter.

Design Reward Systems to Motivate

The basic logic behind designing a reward system that motivates people to perform is quite straightforward. We discussed the key points back in Chapter Three, where we talked about the role of rewards in fueling motivation and performance. We noted that people have needs that must be met by valued rewards and that those rewards must come in a sufficient quantity that people feel they have been properly rewarded. We also saw that people become very motivated to perform if they know that achieving a goal will yield a high level of reward.

That is the basic logic, but it is not all that needs to be considered. Multiple criteria must be met when designing a reward system. We have mentioned several of these other criteria in other chapters, but they are worth repeating and reinforcing now as a holistic set of principles to guide you.

First, organizations must establish a clear line of sight between the performance outcomes they want and the rewards they are offering. It is not good enough simply to offer valued rewards and say that they are based on performance. The organization needs to clearly identify the outcomes desired, as well as the measures for assessing whether or not they are achieved. It also needs to specify how the performance measures affect reward levels. If there is any lack of clarity about the measures of performance and the allocation of rewards, it blurs the line of sight. When people do not know what is expected of them and how they are rewarded, they are not motivated to perform in the way the organization wants and needs in order to achieve its goals.

Second, organizations must give serious thought to the issue of reward size. Many reward systems are designed with a basic flaw: the rewards are far too small to capture the attention of people and make a difference in their motivation. For example, many organizations offer merit increases of only 3 or 4 percent. Organizations need to give much larger rewards than this in order to capture people's attention. Raises or bonuses of 10 percent or more are a more realistic estimate of what is needed. In general, this issue can be resolved only by developing alternatives to merit pay, as we will discuss later in the chapter.

Third, organizations need to give the people who are covered by pay-for-performance systems the power, information, and knowledge they need in order to influence their performance. If there are organizational structures, procedures, or skill deficits that effectively prevent people from providing the high performance they have been asked to deliver, the reward system will not be motivational. This is why good job designs and effective human resource management practices are needed along with a good reward system.

Finally, organizations must provide the leadership necessary to create credibility for their reward programs. Any time employees doubt the ability and willingness of management to deliver on its promises or if there is a history of broken trust when it comes to rewards, motivation will take a nosedive.

To summarize, then, a truly motivational reward system must be designed with all these parameters in mind: it must motivate people to perform through valued and truly sufficient rewards, provide them with a clear line of sight, give them the power to influence their performance, and deliver on its promises. In my experience, fulfilling these criteria usually requires that most organizations revamp their existing reward systems in very significant ways.

Use Rewards to Increase Satisfaction and Development

A good reward system can contribute to people's satisfaction and their willingness and desire to learn and improve their skills. Rewards can positively influence both and as a result lead to greater retention.

The kinds and amounts of rewards people get are a major factor in their level of satisfaction. Needless to say, the more highly rewarded people are, the more satisfied they tend to be with their job and with their life. As we discussed in Chapter Three, satisfaction translates into several important outcomes for organizations: satisfied people tend to be less likely to quit, change jobs, join unions, or be absent. In short, organizations are better off when they provide people with a reward level that leads them to feel at least moderately satisfied.

Of course, ensuring that someone is at least moderately satisfied with his or her rewards is difficult. As we discussed earlier, the evidence strongly suggests that people tend to make social comparisons in deciding whether they are being rewarded fairly, basing their decision on how others with characteristics similar to theirs are rewarded. In most cases, rewarding people as well as others who have the same skills and knowledge improves the chances of their staying with the organization and decreases the likelihood that they will be dissatisfied.

However, this is not a rule that works for everyone all the time. Paying people an amount equal to or greater than what similar others get paid does not always guarantee that they will be satisfied. This is because people always tend to make "optimistic" comparisons when they evaluate themselves. They tend to see themselves as high performers, doing complex work. As a result, they feel they deserve not just what the organization judges to be the pay of "similar others" but pay at a level similar to that of the top performers in their field—which is what they feel they are. For this reason, I still caution organizations about assuming that "competitive" rewards will always lead to satisfaction.

Rewards can also contribute to an organization's success in training and developing people. Promotions and pay raises are excellent rewards for motivating employees to learn particular kinds of new skills. This is not to say that people won't learn skills and develop new knowledge without an extrinsic reward, but they may not learn the skills that the organization needs them to learn unless you have a systematic program in place that rewards them for the "right" development. A good reward system will encourage people to learn skills that directly contribute to the organization's core competencies and capabilities. To do this, the reward system must establish a clear link between learning those skills and increases in rewards.

Rewards and Organizational Effectiveness

Since this is a book about virtuous spirals, it stands to reason that a well-designed reward system cannot be designed to support only *individual* effectiveness; it also needs to create *organizational* effectiveness by being aligned with its strategy, structure, and processes.

If it is not, the reward system is likely to cause conflicts and unproductive behaviors.

For example, let's say you design a performance bonus pay system that goes all out to motivate and satisfy the top-performing individuals, but your organization has a strategy and structure based on teamwork. This reward system will clearly be dysfunctional in the context of your organizational strategy and structure.

Here are some key points concerning how to design a reward system to support the entire organization's structure, strategy, and culture.

Align Rewards and Strategy

Designing a reward system to support a specific organizational strategy is not a function of any single feature of the reward system. Instead, a cumulative message needs to be communicated by the reward system as a whole. The entire reward system must reinforce the strategic direction of the organization.

For example, assume that an organization needs to encourage people to develop skills and knowledge that contribute to strategically important core competencies and organizational capabilities. Supporting this strategy means that the reward system must be designed in a way that makes it a powerful force behind skill development. A poorly designed reward system can do just the opposite, sending messages that tell employees to ignore skill development or that fail to attract and retain employees who have high-level skills.

Ultimately, your organization's business strategy needs to drive the reward system, not the other way around. As I often say, in the absence of a well-developed strategy, any reward system will work. However, if there is a well-developed business strategy, the organization needs to carefully craft a reward system that encourages the kinds of behaviors needed to make that strategy work. In fact, a good test of whether a strategy is actually implementable is to determine whether a reward system can be designed to support it. If a reward system cannot be designed, it is very likely that the strategy is flawed and needs to be rethought because it cannot be executed.

A last important point about strategy and rewards: any time one changes, the other must as well; otherwise, there is a good chance that behavior won't change either. This is why changes in your mission or business plans or downturns in the economy require you to reexamine the design of your reward system and determine if it still supports your strategy.

Align Rewards with Organizational Structure

A reward system can serve to either integrate or differentiate people. Integration occurs when people have a common fate with respect to their rewards. This in turn causes them to be cohesive and to feel interdependent. Differentiation occurs when the rewards are based on individual performance. It causes people to separate and feel autonomous.

Your organizational structure needs to dictate which approach is used in your reward system. If your structure needs large amounts of teamwork and cooperation to be effective, the system needs to reward interdependence, integration, and collective performance. But if it requires strong individual contributions, it is best to design the reward system to focus on individual performance and individual excellence.

Here's a good example of the appropriate use of the individual approach. At Mary Kay Cosmetics, salespeople go out individually selling cosmetics to their own list of customers. Clearly, this type of organizational structure requires individually differentiated rewards. Each person's efforts and performance should dictate the amount of reward earned.

In contrast, consider a product design team in a high-technology company, such as Sun Microsystems or Cisco. Assume that the team's working relationship requires members to be highly integrated and interdependent in order to produce a complex new product or series of products. In this case, individual rewards for performance will be counterproductive because they discourage cooperative effort. Instead, collective rewards that give every member of the team a similar outcome based on the team's success or failure is the correct reward system approach.

Align Rewards and Culture

Reward systems greatly shape and color an organization's culture. Choices about what behaviors get rewarded, who gets rewarded, what rewards are given, and what level of reward people receive—all send a message to employees about whether the organization values excellence, whether it is a good place to work, whether it values entrepreneurial behavior, and so on.

The ties between the reward systems and culture are so strong that once an organization has been in existence for several years, its culture and reward systems become quite interdependent. This makes it nearly impossible to change one without changing the other. Many well-known large-scale organizational change efforts have failed precisely because the rewards they offered were "countercultural." As soon as people see an inconsistency between the verbiage concerning the desired new culture and the behavior of the organization in doling out rewards, they will shut down the changes desired.

One critical implication of this when it comes to creating a virtuous spiral culture is that the reward system must communicate to people that a win-win relationship exists between the organization's desired performance and how its employees are rewarded.

Best Practices in Designing Reward Systems

Reward systems in large corporations have traditionally supported the loyalty contract. They tied rewards to seniority so that people were rewarded for long-term membership in the organization. In many cases, all people had to do to get a raise was pass the metaphorical "mirror test"—fogging a mirror showed they were breathing and deserved the raise. Their actual performance was usually a minor factor in rewards, and organizational performance had even less impact.

People were rewarded for learning new skills largely through vertical promotions, that is, attaining higher-level management jobs. This created a strong incentive for people to move up the organizational hierarchy because it led to higher pay, higher status, and additional perquisites and benefits. However, it did not necessarily foster learning the right skills to support the organization's core competencies or organizational capabilities.

The reality of the traditional pay system was that it excelled at developing hierarchical, bureaucratic, stable organizations. It did little to differentiate one company from another, little to create companies with a particular set of competencies or capabilities, and little to motivate people to be involved in their business or implement the business strategy, and it certainly did not lead to a virtuous spiral.

It did, however, generally create a level playing field with respect to labor costs, since most organizations paid essentially the same rates as their competitors. It also did a reasonably good job of retaining people for a career. Those who left were typically excellent employees who became frustrated with the slow upward movement in their pay and career. They sought a virtuous career spiral and as a result either joined other companies or started their own businesses. Finally, the old system often served top management well; during the 1980s and 1990s executive compensation levels climbed as executives received more and more compensation and expensive perks.

I could go on for quite a while analyzing and critiquing the traditional reward practices of organizations, but that would not be particularly helpful. What is important at this point is to discuss alternatives that are more supportive of strategically driven organizations that are focused on creating a virtuous spiral. Thus the remainder of this chapter discusses reward system practices that have the potential to create win-win situations because they foster both organizational effectiveness and higher reward levels for individuals.

Bonuses Instead of Merit Pay

Correctly rewarding performance is one of the most difficult human capital management objectives to accomplish—perhaps the most difficult of all. Before I talk about what works, I want to be absolutely clear about what does not work: merit pay programs, which base salary increases on assessments of performance.

Merit pay does not work for many reasons. It fails to motivate people to perform well; it fails to pay outstanding performers highly enough to retain them; and perhaps most important, it lacks the flexibility to reward truly outstanding performance.

This leads to one very important conclusion: any organization that wants to motivate performance with cash rewards must use bonuses.

The hard part, of course, is figuring out how to design an effective bonus plan. You must decide whether or not to reward based on individual, group, unit, and organizational performance, as well as what specific metrics to use and how much of a bonus to award. These decisions can be quite complex and need to fit each organization's strategy and design, so I cannot specify an "ideal" approach. However, I can provide several general guidelines to keep in mind when designing bonus programs.

First, remember that individual bonus plans are the most effective way to drive individual performance because they can develop the clearest line of sight between performance and reward. However, they do a very poor job of integrating people's behavior. If your organization uses teams and has a highly interdependent work environment, it requires a bonus plan that rewards collective performance, not individual performance.

Second, if a line of sight can be established between what an individual does and the performance of the entire business or business unit, then basing part or all of any bonus payments on organizational performance can make sense. In general, a bonus plan based on the performance of an entire business has many advantages. It both motivates individual performance and causes people to integrate themselves into a high-performing unit—a key step in creating the kind of virtuous spiral that every organization would like to have.

In the best of all worlds, business-based bonus plans lead to pay well above market rates because the organization's performance is above average. This occurs as a result of the plan's effectively motivating everyone's performance as well as attracting and retaining top-performing people—a true virtuous spiral situation.

Third, maintaining an effective organizationwide performance reward system requires that people be thoroughly educated in the bonus plan. They need to know how their performance is measured, how their behavior affects the entire organization's performance, and at what level the organization will reward them if it performs well.

A poorly designed bonus plan can quickly lead to a death spiral situation. The organization can end up overpaying people relative to their performance, thus sending the wrong message to them as well as incurring high compensation costs. Alternately, it can end up having inspired good performance but paying reward levels below people's expectations, a condition that drives away the best performers and can be fatal to a virtuous spiral.

Raises Based on Skills, Not Performance

Individual performance appraisals have traditionally been the main tool to determine merit salary increases for people. However, in my view, individual performance appraisals are the weakest link in most human capital management systems. They too often produce bad data, and they frequently strain the relationship between managers and employees.

For purposes of determining pay increases, a smarter alternative is to measure skill acquisition, not individual performance. This approach allows people to still have their pay augmented annually to ensure that it keeps pace with the market value of their skills while eliminating the performance ratings that people so often resent. A skill-based approach makes particular sense when the work environment is heavily oriented toward teams or collective performance. In these cases, a strong emphasis on individual performance is actually counterproductive to building the right amount of integration and cooperation. A skill- or competency-based approach is particularly appropriate in knowledge work situations where the worth of individuals is in what they can do, not in the work they are doing at any moment.

Of course, there still are certain situations where it makes sense to measure individual performance and to reward it. In these cases, an effective performance management system needs, at the least, to differentiate between the very best employees and those who are failing and need to be counseled or eliminated.

Identifying the best and the worst performers is often the most difficult part of a performance management process. Among the reasons for this are that most managers are untrained and not naturally skilled at doing performance appraisals; the performance appraisal system is not supported by senior executives; the measures that are developed are poor and may only refer to general traits such as being friendly, kind, and hardworking; and the systems are poorly communicated and understood.

Effective Performance Appraisals

So what can be done if you need to do individual performance appraisals? Here are several practices that, in my view, can make the process run smoothly while producing good data and avoiding resentment.

Individual Appraisals

Individual appraisals of performance should be done only for people who are expected to carry out their activities autonomously and accomplish major measurable objectives on their own. Particularly when the jobs are enriched, individual appraisals can be important sources of feedback and should be an integral part of the reward system.

Top-to-Bottom Appraisals

Performance appraisals need to be done well, starting right at the top of the organization. All too often, the senior executives in an organization are not appraised and do not appraise their subordinates. The result is that performance appraisals become something senior executives tell middle management to do to lower-level employees. Needless to say, this sets up a negative dynamic with respect to the way appraisals are thought of and done. Among other negatives, no senior role modeling is present, and senior managers are not held accountable for their performance. For these reasons, performance appraisals need to be done and done well from the top of the organization to the bottom.

Measures of Appraisal Effectiveness

Evaluating the effectiveness of appraisals makes a significant statement about their importance to the organization. It is also a way to motivate managers to do a good job and give them feedback about how well they do the appraisals. Systematic measurement of appraisals should include three elements: an audit of the quality of the written documents produced in the process, a gathering of survey data on how people feel about the appraisal events, and measures of the timeliness of the appraisal meetings and reports.

Goals Set in Advance

A sound appraisal process requires that specific and quantifiable goals for acceptable levels of performance be established in advance. Managers and their subordinates need to sit down before the performance period begins and establish what measures will be used in the evaluations and what performance levels the subordinate needs to achieve. Research suggests that the more mutual the goal-setting work is, the more likely people are to accept the goals, be motivated by them, and see performance appraisal as a fair and reasonable process. Furthermore, when you are setting goals, keep in mind that goal difficulty is a key determinant of performance. Easy-to-achieve goals tend to lead to poor performance, but so do goals that are too difficult. As I pointed out earlier, when goals are set too high, people give up because they do not believe they can achieve them or they cheat in order to give the impression of achieving them. Developing goals that are perceived to be achievable should therefore be the objective.

Input from Individuals Being Appraised

People who are being appraised should have an opportunity to respond and provide input at the end of the performance appraisal period. They should have a chance to present their version of how well they have performed their work assignments against their preset goals. My research suggests that it is important for people to have this opportunity *before* their appraiser reaches a final performance judgment.

Separate Development and Reward Discussions

It is best to separate the discussion of pay for performance from the discussion of development needs and activities. This means two separate discussions between the appraiser and the person being appraised—one in which past performance and the resulting pay increase or bonus is discussed, and a second, separated by a significant time period, in which the future development and career situation of the individual is discussed. When a knowledge-and-skill-based pay system is in place, pay changes related to skill development need to be discussed at the first meeting, or perhaps at a third meeting that focuses exclusively on skill certification and pay. These meetings may also need to include subject matter experts in addition to the supervisor.

Objective Performance Measures

Many appraisals fail because the performance measures consist of vague rating terms such as "excellent" or poorly defined general traits or personality dimensions such as "reliability," "communication skills," "customer focus," and "leadership." These traits are difficult to judge and almost always lead to communication breakdowns and misunderstandings between appraisers and subordinates. A better alternative is a balanced scorecard of behavior- and outcome-based measures that quantify, or at least clearly identify, what performance is being judged. For example, rather than assessing the general dimension or personality trait of "reliability," the appraisal should focus on whether work has been completed on time and whether the preset goals were met.

Let me give you a simple example of how agreement between rater and ratee can be increased when the appraisal focuses on observable behaviors and the business outcomes they produce. Assume that growth is an important business objective for a certain company; given this, the behaviors that lead to growth need to be identified and each person assessed against those behaviors. Based on this linkage, for instance, a saleswoman in the company would be appraised on behaviors such as the proportion of her sales that come from new products, the number of suggestions she made for product innovation, or her opening of new sales territories and customer accounts. These types of specific measures establish the strongest link between the organization's business strategy and the appraisal process.

Meaningful Rating Scales

Having an overall rating of each individual's performance can be useful. Overall or summary ratings of performance can be used as a basis for the allocation of bonuses, as well as to determine promotions, work assignments, and terminations.

Unfortunately, organizations often use poorly designed rating scales. Many organizations ask supervisors to make appraisal judgments using one of two common types of rating scales. In the first method, supervisors rank their subordinates in sequential order from best to worst. In some companies, the rankings are even done on a companywide basis so that employees are ranked from 1 to a number equal to the total number of employees. In one company I studied, this resulted in one employee being ranked number 1 and another ranked number 3,038. This is silly, to say the least.

I have found that ranking is particularly popular in organizations that employ large numbers of engineers and scientists. I am not sure why this is true, but one possibility is that they like precise measures. I do too, but sometimes you can go beyond the precision of the measurement instrument. Ranking hundreds or thousands of people is like trying to measure the length of an object to the closest one-thousandth of an inch using an ordinary ruler.

I believe that ranking has no place in most organizations for the simple reason that the data needed to compare people so precisely are not available. When many people are ranked without precise performance data, error and randomness come into play, and as a result, ranking is always unfair.

The second common type of measurement scale involves rating people according to categories, from high performance to low performance, like grades in school. The problem is, organizations are often confused about how many categories to use. After years of studying performance-rating systems, I believe that in most situations, the correct answer is three. A three-tiered rating system (for example, "walking on water," "swimming," "drowning") typically provides all the information needed to handle pay increases and to identify who is a core employee and who is a candidate for promotion. In certain instances, it may be useful to have a fourth category ("too new to judge") for employees who are new to the job and just learning how to perform it.

PECO Energy Corporation uses only three categories: "great," "OK," and "needs improvement." This simple system provides all the information the company feels it needs to manage its employees. It replaced a five-point scale that produced ratings that were much more complicated but not more useful.

No Forced Ratings
One rating practice I especially dislike is forced distributions. Many organizations require their managers to identify a certain percentage of employees who are failing, often 5 to 10 percent, and a

certain percentage who are doing particularly well, often 15 to 20 percent. Jack Welch used this practice at GE, and he has argued that others should use it as well. He also goes on to say that in his view, organizations should fire the employees who fall in the bottom category.[2]

I believe that the forced distribution approach is a bureaucratic solution to a serious leadership failure. It ignores the reality that in some work groups there are no poor performers and in others there are no good performers. It causes managers to disown the appraisal event and to essentially say, "I was just following the rules." Finally, it leads to a kind of unfair and unreasonable treatment of employees that moves the organization significantly away from a virtuous spiral environment toward one that fosters survival of the most political or luckiest. It also can lead to lawsuits because it can be considered unfair to whomever ends up in the lowest-rated group. After lawsuits were brought against Ford and Goodyear on this charge, both companies abandoned their forced distribution systems.

Given these problems, why do companies use the forced distribution approach? The answer is simple but not particularly flattering to many managers. It represents an easy answer to solving a classic problem: rating inflation. Just as in universities where professors tend to give high grades to everyone, many managers find it easier to be generous with high ratings, and as a result, many organizations suffer from top-heavy performance appraisal scores.

Because it is a leadership problem, the best solution rests in creating effective leadership rather than the top-down bureaucratic mandate of a forced distribution system. Mandating a certain distribution is a second leadership failure that just compounds the problem.

To prevent rating inflation, senior managers can take several actions. They can hold each individual manager accountable for the ratings he or she produces, making it clear that high ratings have to be justified by operating results that are correspondingly high. They can also set up cross-organizational meetings in which managers have to justify their ratings to their peers. Capital One and Intel call these "cross-calibration" meetings. Both companies have effectively used them to control rating inflation and to develop consistency in how managers use the rating scale.

In short, the best solution to rating inflation is not a bureaucratic rule; it is a set of behaviors and processes that are put in place by the leadership of the organization.

Stock Ownership

Broad-based stock ownership is almost essential for virtuous spiral organizations. The advantage of stock ownership is that as organizational performance improves, everyone's reward level increases.

Ironically, one of the greatest dangers with broad-based stock ownership is that when it is combined with high organizational performance and an exuberant stock market, people can become "too" wealthy. This can cause them to "call in rich" (stop showing up at work), as happened in the case of many dot-com companies during the 1990s. But for most organizations, this is an unlikely outcome and a risk well worth taking.

Two basic methods of fostering stock ownership are worth using. The first is to have employees own stock through a company-supported program, and the second is to award them stock options. Organizations can use either method or both. They deliver somewhat different results that in several ways complement each other. Thus there is a strong argument for using both methods.

Stock that is owned tends to retain some value even in a down stock market. And if you require people to continue to work in order to earn it, it can be a powerful retention device as well as an incentive. Meanwhile, stock options have the advantage of allowing tremendous gains with little risk. Of course, the weakness of options is that they can lose all of their value if the market declines and hence cease to have an effect on motivation and retention. They can also create large windfalls simply because the overall performance of the stock market is strong.

Together, options and ownership can create a virtuous spiral in which employee motivation leads to high levels of organizational performance. This in turn drives stock values higher, which makes it desirable for people who are already employed to continue with the organization and also makes the organization attractive to people whom the organization wants to hire.

A few words of caution are needed here. Employee stock ownership is not necessarily a powerful motivator of performance. The line of sight between individual performance and stock price is usually quite weak, particularly in large organizations. A downturn in the general market also runs the risk of prompting employee flight if too much of an individual's total compensation is based on stock. This is just what happened in dozens of dot-coms at the end of the dot-com bubble, and for them it triggered death spirals that many were unable to survive. As a result, it is best to have a fixed, or base, pay level for people that is at least in line with market rates to serve as a reliable retention device.

Finally, it is important to avoid stock plans that concentrate stock ownership at the top. These plans create classes of haves and have-nots in organizations and undermine the very foundation of virtuous spirals. Not surprisingly, a growing body of research shows that it leads to poor corporate performance.[3]

What broad-based employee stock ownership can do is create a culture of ownership and cause people to focus on the strategic, business, and financial objectives of the organization. As a result, it can be a powerful integrator.

Person-Based Rather Than Job-Based Pay

Financial and status rewards in most organizations are based on the types of jobs people do. This approach is based on the assumption that job worth can be determined and that the person doing the job is worth only as much as the job itself is worth.

Part of this assumption is valid in many situations. With the use of comparative techniques such as job evaluation and salary surveys, it is possible to determine what other organizations are paying people to do the same or similar jobs. However, in my view, it is not clear that the worth of people can be equated to the worth of their job. This approach clearly does not fit with a company that depends on people for its competitive advantage.

The alternative to job-based pay that is being increasingly adopted is person-based pay. It bases pay on each individual's skills and competencies. It does not necessarily pay people rates that are dramatically different from those produced in a job-based pay system because skills sometimes correlate with jobs. However, switching to this system often results in some employees being paid more than they would be paid under a job-based system while others receive less because they don't have the skills they need to do their work.

The benefit of person-based pay is in the kind of culture and motivation the system produces. Instead of being rewarded for moving up the hierarchy, people are rewarded for increasing their skills and developing themselves. This creates a learning culture in which personal growth and development are prized. Paying the person rather than the job is particularly popular in high-tech companies and team-based manufacturing operations. I have helped develop these plans at Procter & Gamble, Frito-Lay, International Paper, General Mills, and a number of other companies. The results are always positive both for the organization's performance and for individuals.

Individualized Reward Packages

First appearing in the 1960s, flexible, or "cafeteria," benefit plans have increased enormously in sophistication and popularity. Today, more than 80 percent of major U.S. corporations give people choices in their benefit coverage. The advantages of flexible benefit plans are many, but two significant ones are that they allow people to choose the benefits they want and they prevent the all-too-common problem of organizations offering benefits that cost more than their value to employees.

Individualizing reward packages is a valid approach to creating a virtuous spiral because it is good for both people and organizations. In fact, as was discussed in Chapter Four, individualized reward programs can be greatly expanded beyond the scope of fringe benefits. Organizations can allow people to choose the types of incentive plans that they want, such as whether they get cash or stock. They can give people trade-offs among compensation levels, vacation time, work hours, and a host of other potential features of their employment deal.

The only note of caution I would add is that a program that offers a great deal of choice may cause organizations to lose some of the power that results from having a unified, systemwide reward system that produces a common culture. Overindividualizing by giving everyone a separate deal can sacrifice cultural unity.

Public Pay

Creating a high-performance organization requires that information about the pay system be available throughout the organization. Without open information, employees are not likely to develop a good understanding of how performance is rewarded, nor will they have a great deal of trust in the reward system's operation.

Historically, most organizations have cloaked pay policies in secrecy, with information made available only on a need-to-know basis. While some general information about the pay systems, such as pay ranges, may be known, it is seldom public how much specific people earn. In most cases, employees also do not have salary survey data or information about what is behind the determination of merit pay increase amounts and bonus amounts. They are asked to trust the organization to deal with them fairly. This policy fits well with a loyalty relationship in which organizations promise to look after their employees and treat them fairly.

However, it is clearly time for a change. Organizations need to be much more open about how they manage and administer pay. They need to assume that employees are sophisticated and knowledgeable consumers of company pay information and practices.

Research suggests that secrecy may create more problems than benefits.[4] Keeping pay secret often leads people to make inaccurate judgments about the fairness of the pay system and how well others are paid. Because people tend to overestimate the pay of others, they often feel more dissatisfied than they would if they had accurate information.

Secrecy clearly limits the degree to which the pay system can support a virtuous spiral. To be motivated to perform well by it, people need to know how the pay system works. They need to believe that what is good for their organization is good for them. Secrecy stands in the way of establishing this trust and understanding.

In several respects, secrecy almost doesn't matter anymore, as a number of factors have converged that make it obsolete. First, the media in the United States and other parts of the world have revealed many details of executive compensation packages, company-wide stock option plans, gainsharing plans, and a host of other compensation practices that allow people to compare these types of rewards from company to company.

In addition, dozens of books and consulting services are available that tutor employees on how to bargain for pay when they join a new company, how to get a pay increase, and how to manage their finances given the increased prevalence of variable pay plans and stock option plans.

Most important, the Web is transforming the whole process of salary communication in dramatic ways. Thanks to the Internet, employees can get a great deal of comparative information about what the job market pays for their skills. Web sites abound that provide pay data, allowing people to have almost an equal footing with companies concerning the market pricing of jobs and skills. Many executive recruiters and job placement services maintain Web sites documenting job openings and pay rates. And many Internet-based services are available to help people assess their skills and career opportunities and to determine what their market value is.

Many compensation managers I talk to say that we are in the era of "dot-com pay," which means that everyone has access to salary survey data and that employees use these data to assess their own pay and to bargain for better pay. Most managers see this as a problem and will not look at dot-com pay data. I think this is a mistake. In my view, it makes sense for organizations to encourage employees to provide any valid salary data that they have. It is clearly better for organizations to find this out as a result of their employees raising the issue than as a result of having employees leave to join another organization with better pay and rewards.

Because so much market and career opportunity information is readily available, it is inevitable that employees will assess whether they are paid relatively well or poorly. As a result, companies should join the parade. They need to provide a clear public statement of the value proposition they offer employees and to back it up with credible reward data that show they are delivering on their value proposition. This is fundamental to their ability to attract, retain, and motivate employees who fit their strategy and their approach to organizing and managing.

Perhaps the only remaining question about pay openness is whether the pay of individuals should be made public. In fact, much of it is already public. In the United States, the pay of senior executives in public corporations must be put into proxy statements. The pay of most government employees and union members is public. Salaries are also known in many corporate settings where self-managing work teams and other groups decide what their peers should be paid.

Much to the surprise of many traditional thinkers in management and personnel administration, making pay public has not caused a massive uproar or revolution. Sure, employees are not always happy with what they find out about what others are paid, but when explanations are offered and appropriate changes are made, it has not proved to be a particularly contentious issue. In many cases, in fact, the public information has led to a better understanding and acceptance of the pay system and to positive changes in the pay system. In other cases, it has led to the correction of problems that might otherwise have gone undetected.

In the future, as organizations increasingly operate with teams and business information that is shared through intranets, it is logical to make public the pay rates of more and more people. In general, I believe that greater openness will have a positive effect on individuals and organizations. It will help attract people with the kinds of knowledge and skills that organizations need and should allow more and more people to make intelligent decisions about their careers.

Particularly if an organization has an effective pay system and pays well relative to the market, there is a tremendous advantage to be gained from making pay rates and pay policies public. Because pay secrecy leads to misunderstandings and perceptions that are more negative than reality warrants, organizations can gain from making pay information public and open to discussion. Openness can increase trust, perceptions of fairness, understanding of the business, and respect for the organization and its management.

Overall, open pay supports virtuous spirals, employability, self-management of careers, the creation of high-trust environments, business understanding, and attracting employees who have a free-agent mentality. In the end, it is not a question of whether your organization should make pay public but rather one of when and on what terms it will occur.

Implications for Individuals

As more and more organizations change from traditional pay systems to ones that support a virtuous spiral, you may encounter new risks, but you have much to gain.

The most fundamental conclusion to be drawn from this chapter is consistent with the theme you have seen in every chapter: it is increasingly important that you proactively manage your career in today's economy.

If you are not comfortable in seniority-driven, job-based pay systems, you definitely should look for an alternative. It is increasingly likely that you can find an organization that stresses skill development and performance while rewarding its employees with stock, variable compensation, and greater individual choice.

If you work for a company that has adopted the new pay systems that I have discussed in this chapter, you can potentially have much more control over how and how well you are rewarded. You can end up with a better and more satisfying total reward package that allows you to create your own virtuous spiral.

The movement toward paying the person rather than the job clearly argues that you should take charge of developing your skills and knowledge. Your development must be managed both in terms of what your organization is willing to reward you for learning and what larger social and business trends exist that may create demand for your particular skills and knowledge. As mentioned in an earlier chapter, it especially pays to seek out mechanisms or devices that certify you as having valuable skills. Certificates and degrees are particularly important in a world where credentials are rewarded and organizations may not have the ability to test people for skills in particular areas.

A significant advantage of a skill-based pay system is that it gives you a certain degree of control over your pay progression. Instead of having to wait for the earth to revolve around the sun for an annual merit review, in many cases you can dictate increases on your own schedule as a result of acquiring new skills. In well-designed reward systems, you can even plan ahead for what skills to acquire

over a period of years and consequently improve your ability to estimate your salary increases. A pay-for-skills system thus allows you
to do sensible career and financial planning. This can be a big plus
if you want to progress in your career by adding to your skills.

Choosing to work at an organization that offers bonus pay and
stock rewards can also be a tremendous boost to your career. It can
give you the opportunity to earn above-market pay and gain more
control over the amount of your pay. But there are some risks to
watch out for.

First, be sure to understand the measurement systems being
used to determine the bonuses and stock allocations and assess
whether the system is fair, reasonable, and likely to deliver the
kinds of reward levels you need in order to be satisfied. Your analysis should involve developing a good understanding of your organization's business strategy and assessing whether it is likely to
produce the results promised. You should read what stock market
analysts say about your company, as well as what trade publications,
customers, and others think. Finally, be sure to look at the histori-
cal performance of your organization to see if it has delivered on
its past promises.

Second, if the reward system uses stock ownership or stock
option plans, be sure you have an in-depth knowledge of how these
plans work and their tax implications. You need to become a knowledgeable investor in your own company and make good decisions
about how to deal with your options and stock. You should carefully
study the conditions that might allow you to profit from the stock
plans, including a careful assessment of the likely performance of
your company and the stock market's general condition. It is also
prudent not to let too much of your rewards be based on stock or
stock options, in case they never reach the values you expect, as
happened to many employees during the stock market decline that
followed the Roaring Nineteen Nineties.

It is also advisable to get professional advice on the tax implications of buying and selling stock and stock options. The failure
of some people to do this has left them with large tax bills and no
cash to cover their liability.

Financial advisers almost uniformly advise stock-rich employees to diversify their risk, particularly when it comes to retirement
plans. Having a tremendous amount of your wealth in a single

company is always a dicey proposition. It is far wiser to sell some of the stock that you acquire from your corporation in order to develop a more diversified portfolio. The collapse of Enron is just one example of how people can lose their retirement income when their retirement funds are concentrated in one company. This is one case where what is good for organizations—having their employees heavily dependent on the success of the company—is not good for people.

As for cafeteria reward plans, you need to carefully analyze your life situation and decide what fits your needs. Organizations have often been very conservative with respect to giving people choices when it comes to their benefit packages. They fear that employees will make poor choices and blame it on the company. In some cases, this feeling is justified, but it should not prevent organizations from giving people choices or prevent you from creating your own mix of rewards. You should understand your personal situation well enough to make intelligent choices about your coverage and as a result construct a win-win situation out of the options you are given.

You need to seek out information about your organization's pay program. Valid information can help you take more responsibility for your career and compensation. With good information, you can realistically assess the options available to you in your own organization and get a clear sense of where you stand. You can validate for yourself what you are told about how the pay system works—an opportunity worth taking.

Pay information is also valuable in career planning and thinking about your development. Good pay information should make it much easier for you to get a sense of where the higher-paying job opportunities are and, of course, to uncover what you believe are any inequities or unfairness in the pay system. If you find that you are indeed paid unfairly or illegally, you can challenge the system both within the organization and in a legal setting. Although this may be uncomfortable for you and your employer to go through, employee challenges can potentially lead to improvements in the pay system as well as to better pay practices for everyone.

You also can benefit from seeking and making extensive use of the publicly available salary information on the Web and from organizations that do salary surveys. Many professional associations, for example, do surveys of their members and provide feedback on what people in their profession make. Having good salary survey data allows you to confirm your market value and to know what you can bargain for either with your present employer or with a future employer.

One note of caution, though, about public salary information. You need to be skeptical about the accuracy of data available over the Web. Although the source of the information may claim it is accurate, it may not be as up-to-date or as accurate as you need. At times, you may have to take a company's word for what your market value is. It is a tough call, but sometimes the organization does know best!

Finally, consider these suggestions about the performance appraisal process. As much as you can, be proactive in regard to your performance appraisal. Admittedly, this is often hard to do because the basic design of most systems puts the person being appraised in a dependent, powerless position. Like a visit to the dentist, the appraisal is done to you, and you are given little opportunity to control it. But the performance appraisal process is absolutely critical to your career, so you should find out as much as you can about it and manage what happens during it as much as you possibly can.

At the very least, be an active advocate for your own performance. Develop comprehensive lists of your performance accomplishments and supporting evidence that documents any exceptional acts on your part that satisfied customers or led to business improvements. Be completely prepared at the time of your appraisal to present a full and comprehensive record of your performance.

If your performance review does not go as well as you believe it should have, you do not need to accept it. Many organizations have a formal appeal process that allows people to challenge an unfair or unreasonable appraisal. If an appeal process is lacking (or ineffective) in your organization, and there is evidence in the appraisal of unfairness based on age, race, or gender, do not hesitate to see a lawyer to determine if a court case is warranted.

In cases where a company's formal appraisal procedure does not have an initial planning and goal-setting process as a starting point for the appraisal cycle, you may find it useful to schedule one with your boss anyway. A solid, comprehensive meeting that lays out mutually targeted results and goals for the year can make the year-end review much more objective and effective. It also can provide you with a strong argument at the end of the year if there are questions about what you were supposed to do or how well you have performed.

If you are a manager and appraise the performance of others, I have two suggestions to make. First, make it a priority to develop your skills in this area. Most managers do it poorly, so this is an area where you can easily differentiate yourself from other managers. You can look like a star when it comes to performance management, and this is an area that many organizations are assigning greater and greater importance to.

Second, place a major emphasis on giving the people who work for you ongoing feedback. There should be no surprises when the year-end appraisal is done. When people are surprised, conflicts can result, and in extreme cases, legal action. So if you want to be known as an effective manager, give continuous ongoing feedback.

Overall, the new approaches to pay discussed in this chapter offer tremendous opportunities for you to better your financial situation—but with those opportunities comes risk. If you do not understand the way pay systems work and you fail to proactively manage your career, you may lose.

Remember, you can no longer count on organizations to manage your career and provide you with a secure pay and reward package. The more proactive you become in gathering information about how you are paid and what you need to do to receive the level of pay that you deserve, the better you will be able to manage whatever reward system you face.

Above all, focus both inside and outside the organization you work for. You need to follow the trends in the labor market and gather salary data in your field. Examine the financial performance of your company, and get advice on how you should behave with respect to your company's stock, profit sharing, and other variable compensation vehicles. Above all else, seek organizations that are committed to creating a virtuous spiral—and be alert for organizations that may be heading toward a death spiral.

Chapter Ten

Lead People Right

Treat People Right Principle #7

Organizations must hire and develop leaders who can create commitment, trust, success, and a motivating work environment.

To say that effective leadership is critical is an understatement. The leadership of managers at all levels in an organization has an impact on both individual and organizational effectiveness. It determines the types of relationships that people develop with the organizations they work for, how motivated they are, how long they stay, and how they treat customers and other employees. Leadership behavior at the top has a particularly strong impact on the strategic direction of organizations and their operating effectiveness.

So what exactly is effective leadership? What characteristics do great leaders have? What can organizations do to create good managers?

Judging from the more than eight hundred books on leadership that are published each year, the jury is still out on these questions. How else can you explain the never-ending parade of theories, ideas, and personal experiences that attempt to identity the characteristics of effective leadership? There are tomes delving into the leadership styles of ancient warriors, the managerial behavior of Shakespearean characters, and the personality archetypes of our greatest political leaders. We also have the biographies of such larger-than-life "star CEOs" as Jack Welch and Andy Grove.

The findings of the Ohio State University leadership studies in the 1950s are very close to the answer I have been espousing throughout this book: great leaders set up a win-win situation, a virtuous spiral.[1] These studies showed that the most effective managers lead in ways that focus both on organizational results and employees. Rather than seeing these as conflicting, the research found that skillful managers learn to combine them in ways that foster a win-win situation.

What was true half a century ago is even more true today. Organizations need effective leaders to attract, retain, and motivate good employees in this new world where human capital is a critical determinant of organizational effectiveness. People need effective leaders in order to have satisfying work experiences and become part of winning organizations.

As for the details of what constitutes effective leadership behavior, this chapter examines leadership from the dual perspectives of what employees need and what organizations need. As you will see, there is a relatively high degree of overlap between the two views. In fact, it is in this overlap space that organizations and employees have the opportunity to create a virtuous spiral. Following this analysis, I will enumerate and discuss several practices that organizations need to implement in order to grow and nurture effective leadership in a world in which not all managers are or need to be leaders and not all leaders need to be managers.

What Employees Want and Need from Leaders

What employees want and need from their leaders is nicely summarized in a simple statement: they want a work environment in which they can reach their goals. In reality, managers have the power to shape this environment because they control the very features I have identified in this book as the most critical determinants of motivation and satisfaction: work structure, mission, goals, and rewards. When managers use their power wisely, they can be very effective leaders; when they don't, they are neither effective managers nor effective leaders.

Consider work structure. In our discussion of job design, you saw that the key elements in creating motivating and satisfying enriched jobs are meaningfulness, responsibility, and feedback.

Managers influence each of these and can often design jobs that are highly enriched and motivating or jobs that are not. This is especially true when it comes to autonomy. In most work situations, managers can either give employees lots of decision-making power or they can micromanage and nitpick. They can either create jobs that are highly autonomous—and thus enriched from a motivation and satisfaction point of view—or they can design jobs so that employees have little or no control over their decisions and activities.

Of course, managers also control many of the rewards employees can receive. In addition to financial rewards, they can directly reward employees by giving praise and choice work assignments. They also play a major role in creating the conditions that make it possible for employees to do their work well enough so that they can earn the rewards that come with high performance. This translates into many types of managerial behaviors, such as fighting for resources so that an employee has the budget or the technical support he or she needs to champion a project or ensuring an employee's attendance at a much-needed training program.

Employees want managers who are focused on human capital, not their own egos. The manager who is always front and center, monopolizing the credit for all good things that happen, is not valued by the employees who work for him or her. To be effective leaders, managers need to share the successes and the limelight in many ways. One of the most critical of these is sharing financial rewards, but others include staging public recognition events, recommending employees for special awards, or simply commending employees in conversations with more senior managers.

Employees want managers who are willing to support their development. Effective managers notice when formal training experiences or opportunities for on-the-job training and coaching can help their employees. They give employees the time and space needed to learn new skills. Even more important, good managers provide coaching, advice, and feedback to help employees develop into strong contributors to the organization's virtuous spiral.

Good managers also play a critical role in promoting their people to new jobs and expanding their skills and knowledge. They make sure their employees don't miss out on development opportunities. They think constantly about how to help their employees grow in ways that take into account their needs and desires—and what will add to their future employability and their virtuous career spirals.

Employees want managers who behave in ways that are respectful, fair, and ethical. Let me be specific about what I mean by each of these characteristics. Only by doing this can we move beyond generalities.

Respectful. People come to work wanting to be treated with respect and dignity. In general, respect means listening to what employees have to say, honoring their input, and getting back to them with answers if they have made requests or suggestions. It also means avoiding all public criticism and rumor-mongering, both of which create a negative work environment. Finally, it involves being sensitive to the differences that exist among people, taking this diversity into account when coaching, assigning work, and rewarding performance.

Fair. Employees want managers who are fair in decision making and in allocating scarce resources. They do not always expect to be winners, but they want to be sure that a fair process is used to reach decisions. For example, if a training opportunity develops or a new piece of equipment is to be allocated, employees need to feel that the decision-making process is handled fairly. Respect and fairness are perceived to exist when managers consider all the relevant information, when they involve people in the work area in decisions, and when the reasons for the decision are made public.

Ethical. Employees want to work for managers who are ethical and operate with credibility. Ethics and credibility start with managers doing what they say they will do. They require that managers make their principles clear when dealing with employees. In the best of all worlds, the behavior of every manager is guided by a set of corporate principles and ethical standards concerning how the organization will be led and how employees will be treated.

Finally, a critical trait that employees want is managers who are leaders. It is not realistic to expect every manager to be a leader, but it is not unrealistic to expect every organization to have leaders in most senior management positions as well as in many other management and perhaps some nonmanagement jobs.

Particularly in organizations that are mission-driven, employees want either a supervisor who is an effective leader or a senior manager who provides the entire business or business unit with a strong sense of mission, direction, and vision. Through actions and deeds, a leader is needed who creates an environment of commitment, in which all employees understand how their behavior is directly linked to the organization's success in achieving its mission.

What Organizations Want and Need from Leaders

What organizations want and need from managers parallels in most respects what employees want and need. Organizations need managers to have the same set of skills and competencies that employees desire—the ability to design motivating work, distribute rewards fairly, train and develop people, treat people with respect, and provide leadership and a sense of mission and commitment. In most ways, there couldn't be a stronger convergence of needs and wants.

Perhaps the only significant difference between what employees and organizations need is that organizations especially count on managers to help provide goal setting, strategic direction, and leadership.

In terms of goal setting, organizations need managers who are good at establishing clear goals. In the Ohio State studies mentioned earlier, this characteristic was referred to as the "initiating structure" side of leadership, although I prefer to call it performance management. It refers to the manager's responsibility for establishing what people are supposed to accomplish, giving them the support that they need to accomplish it, and finally holding them accountable for results and rewarding them when they are effective.

The second critical aspect of what organizations need managers to do concerns the strategy point of the Diamond Model. Managers need to engage in high-level strategic thinking about the direction the organization should take. Senior managers especially must be able to identify new business opportunities and analyze which ones the organization should pursue. In short, organizations need managers to be effective at taking responsibility for their business model and strategy.

Last, organizations need leadership from managers at all levels. This is not to say that every manager needs to be a great leader, but the truth is that it is an enormous plus for an organization to have many managers who are effective leaders. When an organization has a broadly shared leadership capability, it is far more effective in enrolling people in its mission and vision and creating a satisfying work environment. This is why one of the key issues in most organizations is developing leadership skills and knowledge in as many employees as possible.

I don't think organizations need what might be called a "cult" type of leadership, in which people follow a single leader. This can sometimes be effective. Hero CEOs like Lee Iacocca at Ford, Walt Disney at Disney, and Edwin Land at Polaroid were very effective in mobilizing a large organization through their charisma and ability to enroll employees in the mission. Such leaders take on a larger-than-life image in their corporation and in essence develop a following of employees who are eager to please the leader and act on the leader's wishes and desires.

However, in my view, cult-type leadership behavior has significant downsides. First, most organizations cannot sustain success once the cult leader leaves. The next leader almost always fails to provide the same leadership and to develop a cult following of his or her own; as a result, the organization's virtuous spiral ends. There is also evidence that cult-type leadership responds poorly to rapidly changing business conditions that are best handled by sharing decision making and power across all levels of the organization.

There is also a very dark side to cult leadership that all organizations need to remain vigilant in avoiding. All too often, cultlike leaders take advantage of their power and position. Perhaps because of the "high" that comes from being powerful, they become focused on enriching themselves. They become imperial CEOs who run companies as if they exist merely for the benefit of the senior executive or executives. Compensation levels soar, and executive perks proliferate.

I believe that most executives, even imperial CEOs, are honest, but not all are. A small percentage tolerate or engage in unethical and illegal behavior. The recent examples of the abuse of executive power (as by Jeff Skilling of Enron, Bernie Ebbers of WorldCom, Dennis Kozlowski of Tyco, and Gary Winnick of Global Crossing) are sad reminders of how the temptations of personal greed can destroy individuals and organizations.

Best Practices for Effective Leadership

I have researched a number of organizations that in my view have implemented effective practices to ensure they have effective leaders. These practices include establishing a clear leadership brand, developing a broad cadre of leaders, and regularly assessing and developing managers. I will discuss these and several other best practices next.

Developing a Leadership Brand

Just as it is useful to brand your organization's value proposition, branding its leadership style is an effective practice to distinguish your company in the marketplace. Having a clearly identified leadership style can be a powerful factor in attracting, retaining, and motivating the right employees. A positive leadership brand that permeates the organization can also serve as a touchstone for all current employees who are managers or desire to be managers, guiding them toward your organization's "true north" with respect to the leadership behaviors and skills expected of them.

Every organization needs to develop its own leadership brand; no formula exists to indicate what is right. However, there are several characteristics that in my view are critical to strengthening your leadership brand and making it effective.

The most important characteristic is that your leadership brand needs to apply across the entire organization and at all times; it should not involve what is often called "situational leadership." Some leadership gurus have suggested that the most effective managers consider each work situation and then decide how to behave.[2] They argue that managers should take into account such things as the experience of employees, the time available to make a decision, and the type of work that is to be done. I agree that these should have some influence on how a manager behaves, but I believe that all too often situational leadership results in confusion and alienates people. Employees don't want to be uncertain about how they will be treated or not be able to count on being involved in decisions or informed by their manager.

In my view, it is far wiser to develop a leadership brand based on general principles and characteristics that are universally applicable to all managers and all leadership situations. For example, General Electric promotes companywide its "Four E's" of leadership. All leaders at GE are expected to have the personal *energy* to welcome and deal with change, the ability to create an atmosphere that *energizes* others, the *edge* to make difficult decisions, and the ability to consistently *execute.*

Motorola adopted these same Four E's as part of its leadership brand but added a fifth "E"—*ethical behavior.* Both GE and Motorola use their leadership brand as a management credo throughout the entire organization. In essence, they guarantee that employees will have a manager who practices the Four or Five E's of leadership.

The retail clothing company The Limited is another example of a company that is developing a powerful leadership brand. It has created a set of operating principles and specific behaviors to define what types of leadership it deems appropriate and desired. A few of its guiding principles include treating others with respect, keeping promises and commitments, being accountable for decisions, reporting information honestly, admitting mistakes, maintaining a safe and healthy workplace, and standing up for strongly held beliefs and principles. The Limited also stipulates that at all times customers and employees are to be treated with dignity and that people at all levels should be appreciated and recognized.

GE, Motorola, and The Limited have done a good job of taking the idea of a leadership brand and translating it into behaviors. The next step is to develop leaders who can "walk the walk and talk the talk."

Building Leadership Capability

Given the role leadership plays in determining success, organizations need to build leadership capability on an ongoing basis. Two approaches to grooming leaders can be followed: top management-focused or shared leadership.

The traditional top management-focused approach begins by identifying a group of "high-potential" executives who exhibit the skills and competencies that senior executives need. These executives are moved rapidly throughout the organization to gain experience in all aspects of the company's business. A few are then selected for very senior management positions, and ultimately, one is chosen to be CEO.

This approach has been used for decades by large organizations around the world. IBM, GE, and PepsiCo have been admired and imitated for their ability to make this type of leadership development process run smoothly for generation after generation of leaders. Building leadership in this way is clearly the right model for highly centralized, hierarchically structured organizations.

As a result of its commitment to senior leadership development, GE has become an "academy" company that provides leaders to other companies. In recent years, a number of GE alums have become CEOs of Fortune 500 companies. Does GE gain by being a net exporter of management talent? After all, it obviously costs the company quite a bit. I think it does. First, it makes GE an attractive place to work for individuals who want to be leaders. But second and more important, the company gets the best shot at the "pick of the litter" when it comes to employing the best management talent.

The top-management-focused approach is not right for all organizations, especially companies that want to develop a virtuous spiral by practicing and encouraging internal entrepreneurial initiatives and innovations. These organizations require a shared leadership approach that develops leaders at all levels of the organization. In essence, the shared leadership approach encourages people throughout the organization to develop leadership skills and to take on leadership roles and responsibilities.

The shared leadership approach to building leaders operates best from the bottom up. Rather than identifying and grooming a select group of potential leaders from the top, the company uses its corporate structure, work designs, and development programs to open the way for the emergence of leaders at all levels. This requires making leadership training and development programs available to people throughout the organization and opening up information about business results and business strategy to create a shared sense of mission and direction.

In its 2002 annual report, Procter & Gamble CEO A. G. Lafley describes his view of what has made and will continue to make P&G a virtuous spiral company. He argues that it is developing leaders at all levels and creating a culture that values and embraces leadership. According to him, this leads to a "passionate sense of ownership" of the business by employees.

The shared leadership approach requires a commitment to innovation and creative thinking from everyone. Emerging leaders need to be able to propose new projects or initiatives and get the budget authorization and support needed to make them happen. For example, 3M has a well-developed process that allows people who want to take on a leadership role to get support for projects they initiate. It has special budgets for such new projects that give aspiring leaders the ability to apply for money outside of the normal hierarchy of approval.

One caveat is that poorly implemented shared leadership can lead to chaos. Leaders need guidelines, rules, and an overall direction that guide them but do not undercut their initiatives. They need to have room to operate, but they also need to know where the boundaries are that they cannot go beyond without seeking approval and permission. Ultimately, a balance must be achieved that encourages emergent leadership without stifling it—a system that is simultaneously tight and loose, that allows initiatives but has solid checks and balances.

The last critical element of the shared leadership approach is that it must include significant rewards for those who are successful in becoming leaders. As we have seen throughout this book, rewards motivate people to take risks and achieve goals. Without rewards, the best potential leaders may not emerge, or they may look for a company that will reward them for their skills.

Years ago, I was interviewing employees at a large oil company and asked managers throughout the organization what happens to people who step forward to lead new ventures. The answer was unanimous: if they succeed, the chances of their being rewarded are slim, and even if they are rewarded, the reward is small. Meanwhile, if they step forward and their leadership effort fails, punishment is certain and almost always fatal. Not surprisingly, this company had few emergent leaders, little innovation, and a high propensity for people to look to the top for direction.

In contrast, W. L. Gore is an excellent example of an organization designed to support the emergence of broad-based leadership. This company with a staff of eight thousand produces textiles for manufacturers of consumer products, particularly clothing, where their Gore-Tex fabric is well known. Bill Gore, the founder of W. L. Gore, intentionally built an organization that relies on teams and emergent leaders, rather than on hierarchical bureaucratic management.

The company's leadership growth process begins right at the bottom. Everyone at Gore is considered an associate, and there are no hierarchical titles. Becoming a leader is not a matter of being promoted but rather a matter of finding a new business opportunity and convincing others to pursue the venture. Gore does not make the process easy, though; all emerging leaders must compete for talent and resources.

Gore believes that the advantage of its process is that its emerging leaders must show they can overcome challenges to earn their stripes as true leaders. The company makes the rewards for doing so worthwhile; any associate who succeeds in growing a business opportunity can end up running his or her own mini-enterprise within the company.

Admittedly, the Gore model is an extreme case of structuring an organization to encourage emergent leaders and leadership. The program depends on individuals proving that they can run a business entity. People are rarely singled out by senior managers for leadership or are assigned leadership responsibilities. Instead, everyone takes a one-week course on how the company operates and is assigned a sponsor. Emerging leaders get a great deal of feedback about how effectively they are contributing to the company. They are rated by their peers and given regular feedback on their leadership skills and their development as leaders, but it is up to them to actually become leaders.

Identifying and Hiring Potential Leaders

Organizations need to proactively manage their supply of leadership talent. The place to start is with the hiring process. Although there is no magic test to prove how effective someone will be as a leader, there are a number of ways to get a good reading on potential.

First, look at people's behavioral history and assess whether they have demonstrated effective leadership already in their academic career or previous work. Use the interview process to identify the scope and nature of their leadership, whether they initiated projects or were asked to head them up, how many people they led, how they managed resources, and the results of their leadership.

A second powerful way to gather information about how people will perform as leaders is to put them into realistic job previews or simulations that allow you to observe them interacting with others, tackling problems in teams, and generally behaving in situations that require management and leadership skills.

The start of people's careers as managers is a particularly critical period of time to develop them as leaders. You want to be sure that new managers behave in ways that are consistent with the leadership brand of the organization. Dell Computer, for example, takes the onboarding process very seriously for its new managers. They are provided with several types of training experiences at the point of initial hire, as well as at thirty, sixty, and ninety days after joining Dell. The training includes classroom learning and meetings with senior executives to talk about managerial behaviors and how Dell operates as an organization. The training especially emphasizes Dell's culture—how it is developed and sustained through Dell's brand of effective management.

Ongoing Leadership Development

Leader development needs to continue well beyond an employee's initial year or two with your company. People should have access to learning experiences throughout their careers. Especially in organizations that want to create shared leadership, development experiences must be made available to a broad range of employees within the organization, not just a select few who have been chosen as candidates for senior management positions.

However, as I mentioned earlier in discussing development, there are some risks and costs associated with developing people. Particularly with respect to developing leaders, there is the risk that they will leave. Nevertheless, leadership is important enough that organizations need to take this risk.

Although formal classroom training is helpful in developing leaders, a considerable amount of research suggests that the most effective training arises from experience.[3] Emerging leaders learn most from challenging job assignments that force them to examine their capabilities and improve their behaviors. Overall, the best leadership development efforts are those that combine classroom education, coaching, and strategically timed and designed job changes.

One last issue to emphasize about leadership development is the importance of creating leaders at the top who are role models and can educate and communicate well. It is particularly hard— and may in fact be impossible— to get managers throughout an organization to adhere to a leadership brand if senior managers do not follow it and teach it to others. Both the development of the brand and a consistent leadership style need to start at the very top. At the very minimum, senior managers must be able to articulate the organization's leadership brand in an "elevator speech."

Top-level managers in particular need to be excellent communicators and educators who never miss an opportunity to teach everyone in the organization about the company's business and to dialogue with employees about how the company is doing. Two CEOs I have worked with do this particularly well and are models for how top leaders need to behave. Rich Teerlink, the now-retired CEO of Harley-Davidson, took every opportunity to talk with employees about what they were learning and how the company was performing. Bob Eckert of Mattel is cut from the same cloth. He is always ready and able to talk about the toy business and to learn about new developments in management. Given the turnarounds that both these leaders orchestrated for their companies, both have clearly demonstrated that a commitment to communication and education can produce enormous benefits.

Regular Assessment of Managerial Performance and Behavior

For any approach to managerial development to be taken seriously, organizations must regularly assesses managers against leadership, behavioral, and performance criteria.

Fortunately, assessment technology, particularly with the growth of the Internet, makes it increasingly easy for organizations to gather information about the leadership behaviors of their managers. Using technology, much of the paperwork and forms associated with appraisals can now easily be handled via intranets and e-mail communication.

One useful leadership assessment technique is the "360-degree appraisal" approach I mentioned earlier. When leadership is assessed, customers, employees, peers, and bosses should all be asked to offer their views of a manager's performance. This breadth of feedback creates a far more useful appraisal of someone's leadership behaviors and skills than is derived from a single boss's appraisal.

All too often, managers develop the ability to manage upward and as a result get good performance reviews from their bosses, even though their ability to manage downward or laterally is poor. As a result, poor managers are rated highly simply because they manage upward well.

A good leadership assessment needs to employ well-designed rating forms that focus it on specific behaviors and on the leadership brand that the organization wants its managers to follow. Rating categories that use general terms are insufficient to provide detailed, meaningful feedback. For example, rather than having a rater assess a manager on "communicates well," it is far more useful to have the rater evaluate very specific kinds of communications, such as how the manager runs meetings and whether he or she presents business results clearly. When specific behaviors are not asked about, raters often succumb to the "halo" effect, giving managers the same marks on everything because the rating questions are loose and general.

Keep in mind that in any appraisal process, reviewers may have personal issues that can cause them to give invalid or biased reviews. They might be competing with the individual for a promotion, or they might have seen only a small sample of the individual's behavior, not enough to have a good basis for judging performance. And many a review can be tainted by a personal friendship between rater and ratee.

Ultimately, 360s are useful, but they should never be the sole source of information about how effective a manager is as a leader. They need to be one input, combined with more objective measures such as the turnover and absenteeism rates of that manager's employees and his or her operating results. They are often most useful as a source of development feedback to managers who want to improve their skills.

Rewards for Effective Leadership

Organizations sometimes practice an unconscious hypocrisy, preaching a human capital–focused leadership style while rewarding their managers solely on the basis of their financial and operating results. The problem is that this can cause managers to focus more on the bottom-line results than on the process of obtaining them. Often this leads to a number of counterproductive outcomes, such as managers resorting to demanding, autocratic, or punitive leadership in order to get short-term results. Of course, the long-term consequences of this type of leadership are horrific, including alienating good employees and driving them away.

A "results are all that counts" approach to leadership is especially prone to arise in companies that frequently rotate managers from one job to another. Because the negative effects of their behavior do not show up until they have left, autocratic managers are often not held accountable for the long-term impact of their management style. Furthermore, all too often, new managers who follow them end up failing as a result of inheriting the bad situation created by their predecessors.

GE was one of the first organizations to tackle this management issue squarely. To be rewarded and valued at GE, managers must both produce good results and demonstrate managerial and leadership behaviors that are consistent with the company's leadership brand. The company uses a two-by-two matrix, as shown in Figure 10.1, to make sure managers both get the right results and get them in the right way. Anything less leads to dismissal.

When GE first articulated this policy, many organizations saw it as radical. However, some of these same organizations are now adopting it, realizing that it takes a strong stand in order to ensure ethical management and adherence to a clear leadership brand. This type of policy also fits well with the argument made at the beginning of this chapter that to enjoy a virtuous spiral, organizations have to manage in ways that both accomplish their objectives and create a positive experience for employees. This approach rewards only managers who treat their employees with respect and dignity while focusing on the business outcomes that need to be produced.

Figure 10.1. Leadership Performance Matrix.

		Behaviors	
		Incorrect	Correct
Results	Good	At risk	Star
	Bad	Fire	At risk

Limits on Executive Perks

Executives can and often do receive a wide variety of perquisites. Some of these are justifiable from a business point of view because of the unique demands senior executives face. For example, in some corporations, security for executives is a necessity. Private jet transportation is increasingly important, given the difficulties and potential risks of alternative means of travel. That said, it is very easy for executives to let self-indulgence and self-importance lead them to create excessive perk packages.

All too often, perk packages include multiple residences and wastefully large office spaces that intimidate employees and dramatically separate the executives from the rest of the workforce by their grandeur and location. Many perk packages also include less visible perks, such as country club memberships, tickets to sporting events, catered meals, concierge services, personal use of corporate jets, and just about anything else an executive wants.

What is the problem with excessive perks? The problem, I believe, is in the message that it sends to the rest of the workforce. It sends a message that executives are special, distant, and imperial leaders. This is in direct contrast to the idea of shared leadership, a common fate for all members of the organization, and a virtuous spiral that benefits everyone in the organization. It also is in many ways an affront to shareholders, who end up absorbing the costs of the perquisites that executives receive.

A number of CEOs have done a good job of using the elimination of excessive perk packages as a way to establish their leadership brand. They have eliminated many of the visible perks that their predecessors received as a way of sending a message to the rest of the organization that they are going to be a different kind of leader.

For example, when A. G. Lafley took over as CEO at Procter & Gamble, he altered the eleventh-floor executive suites at P&G's Cincinnati headquarters. Oak-paneled walls were torn down, and nineteenth-century oil paintings went to a local art museum. The CEO and his top brass moved into cubicles on half of the eleventh floor, and the other half was turned into an employee learning center. This is a great example of symbolism that says Procter & Gamble has leaders who are more focused on human capital development than on a lavish lifestyle for themselves.

A Focus on the Competitive Environment

This last best practice reflects another skill that organizations must develop in their managers—adjusting to the competitive environment. Some managerial behaviors that are appropriate in a booming economy are not appropriate in a business downturn. Effective managers need to adjust their leadership behavior to the economic times. They need to do things differently when the economy is booming than when it is declining, but they must remain true to the basic leadership brand of their organization.

For example, in an adverse economic environment, what my colleague Jim O'Toole calls "yellow-light leadership" is appropriate. Managers need to make tough analytical decisions about cost controls, investments in new products and services, and especially the treatment of their human capital. Above all else, they need to avoid triggering a death spiral. If they have to downsize, it must be done in a way that remains respectful of their staff, with a positive long-term vision. As mentioned earlier, Cisco, Applied Materials, Intel, and several other leading high-technology companies have done a particularly good job of managing during the downturns they have experienced. Their leadership has focused on performance and skills as a basis for workforce reductions and has placed a particularly strong emphasis on giving people a soft landing.

Difficult times are not usually a period in which to focus on growth opportunities and developing visions of where the organization is going to go. But leaders must not lose this emphasis entirely. There are often great opportunities in a downturn for organizations to improve their competitive position and continue their virtuous spirals by outperforming their competitors. They can, for example, build new capabilities and improve their relationships with customers by offering superior services during economically stressful times. They can also position themselves to rebound quickly when the economy changes.

Regardless of the economic times, organizations need to train leaders to communicate truthfully and openly with their employees about what is going on in the business. Managers quickly lose credibility when they withhold critical information from employees or, worse yet, give them inaccurate information. Sometimes the best answer is "I don't know"; at other times, it is letting employees honestly know that conditions are worsening and changes will need to be made. And whenever bad news about the company must be delivered, it is best to frame it in terms of what is happening in the external environment and how this causes the organization to make changes in its behavior.

Above all, what should never be lost are the principles that support a virtuous spiral approach to human capital management. These principles can easily go by the wayside whenever management stops focusing on acting in ways that are good for both the organization and its people. This often happens in downturns, when leaders make short-term decisions that destroy the relationship between the people and the organization. As a result it becomes extremely difficult to relaunch a virtuous spiral when the economic environment improves. It can also easily happen in an upswing, when leaders become arrogant and cease to focus on the importance of their human capital's sharing in the success of the organization.

In short, organizations need to maintain their leadership brand regardless of the economic conditions they face. What they need to change when the business environment changes are their tactics, business practices, and business models.

Implications for Individuals

The changes that are taking place in organizations with respect to leadership have a number of implications for you as an individual. Fortunately, most of these implications are positive, in two ways. First, they can help you learn how to assess the kind of leadership you will experience when you join an organization. Second, they can provide you with a much better opportunity to develop your own leadership skills and to become a leader.

Just as we discussed with value propositions, ferreting out an organization's leadership brand is very useful when you are trying to decide whether to join it. Although there are individual differences in how managers implement an organization's brand, the more you can know about an organization's leadership brand, the better sense you will have of the way an individual manager will treat you.

It makes good sense for you to do research on your own and to ask questions during interviews to determine whether the organization has a leadership brand and if so, what it entails. You can then assess whether you want to be led and managed in that way, as well as whether you might grow into a leader in that organization.

The tricky point here involves understanding your own feelings and reactions to leadership and management approaches. If you are new to the workforce or have not worked in a large organization, you may not be aware of your preferences for different leadership styles. This is another area where you can improve your self-awareness by taking psychological tests and going to assessment centers. The bottom line is that you will be doing neither yourself nor the organization a favor if you join when there is an obvious mismatch between the organization's leadership brand and the way in which you want to be managed.

The second major implication of this chapter is important if you are interested in being an effective leader. As I have said throughout this book, self-managing your career is critical; this is particularly true of your career as a leader. There are many actions that you need to consider, both outside of work and on the job, in connection with managing your growth as a leader. Some of these actions depend on where you are in your career—new manager, low- to mid-level manager, or a senior manager—so let me walk through these separately, even though some of the implications overlap from one career phase to the next.

Implications for New Managers

If you are an aspiring leader or in the earliest stages of being a manager, the first task for you to tackle is to reflect seriously on your potential to develop as a leader and what type of leadership situation fits you best. Psychological tests and going through various assessment programs are two ways to get a sense of whether you have the skills, desire, and motivation to be a leader, as well as what kind of leader you are likely to be.

Another way to get a handle on your leadership abilities is to look back and analyze past experiences you have had in leadership roles, whether in school or in volunteer organizations. If you have never been a leader before, perhaps you might want to recognize that you do not automatically gravitate toward leadership roles and that management is not a good career for you. On the other hand, if you have worked in any volunteer organizations or in civic activities, these environments may have already taught you some lessons about the extent and nature of your leadership skills, as well as how satisfying you find leadership positions to be.

If you have not worked in a leadership capacity in a volunteer organization, now is a good time to consider doing so. It actually takes exceptional leadership skills to be successful in volunteer organizations because many of the traditional power and structure supports for managing that are present in a for-profit organization are absent. Thus if you can get things done in this environment, it is usually a good sign that you can be a successful leader in a more structured organization. Indeed, a good guess is that people who like leading in volunteer organizations and less structured situations are particularly likely to be successful in organizations that practice participative leadership and employee involvement.

Implications for Low- to Middle-Level Managers

As you move up the ladder in management, the importance of managing your own career becomes even more pivotal. You need to take many actions outside of your work as well as on the job to ensure that you grow into an effective leader.

Off the job, I highly recommend that you take courses and go to conferences on leadership development. Consider getting an M.B.A. or other degree that can help you in your management development.

If you have time constraints, you might prefer to attend one of the executive programs that are offered by many business schools. They are tailored to managers who want to learn about and develop leadership skills in a short period of time. Though these executive training programs do not grant an M.B.A. degree, you receive a certificate of completion that can act as a useful credential in your career growth.

Meanwhile, assess how committed your organization is to growing its leadership capability and to providing you with the resources you need to develop your leadership skills. Also evaluate what methods your organization uses to develop its leaders. Does the company foster shared leadership? Does it provide coaching or perhaps classroom training? Does it encourage development moves that can help you expand your skills? Do you receive assessments with feedback about your leadership growth? All of these are important questions to explore if you want to be an effective leader and to develop your leadership skills.

Remember that in general, your leadership skills are more likely to be developed in an organization that operates on a shared leadership model. But this requires that you must want to be in an organization of many leaders rather than an organization of followers and a few leaders. On the other hand, if you prefer to be in an organization led from the top down, staying in an organization with a shared leadership model is a prescription for frustration.

A helpful way to grow your leadership skills as you rise through the ranks is to find a mentor who is interested in helping you develop. As stated in Chapter Six, an informal mentor relationship with someone you respect and admire often proves to be the best type of mentoring.

Since leadership skills develop best through experience, you should look for job assignments that challenge you and help you learn. You can also offer to chair task forces and project teams. If your company has a 360-degree assessment program, use it and learn from the feedback. Even if you don't agree with the feedback you receive, you can still learn from it by examining why the results came out as they did.

One note of caution about taking on new challenges or assignments: be sure to assess every situation not only for its learning potential but also for its success potential. As you take new management jobs, you need to be careful about inheriting situations that put you at risk, such as instances where someone's poor past leadership has created a no-win situation for the next manager.

The higher you go in management, the more important it is that you develop a leadership brand that fits your organization. If your leadership doesn't fit the style of your organization, there are two things you can do: change your style or look for another job. My advice is to look for another job. In almost all cases, changing companies is definitely the best approach, for two reasons.

First, changing your style is usually quite difficult. Most people simply cannot make fundamental changes in how they lead. They may be able to improve their skills and develop, but they cannot transform themselves.

Second, if you stay and cannot successfully change your leadership style, leading and managing in a style that is countercultural is very risky for your career. While I have seen it occasionally lead to short-term success and on rare occasions to long-term organizationwide change, most of the time it results in failure and career derailment. The simple reality is that organizations tend to reject foreign bodies.

One experience I witnessed firsthand provides a good example of what can happen to leaders who don't follow the party line. One of the best leaders I ever had the chance to observe is Ed Dulworth. He was the plant manager of the General Foods plant in Topeka, Kansas, during a time when employee involvement was a "radical" idea. Ed designed the plant to optimize the involvement of employees and created a very effective plant that truly was one of the first virtuous spiral organizations that I observed.

Unfortunately, Ed's success ended up being his downfall at General Foods. He simply didn't manage in the same way as other plant managers, and as a result, he was not regarded as a good team player. Although his plant had the best results in the company, he was not promoted, and he ultimately left the company to become vice president of manufacturing for Topps chewing gum. So for him, the case had a happy ending.

This is just one of many cases that I have seen where a manager does the right things as a leader but is not rewarded for the effort. Organizations often resist changing their leadership style because a different type of leader is a threat to other senior managers who fear a shift in power and a devaluing of their skills.

While staying in one company that develops your management and leadership potential is the traditional way of becoming a senior manager, sometimes it pays to move around from company to company. Working in a variety of settings can provide a wider assortment of learning experiences and challenges and, perhaps more important, help you establish your personal brand as a leader. As noted earlier, establishing your personal brand goes a long way toward sustaining your virtuous career spiral.

If you are very interested in moving from a middle management to a senior management position, it pays to seek out an organization that is perceived to be well led and well managed. Some organizations develop very strong leadership brands, so working for them is an excellent step toward a significant managerial career. As I mentioned earlier, GE is probably the most obvious example of this, given that it has produced at least ten CEOs of other large companies in a span of just five years. But there are others, including IBM, HP, and PepsiCo.

Implications for Senior Managers

If you are already in a senior management position in an organization, the implications of this chapter—and this entire book—are clear: your behaviors are crucial to whether or not your organization follows a virtuous spiral. I would encourage you to review each of the behaviors and strategies mentioned in this book with respect to what you can do to create and sustain a virtuous spiral organization.

Check your leadership behavior against the principles and practices in this chapter and see how you stack up. Talk to your peers and see what they think; this is one situation where 360-degree feedback is very much in order. Assess whether your behavior contributes to the kind of virtuous spiral relationship that is good for your organization and good for yourself. Leaders in virtuous career spirals can gain from feedback just as employees and organizations can.

My final recommendation concerning what you can do if you are a senior manager is to focus on supporting a virtuous spiral in your organization. You can influence most or all of the features of your organization that propel a virtuous spiral. You can make the changes that are needed to begin and keep the momentum of a virtuous spiral going.

If I had to pick one organization design approach from the many that have been mentioned in this book as the key focus for senior managers, I would pick employee involvement. Senior managers are uniquely positioned to communicate with employees about the results of the business and to involve them in the success of the business. My research into employee involvement has made it clear to me that in order for employees to be committed to an organization, they need information about how the business is doing, knowledge that gives them understanding of the information, a say in how the business operates, and rewards that are tied to business success.[4] Only senior management can create an environment in which all of these are present.

Manage Change Right

You have now read about how to design organizations based on the seven principles of treating people right and creating a virtuous spiral. Before you begin implementing the practices I recommended in Part Two, I would like to provide some additional advice on how to create and maintain virtuous spirals.

Experience has taught me that getting organizations to the point where they can develop a virtuous spiral is enormously challenging. It requires a well-planned series of strategic actions to gain the momentum needed to initiate a virtuous spiral. Further, once a virtuous spiral is established, it requires vigilance and careful attention in order to avoid a wide range of potential difficulties and spiral-ending traps that organizations invariably encounter. Nothing lasts forever without care, maintenance, and in most cases, change.

Because managing change right is so difficult, I will devote this epilogue to a range of recommendations concerning what organizations must do to implement and maintain virtuous spirals. I also want to impart some closing advice for you about your personal virtuous spiral.

Starting a Virtuous Spiral

For an organization to create a virtuous spiral, it needs to develop a change strategy. Virtuous spirals don't just occur once organizations decide to treat people right. The entire organization, including its leadership, must become aware that change is needed and then make the changes that are needed.

In virtually all of the literature on change management, the first piece of advice is that change cannot occur unless people are motivated to change their behavior. For this to happen, they must believe that change will make things better for them.

One way to get people motivated to change is to establish a business justification for it by comparing how your organization stacks up against its competitors. Looking at competitors and establishing where your organization stands relative to them can often inspire the competitive spirit in people that I talked about in Chapter Eight on goals. In addition, there are almost certainly better organizations than yours, and bringing this to everyone's attention can create dissatisfaction with the present condition of the organization and a desire for change.

A second way to get people to feel a need to change is to assess the existing conditions within your organization. Attitude survey data, analyses by financial experts, and data on success in hiring are all examples of the kind of information that can provide people with a realistic view of how the organization is performing. Data like these, when brought to the attention of the organization, can be powerful stimulants for change, especially when people can see that the organization is falling short on objective measures and falling behind its competitors.

A third way to inspire change—and perhaps the most powerful one—is to give people a compelling vision of a more attractive world in which they can live. Creating a powerful, attractive vision helps people recognize and see the advantages of being in a virtuous spiral organization. It also helps people see what they will gain from change and understand what their role will be. Developing this vision is truly the hardest work in any change effort; it requires leadership and commitment.

The most effective change efforts usually combine elements of all three approaches. They use the first two to create dissatisfaction with the current condition of the organization. They use a powerful vision to inspire and direct change.

The Need for Leadership

Effective change requires effective change leaders. Note that I used the plural, *leaders*. All too often when people think about effective change leadership, they think primarily about the head of the organization, usually in terms of a celebrity or star CEO who will save the company like a white knight. Despite the popularity of this way of thinking about change, I believe it is an inappropriate wrong conception of change leadership.[1]

There is no question that the CEO of an organization needs to lead the change, but as was stressed in Chapter Ten, shared leadership is critical to the success of most organizational change efforts. The best CEOs lead in ways that develop leaders throughout the organization, not in ways that depend on the CEOs being celebrities or stars.

Managers at all levels need to become leaders. They need to articulate the vision of change and facilitate its implementation in a programmatic, focused effort. Equally important, people throughout the organization need to play a major leadership role in the change effort. They need to be enrolled not just as supporters of the change but also as its implementers. Virtuous spiral organizations come about only when people at all levels see the advantages of the organizations performing well and do what it takes to provide both direction and motivation.

Let me be clear about this. Whether you are in senior management or not, you have a role to play in leading change. Standing on the sideline waiting for somebody else to lead has the effect of preventing a virtuous spiral from beginning. The start of a virtuous spiral requires individuals like you to take a leap of faith and be visionaries.

The good news about change efforts that are intended to create a virtuous spiral is that people throughout most organizations are willing to sign up for them. When an organization articulates a clear vision that includes a virtuous spiral, broad-based support for it will develop.

I am convinced that people in organizations today, more than ever before, are ready for change. After several decades of organizations being run in ways that primarily advantaged shareholders and senior executives, I believe that people yearn for a vision that incorporates the basic principles of the virtuous spiral approach and that benefits multiple stakeholders. If ever there was a time for executives to lead change by emphasizing how organizations can benefit employees, customers, and society, it is now.

To put it bluntly, people are tired of organizations that seem to exist primarily for the benefit of a few individuals. Since the 1980s, we have seen the compensation levels of too many imperial CEOs and senior executives soar to heights that simply cannot be justified.

What should leaders be like in the future? They should be individuals who build organizations that are transparent with respect to their financial transitions, serve multiple stakeholders, and have uncompromising ethics. Who are the leaders I consider good models for what is needed in the future? Let me answer by listing five now-retired CEOs whom I had a chance to observe and work with:

Rick Teerlink of Harley-Davidson

David Kearns of Xerox

Ruben Mettler of TRW

Robert Galvin of Motorola

Max De Pree of Herman Miller

None of them were celebrity CEOs, but they all set directions for their companies that were strategically correct, ethical, and founded on serving multiple stakeholders.

Adopting a Systems Approach to the Seven Principles

Getting people motivated to change and creating a vision are the first steps in launching a virtuous spiral. The next step is to implement the principles of treating people right.

You cannot simply pick and choose among the seven principles. The principles form a coherent whole that only in combination will give rise to a virtuous spiral. Failure to implement all of them runs the risk of making those that are adopted ineffective and potentially dysfunctional. After all, organizations are systems, and all the parts of a system need to work together as a whole to support the function of each part. For example, simply developing people without making the appropriate changes in your reward system or in your work design may end up doing nothing more than increasing your organization's turnover.

Where your organization has choice is in which of the best practices are selected in order to implement each of the seven principles. You don't need to implement all of the practices I described in Part Two, but it is important that you adopt at least some proven practices in support of each principle so that your organization will support the totality of the virtuous spiral approach.

Admittedly, it can be difficult for an organization to immediately install the wide range of new practices that may be needed to support all of the seven principles of the virtuous spiral approach. This can often be simply more change than an organization can handle. When this is the case, the best alternative is to initiate a few changes that address the areas where the organization currently has its greatest problems. Changing the most severe problem areas can build support for installing additional practices and ultimately making a full transition to a virtuous spiral approach.

For example, if the people in an organization are expressing dissatisfaction with the reward system, implementing some of the best practices regarding reward systems that I have discussed in this book can be a good place to start change. You might consider, for instance, moving to an all-employee profit-sharing or stock ownership plan in order to lay the foundation for people's wanting more information about the financial performance of the company and having more knowledge about finance, both of which support the start of a virtuous spiral.

The key to a successful change effort is to start where there is a felt need for change but not to stop there. Ultimately, the change effort has to bring all the elements of organization design in line with the virtuous spiral principles.

Avoiding False and Fraudulent Spirals

As you go about creating a virtuous spiral in your organization, I need to warn you about a situation that can wreak havoc with your efforts—believing you have initiated a spiral when in fact your spiral is a false one.

Clear examples of false spirals can be seen in what happened to many dot-com organizations during the 1990s. In essence, the stock market incredibly inflated the market value of dot-coms, and so these companies believed they were on a virtuous spiral. But as soon as it became apparent that their market values were too high, stock prices collapsed, and virtually every one of these dot-coms went into a death spiral. Although a few companies managed to survive the carnage—eBay and Amazon.com are two examples—most dot-coms ended up failing.

Part of the reason so many of the dot-coms failed is that they spent money and behaved as if they were on a virtuous spiral, but in fact the economic reality simply was not there. The result was that companies like eToys, Excite@Home, and Webvan.com ended up as nothing more than footnotes in the history of the U.S. economy. Had they made a realistic assessment of their performance and behaved accordingly, I believe many more of them would have survived.

The second kind of spiral that can be mistaken for a virtuous one is the fraudulent spiral. In the past few years, we have seen numerous companies appear to have created virtuous spirals, only to discover that the senior leadership of the company was simply finding ways to create fraudulent spirals. I'm referring specifically to Enron, WorldCom, Global Crossing, Adelphia, Sunbeam, and other companies that falsified their financial reports so that they would appear to be performing well when in fact the opposite was true.

Fraudulent spirals are often the result of greedy executives. They create the perception that their companies are on a virtuous spiral by reporting false performance numbers. Until their fraudulent behavior is discovered, they are able to please their shareholders, Wall Street, and their employees and of course to exercise their stock options and enrich themselves.

When large-scale fraudulent spirals are uncovered, it almost always puts an organization into a death spiral. Stock options are suddenly worthless, bonuses are hard to pay, good employees no longer want to be associated with the organization, and customers flee. The upshot is a sharp decline in the organization's ability to survive. The deaths of fraudulent-spiral organizations can be particularly dramatic when the company relies heavily on human capital and its knowledge for success—witness Enron, Arthur Andersen, and their ilk.

Unfortunately, there is no surefire way to prevent organizations from entering fraudulent spirals. There are a few safeguards, however, that can make a difference. First, the composition of the board of directors needs to represent multiple external stakeholders. A diverse and independent board is much more likely to detect and report fraud than boards dominated by insiders.[2]

The incentive structure of an organization is another key to preventing fraudulent spirals. Overusing stock options as incentives is particularly a problem because senior management has the chance to profit enormously if they can increase the price of the stock, even if only for a few days. When executives can make millions and millions of dollars out of increases in stock prices, they can become obsessed with making positive public reports on the financial condition of the company and manipulating the investment community. This can in turn lead to inaccurate reporting of financial results and to overemphasizing the potential of the company.

Often the perpetrators of fraudulent spirals fall into the same trap that embezzlers do. They think that if they take a little bit of money (or in the case of many of the fraudulent companies mentioned, if they hide some costs or inflate some revenues), it won't be noticed and that it can be covered up and paid back at some point in the future. The problem, of course, is that their fraud quickly escalates out of control to the point where there is so much embezzling or so much false reporting that there is no way to make it up, and the fraud is exposed.

I am not suggesting that the solution to inappropriate compensation policies is to totally abandon stock ownership as an incentive; quite the contrary. However, there should be some reasonable rules about stock ownership and compensation levels. For example, executives should be required to own stock in the company, not just to have options, so that their personal money is at risk. In addition, they should be required to own any stock they receive for at least five years. This safeguard will help encourage them to think about the long-term success of the company, not just short-term or quarterly profits. In addition, executives should be required to report to the public before they sell any stock, and options should be exercisable only after a substantial holding period.

Finally, organizations need to improve the clarity of their financial reporting. Poor auditing and confusing accounting methods increase the potential for fraud and decrease the chances of organizations developing the kind of trust and commitment they need in order to have a virtuous spiral relationship with their employees.

Threats to Keeping a Virtuous Spiral Alive

Once organizations have begun a virtuous spiral, there is no guarantee that they can sustain it. In the past few years, numerous organizations have come to the end of their virtuous spirals. In my experience, there are both external and internal threats to the existence of virtuous spirals. I will review them next and in each case consider how they can be defended against.

The Threat of Environmental Change

Environmental change can be a serious threat to virtuous spirals because it often calls into question the very core of an organization: its strategy for success. Simply put, changes in the environment may call for new strategies.

In fact, the importance and increasing prevalence of environmental change prompts me to modify the virtuous spiral model I presented in Chapter One (Figure 1.1) in order to recognize the importance of change. If you notice in Figure E.1, I have included *strategy change, organizational design change,* and *performance change.* Environmental changes call for new strategies. New strategies call for different kinds of performance and therefore different organization designs.

There is no rule concerning how often companies need to make major changes in their strategy. It depends on the type and speed of changes in the environment. Some virtuous spiral companies have never needed to alter their strategy. Consider Southwest Airlines, which has essentially executed the same strategy for over thirty years, and that strategy has continued to be a successful one for them. As a result, Southwest has been able to sustain a virtuous spiral relationship with its employees without making major changes in its organization design. Can Southwest continue forever without changing? I doubt it. Eventually, it will have to change its strategy because of the appearance of new competitors, regulatory changes, or some other environmental change.

IBM is a very different case. It started as a time-card company, but environmental changes (technology) ruined that business. It was able to transform itself into a computer company. As a computer company, IBM developed a long-term virtuous spiral relationship

Figure E.1. Dynamic Virtuous Spiral.

with its employees, but then its business model began to fail in the 1980s when major environmental changes occurred. IBM reacted to the decreased profitability of its computer hardware products by breaking the loyalty-based employment relationship it had established over many decades. Extensive layoffs were ordered, and commitments to employees in the areas of retirement and careers were broken.

Only in the 1990s, when IBM established a credible new business strategy that emphasized computer services, was it able to improve its performance and reestablish a virtuous spiral. For the past few years, it has done an impressive job of creating a virtuous spiral that relies on an employment relationship based more on skills and performance than on loyalty, a relationship that fits its business strategy.

A number of other virtuous spiral organizations have successfully made strategy changes by reinventing themselves in ways that improved their competencies and added new capabilities. A great example here is the Dayton Hudson Corporation, which recognized that traditional department stores were not the best place to be in the retail market. They followed up on this conclusion by creating Target, which today is among the most successful retail businesses in the world. Indeed, Target is perhaps the only major competitor for Wal-Mart at this point. It has been so successful that Dayton Hudson adopted Target as its corporate name.

Changing its strategy in the retail business required Dayton Hudson to become more focused on costs and the way it managed its inventory and purchasing. However, the company maintained one constant from its earlier days: its approach to corporate governance and human capital management. It had and still has a very strong emphasis on building a virtuous spiral relationship with employees. As a result, the organization has been honored both for its excellence in corporate governance and for its human capital management practices.

Intel is another virtuous spiral company that was forced by environmental change to make a major strategic shift. Once very successful in the DRAM memory chip business, Intel realized in 1985 that it needed to exit the DRAM business because with its cost structure it could not win against its Asian competitors. It switched to microprocessors, and the rest is history. As we all know from its memorable marketing campaigns, Intel has now become the major supplier of microprocessors to PC manufacturers. It is one of the few Silicon Valley startups from the 1960s and 1970s that is still thriving.

Unfortunately, most organizations are unable to make one, much less two, major transformations in their business models. Major change of this magnitude is usually extremely difficult because it often requires the development of new core competencies and organizational capabilities. Indeed, economists have come to refer to corporate failures caused by dramatic changes in the political, economic, or technological environment as "creative destruction." The term was coined by the late economist Joseph Schumpeter and has since been widely adopted.[3]

Public policy in the United States has generally favored creative destruction. The U.S. government does little to prop up and support failing organizations. As a result, many have gone out of business and have been replaced by new ones. The same process does not necessarily go on in all countries, however. Some governments favor supporting failing organizations, and socialist governments almost always do.

From an economic growth point of view, it is hard to argue against creative destruction. It clearly reinforces the importance of organizations developing virtuous spirals and learning how to reinvent themselves. The fact is, most traditional bureaucratic organizations are unable to reinvent themselves when faced with major technological, political, or economic change. They typically enter a fast or slow death spiral and eventually go out of business. But this doesn't have to happen. Death spirals can be avoided and reversed. Creative destruction is not inevitable. Organizations can be successfully changed. It is not easy, but it can be done if the design of the organization is one that facilitates change.

The first challenge is to identify what needs to be changed: Is the strategy correct? Is the execution the best it could be? Depending on the answers to these questions, the solution will be quite different. For example, if the organization determines that its strategy does not fit the reality of the competitive environment, it needs to change its strategy and ultimately change the organization so that it can implement the new strategy.

On the other hand, if the organization discovers it has a problem with execution, it needs to focus on the four organizational design elements to determine why the execution is flawed. Is it a question of the wrong people? The wrong reward system? The wrong processes? The wrong structure?

Many of the practices discussed in Part Two support organizational change as much as they help create virtuous spirals. For example, the following all support change: employment contracts that emphasize skills, employability, and performance; compensation systems that tie rewards to the overall performance of the organization; and skill development programs that emphasize training individuals for the business needs of the organization. These and many other practices that support a virtuous spiral can potentially motivate people to change when the business environment changes and give them the capability to change their organization.

The Threat of Economic Downturns

A slowdown in an organization's financial performance can seriously threaten the virtuous spiral it has created, but a slowdown doesn't have to end it. An appropriate response to a slowdown can in fact allow a virtuous spiral to continue or lay the foundation for a new one. The key to success in dealing with an economic slowdown is identifying its root cause. There are two different economic conditions that can cause companies to experience poor financial performance.

The first of these is a general economic downturn that affects the entire economy of the country or countries in which an organization does business. When this occurs, the challenge is to avoid reacting in ways that damage the organization's long-term ability to succeed. A key issue is how the organization handles its human capital during the downturn. It is tempting to immediately cut costs by reducing headcount, but done poorly or inappropriately, this action can lead to many negative repercussions and prevent an organization from performing well when the economy improves. As we discussed in Chapter Four, key actions include not breaking the employment contract and retaining the right human capital.

The second condition is an economic downturn that is limited to a particular industry. In these cases, if the downturn appears to be temporary, your organization needs to respond in essentially the same way that it should respond to a general economic downturn. That is, it should take steps to position itself to be a more powerful competitor when the situation turns positive. It needs to be particularly concerned about retaining its best performers because they may be attracted to industries that are performing better.

Two organizations that I have worked with stand out with respect to managing industrywide downturns, Applied Materials and Intel, which happen to be in the same industry, semiconductors. Both organizations have survived and flourished precisely because they have made the right moves when the highly cyclical semiconductor industry has experienced downturns. During the most recent one, they both were careful to retain their best employees and in fact added employees with key skills so that they would be well positioned to grow and increase their market share when the semiconductor industry turned around.

Jim Morgan, the longtime CEO of Applied Materials, has consistently emphasized that he sees the downturns in the semiconductor industry as opportunities to consolidate the company's position and increase its market share. As a result of his skillful management during downturns, Applied Materials has maintained its virtuous spiral and has become the world's dominant manufacturer of semiconductor manufacturing equipment.

However, keep in mind that some economic downturns that affect just a particular industry are not short-term and may indicate a fundamental environmental change in that industry. The management of an organization therefore needs to look for the clues that distinguish between temporary and permanent downturns. If it is discovered that the downturn is part of a long-term decline in the industry, the organization must look seriously at changing its basic strategy and moving into a new business.

Mistakes and Self-Inflicted Threats

In addition to environmental and economic changes that can cause virtuous spirals to end, organizations themselves sometimes make mistakes that destroy their virtuous spirals. Perhaps the most common of these involves making bad decisions about how to treat employees.

Too many organizations become greedy and sacrifice long-term virtuous spiral relationships in order to capture short-term gains. It can be tempting to change the employment relationship so that at least in the short-term, it is more favorable to the organization than to the individual. For example, organizations may decide to drop profit sharing and other pay plans that benefit employees because they believe they "are paying too much." They may cancel training and development programs in order to achieve short-term reductions in costs, or they may engage in staff reductions that are too extreme and poorly managed.

The danger of all these actions is obvious: they break a virtuous spiral that the organization may have in place. An organization can quickly go from a great place to work with highly motivated employees to one that is regarded as not a good place to work. Once this occurs, the quality of the talent in the organization begins to drop, which diminishes performance, and this in turn makes it difficult for the organization to recruit new employees.

Executive greed can also lead to a virtual looting of corporate assets by senior executives and to the end of virtuous spirals. Executive compensation levels can get dramatically out of control if they go unchecked by the board of directors and the shareholders. In addition to costing the company large amounts of money, excessively high compensation levels and excessive perks can undermine the credibility of senior executives and reduce their ability to lead. In essence, they are perceived by the rest of the employees as simply in business solely for their own enrichment and not operating in the best interests of the company and the rest of the employees. This is an enormous obstacle for any organization to overcome in trying to maintain a virtuous spiral.

There is little doubt that during the 1980s and 1990s, executive compensation levels in the United States reached a point where they were simply too high and as a result damaged the virtuous spirals in many corporations. Some executives literally made tens of millions of dollars a year simply for running good, not great, corporations. Indeed, some became wealthy for running poor corporations.

Many executives who were ousted for poor performance still received severance packages of tens of millions of dollars and extensive, expensive retirement plans. In addition, many executives received benefits and perks that highlighted their "special" status and distance from other employees. This in turn contributed to some CEOs being separated from other employees and feeling that they did not need to pay attention to their relationship with most employees.

Although excessive executive compensation has occurred mostly in the United States, it has occurred elsewhere in the world as well.

Greed is not just a vice of executives. Virtuous spirals can also end, or for that matter never start, because employees become greedy. The airline industry is a classic example of such employee greed. I once interviewed Fred Crandall, the former CEO of American Airlines, who maintained that the airline industry has never been profitable. This, however, hasn't prevented some of the employees from doing quite well, most notably the pilots. With the help of their very powerful union, the pilots have managed to steadily improve their financial situation with virtually every new contract they have negotiated, despite the fact that the industry has performed poorly.

High wages are just one of the problems the airline industry faces, but it is interesting that Southwest, the only consistently profitable airline in the United States, has much lower labor costs than

United, American, and the other major carriers. It is also the only major U.S. airline that has been able to develop and maintain a virtuous spiral.

United is perhaps the best example of an organization whose pilots have simply not been productive enough to justify their industry-leading salaries. They made wage concessions in the early 1990s. In return, they got stock in the company and seats on the board. But instead of leading to a virtuous spiral, it led to increasingly higher wage levels that pushed United's labor costs to the top of the industry. The wage escalation produced another survival crisis in 2002 that could not be solved by a new round of wage reductions, and United went bankrupt.

There is no magic formula for preventing organizations from taking actions that end virtuous spirals. People will make mistakes, but I think the more an organization adheres to the seven principles, the less likely it is to make a spiral-ending mistake. They each help prevent the most common self-inflicted threats.

The Threat of Fads and Fashions

In my view, many management practices can prevent a virtuous spiral from developing or lead to the end of one. The practice of management has now become a consumer product. Thousands of individuals, companies, and publications vigorously market new ideas about how to manage. Books on management can sell a million copies or more (remember *The One-Minute Manager* and *Who Moved My Cheese?*), and magazines such as *Fortune, Business Week,* and *The Economist* regularly report on new management practices. There is also a never-ending supply of workshops on management practices as well as a multitude of consulting firms that claim to offer the management equivalent of better mousetraps. The market for management products is large and seemingly insatiable, particularly if the innovation can be summarized in a short and catchy blurb, taught in a one- or two-day training course, and promises to produce immediate results.

All too often, organizations adopt such ideas as speed to market, total quality management, reengineering, and organizational learning, among many others, on a short-term basis. After a while, new programs seem like the flavor of the month (or perhaps year) to most employees. The net result is that each time the emphasis shifts to the next new program, with its "silver bullet" solution, much of what was learned in the old program is discarded and forgotten. Individuals who did not commit to the previous program feel reinforced for not accepting it and not participating in it. As they so often say to me when I interview them, "I knew it was a passing fad, so why invest my time and energy in it?"

It is impossible to predict what the next fads will be. The only safe prediction is that fads will come and go just as management by objectives, zero-based budgeting, quality circles, T-groups, and a host of other management "innovations" have disappeared because they did not focus on the kinds of fundamental changes that organizations require in order to become virtuous spiral organizations.

Can organizations inoculate themselves against the fad- or flavor-of-the-month syndrome? I believe they can. For organizations, the challenge is to identify the useful new practices and reject the large number of new practices, recycled old practices, and current fads that dominate the management field but are not a good fit for them or are simply not very useful.

The place you can start is to assess whether the practices lead to the development of organizational capabilities that are key to business success. The best way to do this is by asking the following questions that are suggested by the Diamond Model:

- Does the practice support an organizational capability we need?
- Does the practice add to a needed core competency?
- Does the practice fit our competitive environment?
- Does the practice fit the seven virtuous spiral principles?

Literally any management practice can be tested by asking these questions. If the practice does not pass this test, it should not be adopted.

Finally, senior management must play a critical role in preventing fad-embracing behavior. Leaders needs to have a constancy of purpose and a focus on developing only those practices and policies that are part of the organization's long-term business strategy. If senior management has a short attention span and does not act strategically, it is almost inevitable that the rest of the organization will be easily entrapped by the latest fads.

Designing an effective organization is a journey without end. Yesterday's performance is unlikely to be good enough tomorrow, so you must continuously think of ways to improve your performance and that of your organization. This means change, experimentation, strategic alignment, and a willingness to adopt a learning stance toward the development of organizational capabilities. It does not mean a faddish, ever-changing, flavor-of-the-month approach to effectiveness.

Your Personal Virtuous Spiral

I want to make some final comments about creating and maintaining your virtuous spiral. First, you need to recognize that the world of employment is changing rapidly. Most likely, you should think of yourself as "self-employed." You may be working for a large corporation or doing a piece of contract labor on a temporary basis—it does not matter. In both cases, you need to understand that these are temporary, skill-based employment situations.

In the logic of this new world, career management means developing your skills and knowing how much the employment market values and needs them. As a result, you must be able to (1) develop marketable skills, (2) assess and compare your skill levels to those of others, and (3) manage your own career.

In addition, you must recognize that you can no longer reasonably expect most organizations to guide you through the white water of updating your skills or converting from one skill set to another. As I have said throughout this book, you have to manage these tasks yourself. It is no longer realistic to expect companies to absorb the cost of helping you develop your career. The reason is simple: helping individuals develop the right skills is expensive. And although it may produce long-term payoffs for organizations, it may not produce short-term performance improvements. It is usually much cheaper these days for organizations to hire someone who already has the new skills they need; thus they are unlikely to invest in the development of your skills.

The good news is that the increased importance of human capital will give *you* more power. Keep in mind that if you have skills, you are in an excellent bargaining position with respect to what work you do and how you are managed and rewarded by organizations. As a result, the potential exists for you to enjoy a fulfilling and meaningful virtuous career spiral. In essence, you have the chance to earn a higher rate of return on your skills and knowledge capital than ever before. But you can earn a high level of rewards only if you have valuable capital.

Individuals who do a good job of managing their careers stand to prosper in this new world. In fact, they should be able to have more control over their work lives and take advantage of the wide variety of work options available to individuals with marketable skills. Working part time, working through a temporary agency, developing an ad hoc contractual relationship with an organization, creating a virtual organization, joining an organization as a core employee—all these are increasingly possible scenarios. In the future, there are likely to be even more options available as corporations develop new virtuous spiral–enhancing relationships.

Managing Your Career

What can you do to manage your own skill-based career? I have already mentioned many things, so at this point I will limit myself to reviewing the most critical points to keep in mind. You must learn the market value of the educational opportunities that are available. In essence, an individual who absorbs a great deal of knowledge but does not do so in a way a company can easily see or evaluate may have difficulty converting the acquired knowledge into a good job opportunity or a higher pay rate.

It is also critical that you regularly assess your skills to be sure that they are still at a world-class level. How? If you are working full time for an organization, you should be particularly active in gathering feedback about your performance (by asking for it!) and in attending relevant company training courses. If you are a manager, you should attend skill assessment programs or participate in simulations of managerial situations that provide intensive feedback on how effectively you handle a wide variety of situations.

To manage your own career, you also need to stay abreast of the job market. You need to know how to test it, how to identify changes in it, how to stay in touch with it, and how to build a network of people who can help you develop the skills and contacts needed to thrive in it. A variety of resources are available for those who want to develop their skills and understand the job market. There are unions, as well as professional associations and clubs, that bring together people who have common interests in finance, human resources, and other specialty areas. In addition, considerable information about skills, work opportunities, and organizations is available in both the electronic media and the business press. Anyone who is not regularly reading the business press and finding out what is going on in the hiring world is at great risk of being unable to manage his or her career successfully.

You can also help yourself by applying for new positions in your present organization and in others. In many respects, this is the best way to gain data about your market value and to learn what you need to do to further your career.

Finally, I believe that more and more people should use agents and coaches to help them manage their careers. This has already happened in such human capital–intensive industries as sports and entertainment. Senior executives use coaches and have lawyers and search firms who help them. It is only a matter of time before others who have valuable human capital have career coaches and agents.

Commitment Versus Loyalty

The last piece of advice is to be happy and enthusiastic about your current job and employer but be prepared to leave. In other words, see your current job as an opportunity to show what you can do and as an opportunity to increase what you can do, not as a comfortable long-term niche.

A number of articles have suggested that because individuals cannot count on an organization for permanent employment, they should be, and inevitably will be, somewhat less committed and loyal. This may be inevitable, but it is also potentially counterproductive for all concerned. If you fail to fully commit to doing a good job, you may be more likely to be let go and may find it more difficult to get a new job. Failing to perform well may also prevent you from developing the kinds of skills and competencies that will position you to get jobs elsewhere. Besides, a commitment to high performance is different from loyalty to an organization.

If loyalty means staying with an organization regardless of how you are treated or the prospects it offers, then it is clearly stupid to be "loyal." It is smart, however, to be committed to developing your skills and performing well.

One thing you can and should do is clearly establish the nature of the employment relationship with your employer. In some cases, this relationship is obvious—for example, if you are working through a temporary agency. But the relationship may not be so obvious when you have a "regular job" in a large organization. It can be especially confusing if the organization has a "rings strategy" of employment security, which identifies some employees as permanent and others as subject to layoffs and staff reductions. Knowing your position in the organization is crucial to developing a sense of what kind of skills to develop and how to orient yourself toward the external labor market.

The best rule of thumb is that unless the organization says that you are a long-term employee and have a job for life, it is wise to assume that you are self-employed and to behave accordingly.

Final Thought

I began this book by stressing how important it is to create organizations that perform well and treat people right. Throughout I have provided examples of how this can be done and where it is being done.

I would like to conclude by emphasizing that the existence of virtuous spirals depends on organizations recognizing the importance of serving multiple stakeholders. Yes, making the numbers is important, but so is satisfying customers, enriching communities, and helping individuals develop virtuous career spirals.

When all is said and done, organizations are created by people to serve people. Their survival should and does depend on how well they serve people—they do not have a right to exist otherwise.

Notes

Chapter One

1. K. Dychtwald, *Age Power: How the 21st Century Will Be Ruled by the New Old*. New York: Tarcher/Putnam, 1999.
2. C. A. O'Reilly III and J. Pfeffer, *Hidden Value: How Great Companies Achieve Extraordinary Results with Ordinary People*. Boston: Harvard Business School Press, 2000.

Chapter Two

1. D. C. Hambrick and J. W. Fredrickson, "Are You Sure You Have a Strategy?" *Academy of Management Executive*, 2001, *15*(4), 48–59.
2. C. K. Prahalad and G. Hamel, "The Core Competence of the Corporation." *Harvard Business Review*, 1990, *68*(3), 79–91.

Chapter Three

1. E. E. Lawler III, *Motivation in Work Organizations*. Pacific Grove, Calif.: Brooks/Cole, 1973.
2. B. Nelson, *1001 Ways to Reward Employees*. New York: Workman, 1994.
3. A. H. Maslow, *Motivation and Personality* (New York: Harper, 1954); A. H. Maslow, *Toward a Psychology of Being* (New York: Wiley, 1968).
4. D. Feingold, S. A. Mohrman, and G. M. Spreitzer, "Age Effects on the Predictors of Technical Workers' Commitment and Willingness to Turnover." *Journal of Occupational Behavior*, 2002, *23*, 1–20.
5. E. A. Locke and P. G. Latham, *A Theory of Goal Setting and Task Performance*. Upper Saddle River, N.J.: Prentice Hall, 1990.
6. W. F. Cascio, *Costing Human Resources: The Financial Impact of Behavior in Organizations*, 4th ed. Cincinnati: South-Western, 2000.
7. M. W. McCall Jr., M. M. Lombardo, and A. M. Morrison, *The Lessons of Experience: How Successful Executives Develop on the Job*. San Francisco: New Lexington Press, 1988.

Chapter Four
1. E. E. Lawler III and D. Finegold, "Individualizing the Organization: Past, Present, and Future." *Organizational Dynamics*, 2000, *29*(1), 1–15.
2. E. E. Lawler III, S. A. Mohrman, and G. S. Benson, *Organizing for High Performance: The CEO Report on Employee Involvement, TQM, Reengineering, and Knowledge Management in Fortune 1000 Companies.* San Francisco: Jossey-Bass, 2001.
3. Lawler, Mohrman, and Benson, *Organizing for High Performance.*

Chapter Six
1. Lawler, Mohrman, and Benson, *Organizing for High Performance.*
2. Lawler, Mohrman, and Benson, *Organizing for High Performance.*
3. G. Hollenbeck, "Coaching Executives: Individual Leader Development." In R. Silzer (ed.), *The Twenty-First-Century Executive: Innovative Practices for Building Leadership at the Top.* San Francisco: Jossey-Bass, 2002.

Chapter Seven
1. J. R. Hackman and G. Oldham, *Work Redesign.* Boston: Addison-Wesley, 1980.
2. J. R. Hackman and E. E. Lawler III, "Employee Reactions to Job Characteristics." *Journal of Applied Psychology*, 1971, *55*, 259–286.
3. Lawler, Mohrman, and Benson, *Organizing for High Performance.*
4. B. Schneider and D. E. Bowen, *Winning the Service Game.* Boston: Harvard Business School Press, 1995.

Chapter Eight
1. Locke and Latham, *A Theory of Goal Setting and Task Performance.*
2. I. I. Mitroff and E. A. Denton, *A Spiritual Audit of Corporate America: A Hard Look at Spirituality, Religion, and Values in the Workplace.* San Francisco: Jossey-Bass, 1999.
3. Lawler, Mohrman, and Benson, *Organizing for High Performance.*

Chapter Nine
1. E. E. Lawler III, *Rewarding Excellence: Pay Strategies for the New Economy.* San Francisco: Jossey-Bass, 2000.
2. J. F. Welch and J. A. Byrne, *Jack: Straight from the Gut.* New York: Warner Books, 2001.
3. J. Biasi, D. Kruse, and A. Bernstein, *In the Company of Owners: The*

Truth About Stock Options (and Why Every Employee Should Have Them). New York: Basic Books, 2003.

4. E. E. Lawler III, *Strategic Pay: Aligning Organizational Strategies and Pay Systems*. San Francisco: Jossey-Bass, 1990.

Chapter Ten

1. R. M. Stogdill and A. E. Coons (eds.), *Leader Behavior: Its Description and Measurement*. Columbus: Bureau of Business Research, Ohio State University, 1957.

2. K. Blanchard, P. Zigarmi, and D. Zigarmi, *Leadership and the One Minute Manager: Increasing Effectiveness Through Situational Leadership*. New York: Morrow, 1985.

3. D. R. Ilgen and E. D. Pulakos (eds.), *The Changing Nature of Performance: Implications for Staffing, Motivation, and Development*. San Francisco: Jossey-Bass, 1999.

4. E. E. Lawler III, *From the Ground Up: Six Principles for Creating New Logic Organizations*. San Francisco: Jossey-Bass, 1996.

Epilogue

1. R. Khurana, *Searching for a Corporate Savior: The Irrational Quest for Charismatic CEOs*. Princeton, N.J.: Princeton University Press, 2002.

2. J. A. Conger, E. E. Lawler III, and D. Finegold, *Corporate Boards: New Strategies for Adding Value at the Top*. San Francisco: Jossey-Bass, 2001.

3. J. A. Schumpeter, *Capitalism, Socialism, and Democracy*. New York: HarperCollins, 1975. (Originally published 1942).

The Author

Edward E. Lawler III joined the faculty of Yale University after receiving his Ph.D. from the University of California at Berkeley in 1964. Three years later, he was promoted to associate professor.

He moved to the University of Michigan in 1972 as a professor of psychology and also became program director in the Survey Research Center at the Institute for Social Research. In 1978, he became a professor in the Marshall School of Business at the University of Southern California. That same year, he founded and became director of the university's Center for Effective Organizations. He was named professor of research at the University of Southern California in 1982 and distinguished professor of business in 1999.

Lawler has been honored as a major contributor to theory, research, and practice in the fields of human resource management, compensation, organizational development, and organizational effectiveness. He is the author or coauthor of thirty-five books and more than two hundred articles, which have appeared in the *Harvard Business Review, Fortune, MIT-Sloan Management Review, California Management Review, USA Today, Strategy and Business,* the *Financial Times,* and more than thirty other magazines, journals, and newspapers.

Business Week has proclaimed Lawler one of the top six gurus in the field of management, and *Human Resource Executive* called him one of HR's most influential people. *Workforce* magazine identified him as one of the twenty-five visionaries who have shaped today's workplace over the past century. He has been a consultant to many corporations, including the majority of the Fortune 100, as well as governments at all levels.

Index